Bukowski
A Biography

Aubrey Malone

JC Publications
Sacramento, Ca

Bukowski
A Biography

By Aubrey Malone

(ISBN-13-978-0692069394):

JC Publications

Sacramento, Ca

JC Publications.com

Acknowledgements

There have been many excellent biographies of Charles Bukowski. This one isn't intended as a substitute to any of them but rather a footnote. Parts of it were originally published in *The Hunchback of East Hollywood* in 2003.

Quotations from *Ham on Rye* and *Run with the Hunted* by permission of Axis Publishing.

Thanks to James Curl, Don Skirving, Sarah Fordham, Joanna Burgess, Katherine Norman-Butler, Kevin Ring, Rikki Hollywood, Jeffrey Taplin, Cory Nealon, Ronald Hague, Patricia Rodriguez, James Maynard and Charles Wommack. Special thanks to Al Berlinski for his help with both editions of this book and his kindness with photographs.

He might have been just another inhibited child. He might have been just another misunderstood son on a disgruntled milkman and his subservient wife. He might have grown up like anyone else on the street, toeing the line, pocketing his weekly pay-check, raising his 2.2 children and going to the ballgame at the weekend.

But that could never happen. He was different. He knew it was better to be an idiot or a bank robber than to live his life as others did.

Whatever his future was, it wouldn't be predictable. He decided he would be brilliant or a disaster. Or both.

Table of Contents:

Born Into This

It began as a mistake.

Army sergeant Henry Bukowski, a man who resembled the actor Charles Bickford in appearance, proposed marriage to his girlfriend Katharina Fett in the German town of Andernach in 1920. He had German blood in him but he'd grown up in Pasadena.

He met her at a dance the army threw for the defeated Nazis. She was a seamstress, and five months pregnant with what would be their only child when she went down the aisle. They might have stayed in Germany but for the poor state of the economy. He worked as a building contractor after the war ended but the business failed and he decided to go back to the U.S. For him it was a homecoming but for her an uprooting.

They moved first to Baltimore and then Los Angeles. Henry got a job driving a horse-drawn milk wagon. Their child was christened Heinrich Karl. He was born in a building that would subsequently become a brothel, or so the legend would have it. An unwanted child from a country he would soon learn to disparage, born to parents he would also learn to detest, it was hardly the formula for an all-American childhood.

Bukowski grew up in 2122 Longwood Avenue

Graham Greene once said that an unhappy youth is a wonderful inspiration for a writer. If this is true, Bukowski was one of the best, minting poetry out of this pain. He grew up in 2122 Longwood Avenue, an anonymous street in an anonymous suburb. His youth was fraught with misery. There was a kind of fighting with the universe inside him which wasn't helped by his circumstances.

Literary childhoods are awash with experiences of one brutal or unfeeling parent. What made Bukowski's unique was the negative reaction he got from both father and mother alike. A woman with an only child usually confers her maternal instinct on such a child but Katharina Fett didn't, either due to the fact that he was an unplanned baby or from fear of her cruel and abusive husband. She held herself back from expressing the emotions that must have been welling up in her.

Bukowski's emotions also became buried as a result. His parents were the dead hand that stifled his first steps in life. 'Heinie,' as he came to be called, grew up without those random acts of kindness any child is entitled to expect. He was clothed and fed by a couple who seemed to regard these as activities as gifts that were to be repaid when he became an adult

In some ways he felt like an adopted child. They dressed him formally. The house was run like a concentration camp. There were designated times for meals, chores, bed.

Image meant everything to them. Don't walk on the grass. Toe the party line. Work from nine to five. Pay your parking fines. Put out the garbage. Have the relations around on Thanksgiving.

When they took him for drives to the beach there was an air of dutifulness about it. There was no sense of adventure. This was parental sterility transported from an anonymous town in Germany to an equally anonymous L.A. suburb.

There was no magic in their lives, just the routine of making do. For Heinie they were paper people with paper lives. They hated anything life-enhancing. In the poem 'The man with the beautiful eyes' he claimed he was warned away from visiting a neighbor's house once because the person was gentle. When his house burned down afterwards he speculated that maybe his father was responsible because he resented such gentleness.

Bukowski's parents didn't like him playing with the neighboring children. They said they wanted to protect him from the underclass but as far as he was concerned he was already *in* the underclass. Their snobbery had nothing to back it up.

He once said he would have preferred to be Jack the Ripper than Lucille Ball. His heroes growing up were people like John Dillinger and Pretty Boy Floyd. He thought he might rob banks to make a living. It would certainly beat delivering milk. That was his father's job.

His parents, he thought, kept him aloof from others because they were afraid he would discover happiness away from them. They wanted his world to be their world. They sent photographs of him to his mother's family in Germany to show them what a good time he was having in America but even this was pathetic. Almost every photograph taken of the young Bukowski has him scowling.

One year he got an Indian suit from his father. All the other children he knew had cowboy outfits. It was bad being an immigrant with a German name but the Indian suit made him even more of an outcast. At playtime he was surrounded by his classmates with their cowboy suits. They taunted him relentlessly. 'I was an Indian,' he said, 'It was another reason to hate me.'

Bukowski saw his father as a man who ransomed his life to his mortgage. Owning his house was like a holy grail to him. He wanted to get up the capitalistic ladder but he failed at this. He believed in the system even though the system stamped him into the ground. He hadn't the vision to see beyond it or beyond himself. He didn't know the difference between living and earning a living.

His world was 'Yes sir, no sir, three bags full, sir.' You gave grief to those below you on the ladder just as you took it from those above you. And so the circle turned. Each era threw up new demagogues and new victims. The big fish ate the little fish and thus were all the institutions preserved.

His character was flawed too. He cheated on his wife and sometimes beat her. He hated anything good in life, Bukowski said, killing beauty wherever he found it. One day he flung a number of live mice into an incinerator for no reason. Heinie learned to accept this kind of behavior as the norm from him.

A pauper with the soul of a capitalist, this unlikely conformist wanted his son to epitomize the same dull respectability he did. 'If I own one house,' he told him, 'you can own two.' But Heinie

9

didn't want to own anything at all. He just wanted to go from one day to the next without thinking.

His father detected a resentment in him. He made it his business to beat it out of him. Heinie was an easy target. He didn't know why it was happening at the time but in later years he said, 'My father didn't achieve what he wanted in life so he took his frustration out on me.'

One day there was a letter home from school saying Heinie had misbehaved. His mother freaked when she read it. 'Wait till your father comes home!' she screamed. When he did he brought Heinie upstairs to the bathroom with him. (This was a room he would subsequently refer to as The Torture Chamber). He told him to take down his trousers. When he did he beat him mercilessly with a razor strop. The blows rained down on him until he was too tired to continue. It was the first of many beatings that would occur like clockwork over the next few years on trivial pretexts. That night Heinie had to sleep on his stomach because his back was so sore. It was a habit that would last a lifetime.

He tried not to scream as the lashes rained down on him but he couldn't. 'How can you not scream when you're six years old?' he said. His mind told him: This is life, this is what your future is going to be, a future your father is in charge of. The bathroom was like a microcosm of his world and so was the razor strop. His father owned it. He owned everything. 'Even the sun that shone on his house seemed to belong to him,' said Bukowski of these early years.

Because he wasn't allowed play with the other children on the street, he grew up without knowing how to catch a ball. When someone threw one at him in the schoolyard he usually fumbled it. This resulted in more jeers. He got the image of being a sissy because he couldn't play baseball like all the other boys. Some days he was followed home from school and throttled by bullies.

. For years he took this bullying, seeing it as the way things were just like his father's bullying was. But then one day he decided to fight back. When he did, it was with a vengeance. 'I stood up to boys taller than me,' he said, 'and they didn't know what to make of it.' Their reaction surprised him. 'They saw something dangerous in me and it made them back off.' He got a sudden surge of elation from this: 'It made me feel good. It was better to beat than to be beaten.'

Heinie now started to run with the 'bad' gang. With some other hardboiled classmates he targeted a boy called Harold. Harold became the new Heinie for the bullies, one of whom was now Heinie himself. The hunted became the hunter.

They bullied Harold on a regular basis. The usual 'fun' involved a threat to hang him. To escape the noose he either had to 'eat shit or drink piss.' He usually chose the second option. It was the lesser of two evils.

Now that the germ of dissension had been laid, it continued into the classroom for the young Bukowski. He began to speak up to the teachers, to refuse to do what they asked. As a result he was often put in detention. Sometimes he was put in detention when he hadn't even done anything. 'I was always being found guilty of something,' he said in later years, 'and I usually wasn't told what it was. My belief was that it was the rebellion in my eyes I was being punished for.' It was the same sense of rebellion his father had noticed. We can see this in some childhood photographs taken of Bukowski. He usually has a set expression in them, his lips pursed.

Instead of detention sometimes he was put standing in a phone booth outside the classroom and left there for hours. To him this was preferable than the boredom of the classroom. There were usually copies of a magazine called *Ladies Home Journal* in it. Some days he picked it up and started reading it. 'I thought I might learn something about women,' he said.

That wouldn't happen until years later because Bukowski's childhood was very much a 'Boy's Own' one. There were girls in his class but he didn't have much to do with them.

His sexuality, however, was awakening. One of his teachers was called Miss Gretis. Bukowski loved looking at her legs. He used to sit under her desk watching her cross and uncross them. He tried to see what color underwear she was wearing as her dress went a little higher each day. Another boy joined him in this 'ambition.' Sometimes they thought she was aware of them looking at her, or even enjoying it. One day when Miss Gretis lifted her dress up even higher than usual on her thighs, Bukowski said to his friend, 'She's going for the record!' He wondered what wonderful thing lay at the top of the thighs, what Golden Fleece.

Bukowski's youthful friends called him 'Kraut' as well as Heinie. World War 1 had just ended when he came to America and Germans were as hated in Los Angeles as they were everywhere else in the country. It confirmed his outcast status even more. He felt removed from everyone but didn't seem to mind this. A part of him enjoyed being different.

He cycled his bicycle to school and watched the rich people in their cars as they passed him by. They looked as if they had all the answers to life but even this early, Bukowski sensed they didn't. Maybe they were secretly as lost as he was. Maybe they were even more lost because they had to pretend they were something they weren't. He couldn't see anything he wanted in these well-groomed people in their big cars. He identified more with neglected children like himself.

He formed a friendship with a boy who had only one arm and with another one whose parents had no time for him. The outsiders banded together.

At home, meanwhile, things got worse. Every week Heinie had to mow the grass on his front lawn. The first time he was told to mow it he was playing a football game. His father dragged him away from the game, apparently resentful of him having any fun.

Every week Heinie had to mow the grass for his father

Over time the grass cutting ritual became horrific. Directions were screamed out at him as if he was on a military reconnaissance. He was warned against leaving any blades of grass uncut. There were threats of further beatings if he did. When his father inspected the finished work he invariably found such blades.

Afterwards he soundly thrashed his son. Even one blade higher than the one beside it qualified for a beating.

His father seemed to get high inflicting punishment on his son. It became like a drug to him. One day he threw a 2x4 at Heinie when he failed to do a job to his satisfaction. He writhed in agony as a blood vessel burst. It stayed in a jutted-out position for the rest of his life.

His mother supported her husband no matter what cruelties he perpetrated. Not because she thought he was right but because she feared crossing him. Such fear over-rode whatever natural affection she had for Heinie.

He never really understood why she didn't step in to protect him. Was it that she was inhibited because of her Germanic roots? America had conquered Germany on the battlefield and now this tyrant in civvies was doing it again on the domestic front. 'She was German,' Bukowski said in later years, 'Maybe that was all there was to it. In Germany the husband's word is law.'

Even so, he could never forgive her. In many ways she was the root from which Bukowski's subsequent misogyny sprang. When he grew up he expected every woman he met to behave like her. If they didn't it was almost like a surprise to him.

Even when his father wasn't using his fists to subdue his wife and son, Bukowski still hated him. He hated the way he looked, the way he dressed, even the way he ate his food. If Bukowski saw anyone who reminded him of his father in later life it brought all this back to him. He was like a microcosm of all his aversions rolled into one person.

He once described him as a 'sweaty, red faced, angry man.' He voted Republican, he said, and abided by all its dictates to the letter. He worked hard but never seemed to get ahead. He had an 'early to bed and early to rise' philosophy but it made him neither healthy, wealthy nor wise. He had blood pressure and an irregular heartbeat and smoked too many Camels and Pall Malls for comfort.

Every night at eight o'clock he'd send Heinie to his room with the injunction 'Lights out!' Heinie did as he was told – or at least appeared to. He undressed and turned the light in his bedroom off but he didn't go to sleep. Instead he read books under the blankets with the light of a torch. The heat was suffocating to him but it was worth it:

'It made each page I turned all the more glorious,' he said when recalling such nocturnal activities, 'as if I was taking dope.' As the years passed, his reading material turned from comics to more serious literature: 'Sinclair Lewis, Dos Passos, these were my friends under the covers.' The more he read, the more he decided he'd like to write, to see if he could do it as well as they did.

One day in school he wrote an essay about a visit of President Hoover to a nearby town. He wasn't there for it but the way he wrote about it impressed his teacher so much she read his essay out to the class. They were dumbfounded. So Heinie Bukowski had a mind. Nobody expected this of the sour-faced immigrant. It was as if a rock had suddenly found a voice.

**Bukowski's first taste of literary glory
came with an essay on Herbert Hoover**

Years later he wrote about the incident in his book *Ham on Rye*: 'My words filled the room from blackboard to blackboard. They hit the ceiling and bounced off. They covered Mrs. Fretag's shoes and piled up on the floor. Some of the prettiest girls in the class began to sneak glances at me. All the tough guys were pissed. Their essays hadn't been worth shit. I drank in my words like a thirsty man. I even began to believe them. I saw Juan sitting there like I'd punched him in the face. I stretched out my legs and leaned back. All too soon it was over.'

The circumstances of the essay were ironic because it was built around an event Bukowski hadn't attended. He'd got his first literary buzz from a lie. This led him to conclude that lies were the foundation stone upon which the world was built. Just as President Hoover had filled the populace with lies about how the economy was doing, so Bukowski had filled his pages with a different kind of lie. He felt this was going to be the way forward for him. Lies would take him out of his rut. His parents' life was a lie; America was a lie; the whole of life was one big lie. Especially politics. People who believed in politics, he once said, 'made about as much sense as those who thought you could suck wind through bent straws.'

Bukowski's youthful miseries were compounded when he developed a condition called *acne vulgaris* which caused him to miss an entire semester at school. It was so bad the medical establishment almost regarded it as a deformity. Bukowski had a different attitude to it. He saw it as coming mainly from a psychological root. 'It was my mind revolting against my body,' he said. For him it was the externalization of all the suffering he'd undergone since the day he was born. 'I had boils the size of apples,' he recalled, 'They were in my eyes, on my nose, behind my ears, in the hair on my head. The poisoned life exploded out of me. The withheld screams sprouted out in another form.'

When he attended hospital for treatment the doctors told his parents he had the worst case of acne they'd ever seen. After the diagnosis came the treatment. It was painful but, as was the case in 'The Torture Chamber', he tried not to scream. There was no razor strop here but there were needles, machines, ultra-violet rays. The boils were lanced and the pus gushed out. Each time one of them disappeared, another one flared up. They seemed to come from every orifice in his body. What had he done to deserve them? Was it his 'badness' that caused it?

The pain seemed to bother him less than the embarrassment of his body being seen by others. This was more a problem in school than at the hospital. He hated gym because it meant he had to undress to escape the humiliation of his body being seen in public he enrolled in a training corps called the ROTC. His uniform freed him of the indignity of stripping down to his underclothes in the locker room. This usually drew jeers - and gasps – from those looking at him.

Bukowski enrolled in an ROTC corps to avoid having to go to gym

An unlikely advantage of his acne was that it made him look older than his years. That meant he was able to get beer from the local bars despite being under age. He had his first drink when a friend of his, 'Baldy' Mullinax, brought him to his father's house. Baldy's father was a doctor who'd lost his license to practice because of a drink problem. He had a wine cellar in his basement. The first time Bukowski was shown this he put his head under one of the casks and turned the spigot. When the wine gushed down his throat he loved the sensation of it. He was hooked on liquor from that moment on.

When Bukowski drank he discovered a new side to himself, a side that made the world seem a tranquil place. It was a beautiful escapism for him, a happy drug. The second the alcohol touched his lips he seemed to feel a serenity inside himself. He almost felt as if it was waiting for him to discover it, as if it was a kind of mirror image of himself.

Bukowski in his ROTC uniform (University of Buffalo)

'It was love at first taste,' he said, 'As soon as the liquor went down my throat I became twelve feet tall.' It became a friend to him, an ally in the absence of any other ally. He would return to it throughout his life any time he had a problem and use it to work his way through that problem. Other people might have had their lives destroyed by drink but Bukowski always insisted it saved his.

The next crisis in his life occurred when his father enrolled him in Los Angeles High School, an upmarket establishment that only served to intensify his feelings of inferiority with his classmates. Most of them came from well-heeled families. 'He sent me to that rich high school,' he wrote years later, 'hoping that the ruler's attitude might rub off on me.' It didn't.

Here his acne grew even worse. He developed pustules on his shoulders and these necessitated more trips to hospital for painful drainage procedures. Sometimes electric needles were used to drill them. Bukowski drew on all his resources of pain management and suffered it.

After a time he became immune to the pain. One day a doctor said to a nurse who was standing beside him, 'I never saw anyone go under the needle that cool.' It wasn't courage, he thought, just a question of blocking something out of his mind. He'd had a lot of practice at that.

Alcohol helped such a blockage. As his teenage years went on he started to drink more. When he was drunk he continued to feel at home with the world. It was like a journey back to his real self. At these times he didn't seem to mind the fact that his parents didn't love him. He didn't mind the fact that the world wasn't his oyster, that teachers gave him a rough time, that he might never get a girlfriend because of the way he looked. The bottle could be a substitute for all of these things. It gave him a harmony with himself and his surroundings. It was like a surge of electricity coursing through him, like 'kissing God.' Once the magic juice kicked in he was another person, relieved temporarily of all inhibitions, ready suddenly to take the world on.

His father lost his milk run job in 1936. Bukowski's mother had to clean houses to enable them to meet their mortgage repayments. His father pretended to go to work, driving out of the house each morning like clockwork and staying away until teatime to preserve his image. This was another example to the young Bukowski of his father 'living the lie.' It was an unnecessary one because the Depression had made his plight almost ubiquitous in the area.

They qualified for free food because of their circumstances but were too proud to avail of this. Sometimes they went to a market in a nearby suburb to get cheap food instead.

At the age of 17 Bukowski decided to cut loose from his moorings. He sought out the night life of L.A., the seedy underbelly that would define his future work. He became involved with a group who were engaged in petty theft like robbing gas stations. He used to sneak out of his room most nights to be with them. He became the nominated 'leader of the pack' even though the others were older than him.

He drank in derelict houses with them. Some of them carried guns. They liked Bukowski, being impressed with his apparent disgust with everything in life. He had, they thought, a 'soulful bravado.' They also admired his capacity for ingesting vast amounts of alcohol without showing the effects of it.

One night when he came home drunk he found the door locked so he couldn't get in. His father refused to open it when he called out. 'You're not my son!' he roared from the other side. Bukowski lunged at it. It flew open and he went hurtling across the floor. Once inside, his father's 'hideous cardboard face' made him throw up on the hallway rug. His father was disgusted. He told him he was a dog. 'When dogs shit on carpets,' he said, 'We rub their noses in it.'

'Don't do that,' Bukowski said, but it was too late. His father grabbed him and pushed his head down onto the floor. Bukowski wasn't having this. He stood up and hit him with an uppercut. His father reeled back, spouting blood. His mother screamed. She dug at Bukowski's cheeks with her fingernails, begging him to stop. Bukowski stood back. He felt triumphant. His father said, 'I'll see you in the morning.' 'Why wait till morning?' Bukowski countered, 'What's wrong with now?' His father must have realized at that moment that his son had grown up, that the beatings would be no more. There was a long silence. Then he walked away.

Life became different after that night. The hostility between them was still there but it was more muted now. The battle lines were drawn. There was a point beyond which his father wouldn't go. He was wary of the boy he'd raised.

Bukowski started to read more widely in the local library now. Most of the books bored him. When that happened he put them down and left the building. He thought he could do better himself.

One of the first stories he wrote concerned a one-armed pilot in World War I fighting off the enemy with an iron hand. He was German. Too many people, he thought, wrote about American heroes. Too many people also wrote about able-bodied men. The hero of Bukowski's story was a cripple. Maybe he was thinking of his friend with one hand as he wrote it. Or himself.

When he told his father he wanted to be a writer he was advised to come down to the planet Earth. Writers didn't make money, his father told him. Besides, where was his talent going to come from?

He saw the idea as nothing more than a way to try and avoid working for a living.

The prom concert beckoned. It was a seminal night in any young man's life. This was the night when you nailed your colors to the mast, when you came out of the closet with your partner. But Bukowski didn't have one. Even so, he went down to the school. He stuck his nose against the fog of a window-pane and peered in. He was like the poor boy at the feast as he watched the dancing couples inside. He wanted to be a part of it and yet he didn't. Deep down he knew it all meant nothing. He gazed in at the self-satisfied people dancing around the floor and decided he hated them all. He tried to picture a different scenario, a scenario where he was in there dancing around with a woman in his arms. But it didn't work. It wasn't him and it would never be him.

Bukowski's High School Yearbook photograph. (The Poetry Collection of the University Library, University at Buffalo, the State University of New York)

Soon afterwards he left the school. There was no nostalgia, no sentiment. Was he going to something better? He didn't know. A lot of his classmates were headed for college. He would have preferred to dig ditches than do that. What was he going to do with his life? He didn't know. The editor of the school magazine predicted his career would probably involve something like putting holes in doughnuts. 'Henry will put bigger holes in them than everyone else and make more money that way,' he derided. Bukowski wasn't amused.

His father asked him if he had any job in mind. He said he hadn't. Getting a job meant licking ass, he said. He would have preferred to catch butterflies for a living than do that. His father thought this was a convenient excuse. He reminded him of the money he'd invested in him since the day he was born, the money he spent on his clothes, his food, even his medical treatment. All these things added up, he said. He told Bukowski he needed to develop a sense of responsibility. He needed to kick ass, to work his way up the ladder until he became better off than the next guy.

This was the spirit of rugged individualism, the spirit that made America great. It was the ethos of capitalism. Delivered by a white trash milkman on Longwood Avenue to his jerk-off son.

Bukowski listened to his rant with disgust. Was it possible anyone could believe this was a good way to live? He went to his room and brooded. There had to be another kind of world out there.

He tried to conjure it up by writing poems about it. His father had bought him a typewriter and he wrote them on this. He liked the sound it made when he pressed the keys. He hit them hard. The rat-tat-tat reminded him of a rifle.

His poems were tough. They were about misfits, people from the wrong side of the tracks. He couldn't write picnic-in-the-park lyricism. He preferred parables of the gutter, the bittersweet music of bruised love. If you tried to euphemize grief you sanitized it.

24

He enrolled at the Los Angeles University and studied journalism. More and more words poured out of him. When the other students wrote one or maybe two stories, he did a dozen. He wasn't able to stop himself. It was like verbal diarrhea.

He got a job to keep his father off his back. It was with Sears Roebuck. He arrived five minutes late on his first day. When his boss asked him why he was late he said, 'I saw a starving dog and I stopped to give it food.' It was true but it wasn't believed. He had his first black mark registered against him in the white collar world. It would be the shape of things to come. He only lasted a week in the job. That would also be the shape of things to come.

Bukowski now spent his evenings riding streetcars to run-down bars where he could drink in peace. Sometimes when he came home he typed out another poem or story. He found it easier to write with drink than without it. It was as if the alcohol released his muse. He didn't show any of his writings to his parents.

One day his father discovered a story he wrote which had what he called 'foul language' in it. He was so shocked at it he threw it out the window. Then he threw out the typewriter it was written on. Bukowski was out of the house at the time. He met his mother and she told him what had happened. When he came back he squared up to his father 'Why did you throw out my story?' he asked him. 'Because it was disgusting,' his father said.

He looked at his mother. 'You should write happy stories, Henry,' she said, 'nobody wants to read sad ones.' This was the woman who used to tell him to smile when he was a boy so he could be happy. He knew she had it the wrong way round. You had to be happy before you could smile. There was no point in arguing with her, with either of them. They were his enemies, the two of them united in their idiocy. He decided he had to get away from them immediately, to leave home for good.

On the Road

Poverty is a giant. It uses your face like a mop to clear away the world's garbage. (Louis-Ferdinand Céline)

Some authors left home for adventurous purposes. Bukowski left because he had to. He was running away *from* something rather than *to* it. He had no plan in mind. He wasn't Huckleberry Finn or Jack Kerouac. It wasn't the tradition of the wide open plains he fell into. He was a young man on the edge of madness if he stayed.

Another reason for setting out was to store up some experiences he might be able to write about. He knew he had 'the juice,' as he called it, to be a writer. What he needed was a platform, a set of experiences to build on.

Leaving home was like breaking out of a cage for him but he still had no idea what he wanted to do with his freedom. There were too many devils inside his head. Standing between home and the great outdoors he took a deep breath. What would his next move be? There wasn't anywhere in particular he wanted to go. He didn't think any one place was different from any other one. The only thing he knew for sure was that he hated crowds. No matter where he went it would be difficult to escape the screaming masses. But at least it would be a relief from home.

The first place he got to was New Orleans. Afterwards he went to San Francisco, and then St. Louis. The places didn't matter. All that mattered was that he was on the move, exorcising the past.

After leaving St. Louis he went to New York, the place he called 'the rotten apple.' When he got there he had only seven dollars in his pocket. 'I had no job and no friends,' he said. 'The buildings scared me. The people scared me. The women wouldn't talk to me.'

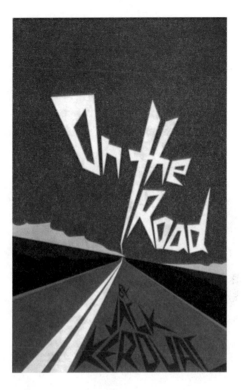

He loved waking up in strange cities and taking in the sights and sounds. 'I wanted to get as far away from my father as possible,' he said. That was the prime motivation.

There was no greater pleasure in life for him than to arrive somewhere he'd never been before and soak in its atmosphere. After spending a while listening to people's voices on the street he'd search for lodgings. When he got a room he'd put his suitcase on the bed and seek out some bar where he could spend a few hours drinking cheap beer.

The lodgings were usually cheap as well. He'd lie on the bed when he came home, usually with a bottle of wine in his hand. If there was a radio in the room he'd try and get some classical music station on it. This was his favorite type of music. It soothed him.

He'd pull down the shades and lie in the darkness as the music and the wine sent him into oblivion. Sometimes he heard mice scratching behind the walls and even that soothed him. He liked the darkness, the anonymity, the wine going down his gullet like liquid gold. He even liked it if the window shades were torn, or if there was a newspaper on the floor where he could keep reading the same headline again and again.

He preferred it if he was the only person in the building but that was rarely the case. Sooner or later someone in an adjoining room would probably put on a television or the landlady would start vacuuming outside his door.

As he lay on his bed drinking wine he liked looking at everything around him: the knobs on the cabinet drawer, the cracks in the mirror, the patterns in the carpet. The writer in him took it all in. Details like these would surface in future poems but he wasn't aware of that then. He was just living the moment.

When the little money he had ran out he'd buy a newspaper and look up the 'Help Wanted' section. If a job was offered that didn't require experience he'd apply for it. He used a reference he had from Sears Roebuck for all of them. 'By the time I got to St. Louis,' he said, 'it was held together by tape. The words were almost faded into nothing.' Jobs weren't too hard to come by because a lot of the male work force was at the front.

Between jobs he lived like a hobo. There was a time he thought such a life might be romantic. Not now. When he got to 'The Row' he found many of the people there were uncomfortably similar to his father in the way they thought. It wasn't that they objected to capitalism. They just failed to achieve it.

Some of the jobs he found himself in were so soul-destroying they were only marginally preferable to life at home. Not for him the zany excitement of a Jack Kerouac or a Neal Cassady. When he booked into the lodging houses he always told the landladies he was a writer. That went down well but then he'd get noisy, or they might find wine bottles under his bed when they were vacuuming his room. Being a struggling author might have been acceptable to them but not a struggling alcoholic one. He was often evicted from these places. He usually went quietly but if he was drunk he might create a scene. There were occasional nights in jail for disturbing the peace. The police would cuff him and take him 'down town' to cool off. The handcuffs were always too tight, he said, the steel cutting into his wrists.

Books came to his rescue. He didn't have enough money to buy them so he went into the libraries to read. Libraries were better than park benches. He could use the toilet facilities there and also recover from hangovers. He could sleep without having to worry about being moved on by a policeman. The sun streamed in from the windows, burning the back of his neck as he read. Many books left him cold but when he found one he liked he got drunk on the words.

He saw libraries like supermarkets of literature. He reached up to this shelf and then that one, plucking books down at random. He had no inkling of what he might find and that increased the sense of anticipation. One book he read at this time was by a philosopher who 'proved' the moon didn't exist. Bukowski loved it.

Dostoevsky's *Notes from the Underground* also impressed him. So did Camus' *The Stranger*. He read Antonin Artaud, William Saroyan, Robinson Jeffers. In these voices he experienced a sense of liberation from the world of Longwood Avenue.

He also loved Ernest Hemingway, especially the early stories. He copied his lean style in what he wrote himself, transplanting it onto his own dysfunctional blue collar world. Hemingway's alienation was also present in *The Stranger*. He empathized with the absurd life of Camus' hero, Meursault. This was a man who could kill for no apparent reason and then be brutalized by the state because he hadn't cried at his mother's funeral. How Bukowski could empathize with that. Camus' book ends with Meursault wishing to be greeted with 'howls of execration.' Extreme language like that spoke volumes to Bukowski.

He also read Knut Hamsun's *Hunger*. Hamsun's poverty-stricken circumstances struck a chord with him. Like Bukowski, he also had some Nazi leanings. This was amazing considering Norway had been occupied by the Germans during World War II. It led to Hamsun being examined by a psychiatrist — another circumstance that would be paralleled in Bukowski's life.

He read all these authors alphabetically, moving along the shelves from A to Z. That meant he would have come to Artaud before Camus and Celine before Hemingway.

At F he found Fante.

Just as some authors feel a book has existed before them and waits for them to discover it, so Bukowski felt *Ask the Dust* was waiting for him. It wasn't so much 'a' book as 'the' book, the end of his search, something that was a touchstone for everything he'd gone through in life up to this. He couldn't believe he'd never heard of him before. Who was he? Was he too good to be known by the masses – the 'crowds' Bukowski despised? Was he too good for the academics – whom he also despised. Maybe once every generation a genius seeped through. Maybe one day Bukowski himself could be that genius.

He found himself able to identify with almost every aspect of Fante's life: his unhappy childhood, his cruel father, his soul-destroying manual jobs, his out-of-control drinking, his brushes with death. Some of these events had their roots in real life. Fante was almost killed in an earthquake in Long Beach in 1933. Six years later he was involved in a car crash that could have been a suicide attempt.

Bukowski could also identify with Fante's volatile relationships with women, particularly his wife Joyce, who tolerated his raging tempers with saint-like patience. And of course his struggle to become a successful writer. .

Arturo Bandini, Fante's alter ego in the book, was like a forerunner of Bukowski's Henry Chinaski. He lusts after women, he drinks, and he's obsessive about writing. These would become classic themes of Bukowski in time. He loved the way Fante could convey a myriad of sensations in a paragraph. His book was scorchingly satirical as well as being heartbreaking. Often the distinctions were blurred. For Bukowski he was a writer who shared his experiences of lostness and longing and he wasn't afraid to let his pen roam wild and free as he documented these emotions.

Ask the Dust reverberates with energy as Bandini, the little man with big dreams, oscillates between writing and sexual infatuation. The two themes are unified in the finale as he casts his precious book at a woman who's just disappeared from his life for good. He's angry at the world and his place in it but he dilutes this with a series of irreverent dialogues with himself.

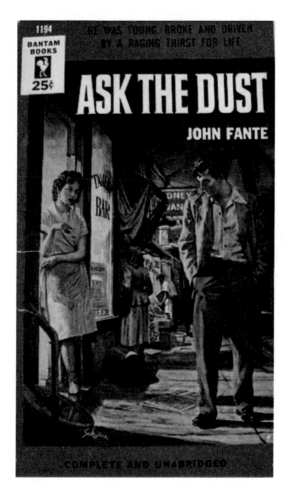

There's also the question of his immigrant status. He mythologizes his status as a writer on the cusp of glory but becomes tortured by the taunts of 'wop', 'dago' and 'greaser' that are thrown at him. Bukowski, aka Heinie the Hun, empathized with this. He also had a more immediate geographical connection with Fante. He often passed by the hotel in the bad end of L.A. where Fante lived, the Alta Vista in South Bunker Hill.

A more spirited delineation of deprivation than Hamsun's *Hunger,* in the end it's the self-mockery of *Ask the Dust* that makes it so distinctive. Fante can't seem to make up his mind if he's writing tragedy or comedy. It was the blurring of such genre distinctions that made it take off for Bukowski.

Fante knew he'd written something important but he was sufficiently versed in the harshness of the writing world not to expect anything to come from it. The reviews were kind but it was seen as a minor work. It had to compete with the likes of Steinbeck's *Grapes of Wrath* and Raymond Chandler's *The Big Sleep*, both of which were published in the same year. Bukowski was annoyed by the way it had been bypassed. For him Fante was the man who captured lowlife L.A. in a manner he himself would spend the rest of his life emulating. He didn't only admire Fante/Bandini: he *was* him.

Another book that influenced Bukowski a lot at this time was Louis-Ferdinand Céline's *Journey to the End of the Night.* This heady chronicle of wartime blues, factory oppression and hedonistic sex touched every possible chord it could for the impressionable Bukowski. He was even seduced by its appropriation of Nazism. (This would eventually destroy Celine after the end of World War II when he was imprisoned for his perceived fascism).

Bukowski relished its acerbic bite, its summary denunciation of the status quo. At last he'd found a writer who agreed that the world was run by jackals and jackasses. He read the book over and over again throughout his life, savoring its free-flowing narrative thrust, its devil-may-care irreverence. Like Fante, Celine was able to tell a story with both barrels blazing. Like Bukowski he had contempt for authority, preferring to play life loose. He said he read the book at a sitting, enthralled by its iconoclasm, its high humor, the manner in which it debunked sacred cows while still managing to have a merry old time for itself in so many alien environments.

Books like this were like food for Bukowski when he couldn't afford food itself. They were like drink when he couldn't afford drink. They exuded life when life itself gave little.

He roamed from place to place with the thoughts of Celine and Fante rolling around in his head. Leaving home had been necessary but life on the road held few delights. He took odd jobs and drank most of his salary, keeping some aside for rent and food (the 'luxuries.').

Landlords took him in grudgingly, bewildered by this quiet man who carried a cardboard case and held his shoes together with duct tape. Nothing hung together about him — not his manner, not his dress, not his occupation.

Who was he? And what was he writing? What could be important enough to justify the ferocious way he banged on his typewriter keys? If he was typing late at night and the other lodgers had to get up the next morning it led to friction. The people living upstairs from him pounded the floor. The people below tapped the ceiling. He found the noise from their televisions equally annoying but this was deemed to be acceptable by the people running the properties.

Under pressure from landlords or landladies he usually agreed to type until a certain hour every night. Then he'd put his typewriter away until the next day. If he still felt like writing he'd do so in longhand, using capital letters so that he could read his work the next day.

Drunk men rarely wrote legibly and he was no exception. If he didn't use capitals his writing resembled the proverbial spider crawling across a page. That was one reason he used them. His poems and stories often had people roaring at one another so that was another one. Arguments in his stories are often punctuated by many exclamation points and lines of abuse from both parties. One imagines Bukowski getting rid of a lot of his own anger in these types of stories. It was the kind of thing he had to listen to from his father in Longwood Avenue growing up.

The only other times he had to write in longhand was when his typewriter was in the pawnshop. That usually happened when he ran out of money and he needed a drink. At times like this he carted his machine to the nearest pawnbroker and hocked it for a pittance. You couldn't drink typewriter keys. He was glad to hand the machine over for the precious few dollars he got to slake his thirst. When he got a job he'd buy it back. And so the process continued. He never grudged losing money on such transactions. They were lifesavers to him.

**Pawnshops often came to Bukowski's rescue
when he had no other source of income.**

If he was too noisy in his drinking he might be ejected from whatever premises he inhabited. Or he might be ejected from failure to pay the rent. That tended to happen whenever a job fell through, or he walked out of one.

Jobs meant nothing to him other than getting the dollar. He could never understand the concept of a career. The idea that somebody would actually look forward to going to work, that it could be in any way fulfilling, was impossible for him to comprehend. His father swore by work and that was part of the reason he revolted against it. Too many people were nailed to empty processes, empty rituals.

Some jobs he left of his own accord. Others he was sacked from, either due to drinking too much or going AWOL. He became surprised if they lasted.

He always looked for the human side of a job, a friendly hand or someone with an interesting story. But he rarely approached people. If they approached *him* he was civil but distant. Nobody would have known all the thoughts that were going on in his head.

He tried to get through to people at a level beyond what they were doing, to get them to keep a distance from the work.

One company he worked for was called Sunbeam. One day when he was bored he started shouting out the word 'sunbeam.' Pretty soon everyone else joined in. They stopped working at whatever conveyor belt they were at and yelled out, 'Sunbeam!' Bukowski felt he'd achieved something. He'd liberated them in a way.

They clapped their hands and called the word out in unison, making fun of it and celebrating it at the same time. It made him feel good. But the following day they were back to themselves. It didn't affect their lives. They were still wage slaves and so was he.

Bosses roared at him to make their presence felt, or maybe simply to justify their existence. Sometimes they made up reasons to get rid of him if they didn't like him. It reminded him of his father all over again. He felt they were often using him as a punching bag for their own frustrations. The more power they had, he thought, the emptier they were inside.

America had become involved in World War II by now. Bukowski was blithely indifferent to his adoptive country's retaliation to the Pearl Harbor bombing.

He refused to join in with the national hatred of Hitler. Maybe he even had a sneaking affection for 'the man with the toothbrush mustache,' as he called him.

The 'evil Hun' was too easy a target for the self-righteous outrage of breast-beating patriots. Germany was his mother country, after all. There was also a lot for him to identify with in Hitler – his outcast status, his hatred for his father, the fact that all the 'stars and stripes' people he knew despised him.

His enemy's enemy was his friend. The fact that Hitler tried to take over the world – and gassed six million Jews – seemed to have been pushed to the back of his mind, or put out of it altogether.

He had an ability to dispense with conventional logic when it suited him. He took part of an argument and made it into the whole one. He would argue black was white just to be different. Hitler was a hate figure so therefore he made him into his hero or pretended hero. That got up peoples backs, especially the backs of smug people. All of this fed into his need to be different, contentious, politically incorrect before that term was invented.

Bukowski had Nazi leanings in his youth.

The war was very far away from this unconscientious objector. He didn't feel like taking up arms to fight an unknown enemy when there were so many known ones around. He hated listening to his father bleating on about things like 'national duty' and so on. His only duty, as he saw it, was towards his own survival. The war was already taking place on his own doorstep, in his own mind. He didn't need to enlist in the army to find it. He liked to quote Fante, 'The only war I care to fight is the one I start myself.'

He didn't object to killing a man, he wrote in his short story 'Life in a Texas Whorehouse,' but he wasn't keen on sleeping in a barracks with a bunch of smelly soldiers who snored. That would have been harder. Killing people in a war situation wasn't courageous, he claimed, because it was legal. He had more respect for those who killed outside that comfort zone. It took guts because there were repercussions.

Being anti-war in the forties, as he pointed out, was different to Jane Fonda wiggling her ass against a tank in Vietnam a couple of decades later. 'They looked on me as a cockroach,' he said, 'I was before my time.'

No matter what political persuasion he espoused, however, he had to hold down jobs. In 1941 he worked at the South Pacific Railway Company cleaning railcars. The following year he drove a truck for the Red Cross in San Francisco. He worked at all sorts of jobs over the next number of years, from a dog biscuit factory to a New York subway where he hung posters. He also worked in a meat packing plant, and he was a shipping clerk in a ladies' dress wear store.

Every now and then he returned home from his travels. Sometimes when he got there he discovered to his horror that he was being charged for his room and board. During one trip home he was dismayed to learn that his father told the neighbors he'd been conscripted and then killed in action. He was more amused than shocked at the revelation.

A more dramatic event unfolded in his life at this time. When he went to Philadelphia in 1942 he was arrested for alleged draft-dodging, having failed to advise the draft board of where he was living. He'd left a forwarding address at the local post office but he was moving so much this wasn't much use.

Two FBI agents pounced on him one night out of the blue. He was listening to Brahms when the doorbell rang. Classical music always soothed him, providing temporary solace from a life that always threatened to spiral out of control.

'What do you want?' he asked them, not being used to visitors. When they said they were from the FBI he became interested. What were they looking for?

When they told him they were taking him 'downtown' his imagination went into overdrive. It was like a line from a movie. He wondered what he'd done to land himself in this pickle. Had he murdered somebody while drunk and then forgot about it? Anything was possible. As he was being led out the door, one of the other tenants shouted out, 'That horrible man — they've got him at last!'

The arresting officers were amazed at his casualness. It was the same coolness the doctor treating him for acne noticed when he went under the needle all those years ago.

What surprised them most of all as they took him to the precinct was that he didn't ask them what his offence was. They didn't realize that being jailed was hardly a threat to a man for whom liberty meant so little. It might almost have been a novelty for him.

He was sent to Moyamensing, a minimum security holding facility in Philadelphia. His cellmate was a notorious criminal called Courtney Taylor. He referred to himself as 'Public Enemy No.1.' Bukowski thought he had a screw loose.

At his trial Taylor had asked the judge for an extra eight years to be added to his sentence. 'They locked me up with a looney,' Bukowski said, 'because they thought I was one. Maybe they were right.'

Before long they were betting with one another about how many bedbugs each could catch. Taylor won with eighteen but Bukowski later discovered he'd cheated. He only caught nine but broke them in half to make them count for double. .

In the course of one of their conversations Taylor starting talking about suicide. He told Bukowski the best way to kill himself if he felt so inclined was to stand in a slop bucket and put his hand in the light socket. 'Thanks,' Bukowski said, 'I'll remember that.'

Moyamensing Holding Facility, where Bukowski was detained for alleged draft-dodging in 1942

After seventeen days in custody the prison authorities came to the conclusion that Bukowski hadn't willfully tried to dodge the draft. They now sent him to an induction center to be examined. He did a physical test there and then a psychiatrist quizzed him. He asked him a few routine questions, and then an unusual one. He said he was having a party at his house, at which there would be artists, writers, scientists and lawyers. Would Bukowski be interested in going? 'No,' he replied flatly.

The psychiatrist thought this showed evidence of maladjustment. He told Bukowski he wasn't going to be called up for active service in the army. Bukowski was delighted. If one could be relieved of military duty on such a flimsy pretext as the unwillingness to attend a party, he thought, three-quarters of the American population would probably have said no to such a request. He said afterwards, 'It was a trick question. I knew what he was doing so I decided to play him at his own game. I gave him mixed signals. I said I'd be happy to go to war because I wanted to die but I wouldn't go to his party because I didn't like socializing. I made him think I was nuts.'

It's more likely the psychiatrist was toying with him here, having already decided he was mentally unstable. In his book *Bukowski in Pictures*, Howard Sounes claimed it was simply his physical condition that made him unsuitable for service. This is possible but it doesn't make as interesting reading as the party story. The most surprising aspect of the whole business was that they didn't quiz him further on his Nazi views. (They'd found *Mein Kampf* in his room when they went through his books).

Bukowski always said that if he'd been sent to the frontlines he'd have killed if necessary. Not from any high-sounding principles but simply because that was what he would have been asked to do. If Uncle Sam said go, he would have gone. He was too indifferent to rebel. He preferred to do nothing. Playing dumb about the war – he said he didn't know the difference between Hitler and Hercules - was his insult to everything it represented. It couldn't hurt him because he refused to think about it.

Released from custody he embraced drinking with a newfound passion. He didn't see himself as an alcoholic because he was able to hold down jobs between binges.

He was also able to write in a drunken condition. To him that meant he didn't have a drink 'problem' as people generally understood that term.

Those who witnessed his intake at this time of his life thought he was doing his best to end it. It was almost like a vocation for him. He often got into fights in bars, waking up the following morning in alleyways wondering how he'd got there. Children poked him with sticks, trying to figure out if he was dead or alive. Dogs sniffed at his feet. Truck drivers pulled up before him and roared at him to get out of their way. It was a miracle one of them didn't run him over.

Some of the fights he engaged in were merely to provide entertainment to those watching, people who needed any excuse at all to keep from going home. Others were simply to get free drinks. Brawlers were 'rewarded' by their audiences. It was never a question of winning these fights as far as he was concerned. He participated in them out of some quasi-macho duty. Besides, what did drunks do for kicks except beat each other's brains out?

This was how they earned their right to the bar stool. Looked at from another point of view, fighting acted as a surrogate form of sex for him. Or at least took his mind off it. It also fed into his idea that life was absurd. When he was getting his head crushed up against the edge of some urinal, he said, he saw the fights as humorous things, sick jokes.

He thought he was better at taking a punch than giving one. Maybe that was because of his small hands. He was always embarrassed about these. He could soak up punishment but he didn't think his left hook – or his right cross – were all that good. He was generally surprised when he won a fight.

That would usually happen if he caught the other guy with a sucker punch he wasn't expecting. When he lost them he was bought drinks but when he won he was ignored, or even told to leave the bar in question. If he was badly beaten the drink acted as an anesthetic – or a sleeping pill.

When he woke up after such fights he often found he'd been 'rolled.' He was an easy target for pickpockets when he was out cold.

Sometimes, in anticipation of this, he hid his money in his shoes. If he was with a woman he also did that. They tended to find it when he took them off before going to bed with them. The kind of women he went to bed with often stole his money as he slept. They were usually older than him. They fell into a pattern: 'Saggy stockings, rouged cheeks, deathly mascara, yellow-toothed, rat-eyed, bellowing hyena laughter.'

He took them because they were society's leftovers, the ones nobody wanted. They went back to tawdry motels with him and a familiar scenario unfolded: 'A fifth on the dresser, a little talk, a kind of dead fuck, then more drink, more easy talk, then another fuck.'

Afterwards he would fall asleep. In the small hours of the morning they helped themselves to whatever he had. Usually it wasn't much - unless they got him on payday. In later years people robbed his books when he was asleep – or drunk – but now it was his wads of cash, the precious billfolds set aside for the next night's drinking.

.

When he woke up, the women would be gone. That in itself was usually a sign. The first thing he'd do after he looked around the empty room was to check the back pocket of his trousers to confirm his suspicions. They were usually justified. When he went back to the bar where he would have picked them up they were rarely there. They'd go under cover until the heat wore off.

Then a few weeks later they'd turn up without warning. 'Hi baby,' they'd say, 'How ya been?' as if nothing happened. And he'd take them back into his life again.

Sometimes the rooming-houses he stayed in were broken into. He lost his money that way too, at least if he didn't bring all he had out with him wherever he went. If he didn't he had to think of places to hide it when he was out - in a book, behind a shelf, even under the carpet. One time he didn't have enough money to pay the rent and he didn't know what he was going to do so he went out for a walk to try and think of something. When he came back the landlady rushed up to him and said, 'I have some good news for you. I found your money!' What happened was that she'd found a wad of notes under the carpet in his room when she was vacuuming the floor. He'd left it there when he was drunk and forgotten all about it.

Another time he drank so much that when he left the bar he forgot the location of the rooming-house where he was staying at the time. He walked up and down various streets in a panic as he had no address for it. All the buildings looked the same. It could have been any of them, he thought, on any of the streets. He tried to think of some identifying thing about his lodgings but he couldn't. Everything he owned in the world was in that room – his clothes, his money, his typewriter. Eventually he thought he saw the building but he wasn't sure. He ran in the door and up the stairs and bounded down the corridor to his room.

As soon as he opened the door he knew he was in the right place. When he saw his cardboard case on the bed he breathed a huge sigh of relief. There was a half-filled bottle of wine on the locker beside his bed and he looked at it almost with love. He slugged it back like someone who hadn't had a drink for months. He was happy to lie down on the bed and swig it with nobody to bother him and nothing to worry about. Life was good.

In 1944 he had his first story published. Appropriately enough it was in a magazine called *Story*. Its title was appropriate too: 'Aftermath of a Lengthy Rejection Slip.' Whit Burnett was the editor. He'd sent back all of Bukowski's other efforts but he was always encouraging to him, suggesting ways he might improve what he sent. 'Even getting a reply in those days was a bonus,' Bukowski said, 'Most of the editors didn't bother.'

He got excited when he saw the magazine on a stand: his name was finally in print. But his excitement was short-lived. When he riffled through the pages he realized Burnett had relegated him to the end of the magazine rather than having him at the beginning of it, where he expected to be. This disappointed him but the fire had been lit. He had, as they say, become bitten by the bug.

The story caught the attention of a literary agent who contacted him after reading it. She wrote to him telling him she loved the story and wanted to meet him with a view to representing him. He knew that wouldn't have been a good idea. He hadn't lived enough: 'She'd have made me write some drivel shit,' he said. He wrote back to her saying, 'Dear Madam, I'm not ready.' He knew he hadn't the right 'stuff' in him to craft a literary career just yet. If he started one too soon he knew he'd have ended up trying to make something out of nothing.

World War 11 ended in 1945. That didn't mean much to him. Johnny came marching home again to the adoration of his loved ones. For Bukowski that was bad news. Now there wouldn't be as many jobs available. If he didn't work he wouldn't have any money to drink.

He was happier during the war than after it for a number of reasons. 'Nothing was the same after the war,' he said once. Food didn't taste as good. Drink didn't taste as good. Everything seemed to be turned to plastic.

He went back to Philadelphia. 'They called it the city of brotherly love,' he said, 'but I found it to be slightly different to that.' When he got there he booked into a cheap rooming-house, as was his practice. Then he went for a drink – as was also his practice. He wasn't long there when a fight broke out. One man said to another, 'You do that again and I'll kill you.'' It was only lunchtime and bottles were sailing over his head.

The two men started sparring. He had to go between them to get to the toilet. As he did so he said, 'Pardon me, gentlemen.' They stopped for a second. When he came back from the toilet they were still fighting. Again he said, 'Pardon me, gentlemen' as he made his way through them. They stopped to let him through and then started again. Bukowski thought to himself: 'This is my kind of place, this is my nirvana. I don't ever want to leave it.'

He went back to the bar the following night to see some more action but nothing happened. There was no fight. The next night he went back again but nothing happened then either. For a long period of time he kept going back and kept being disappointed. He felt trapped by his anticipation: 'It was as if the fight was set up to get me interested.'

He started a routine of going there early so there'd be no problem getting in. The bartender usually admitted him in at 5 a.m., two hours before the official opening time. He gave him free drinks for those two hours. When he opened the doors to the public, Bukowski became a paying customer like the rest. The two-hour gap gave him a head start on the other drinkers and that was the way he liked it.

The bar smelt of 'piss and death.' It was so run down, he said, one night when a prostitute came in to do business the customers felt honored. He liked sitting there watching the optics, watching the backs of people's heads, getting occasional free drinks from the other customers. 'I never ate. I went down from 190 pounds to 130. I was the joke, the discard the madman. The bartender used to fight me at his leisure when he needed a scarecrow to slap around.'

One day he decided to check out a rougher bar in the area. (Definitions of what constituted 'rough' had to be re-evaluated with Bukowski). When he got inside he saw a woman sitting at the counter and they started talking. She told him her favorite song was 'Her Tears Flowed Like Wine'. He said he liked it too. There was a juke-box in the bar so he said he was going to put on a song for her. He put a nickel into it and it came on.

As they sat there listening to it a man who was sitting with another man at the end of the bar came up to him. 'That's my bosses' girlfriend,' he said, 'Do you know what that means?' Bukowski said he didn't. The man said, 'It means get your ass out of here.'

Bukowski ignored him. He continued singing 'Her Tears Flowed Like Wine.' A few minutes later he had to go to the toilet. When he was standing at the urinal the man who warned him to stay away from the woman came up behind him. He struck him across the head. Bukowski spouted blood. He fell to the ground in pain. When it died down a bit he sat up and examined the wound. It didn't look too bad. The man was still standing there beside him. He said to him, 'Is that the best you can do?' Then he stood up and went out the door, leaving the man behind him.

He went back to the woman who was sitting at the counter. 'Jesus!' she said, looking at his head, 'What happened to you?' 'It's nothing,' he said, 'just a little accident.' The man who struck came back to the bar. He looked at Bukowski as if he couldn't believe what he was seeing. He shook his head in disbelief and went back to his friend.

The strange thing about the story is that Bukowski wasn't really interested in the woman at all. He just wanted to prove to the hood that he wasn't afraid of him. The woman left the bar soon afterwards. Bukowski continued singing 'Her Tears Flowed Like Wine.'

After a while the hood came over to him with his friend. He said to Bukowski, 'We love you. You're a madman. You're beautiful.' He told him he belonged to the biggest gang in Philadelphia and that he wanted Bukowski in it. 'You're just what we need,' he said. Bukowski looked at him hard and said, 'I don't fuck with that kind of shit.' All the man could do was laugh. Then Bukowski went off to hospital to have his head stitched. After he was bandaged up he went back to the bar again but the men were gone by now.

This was one of the most concerted periods of drinking in Bukowski's life, and it had some competition in that department. He liked the bar because he never knew what was going to happen in it on a given night. Even if there weren't fights like that first night, or hoods coming up to him threatening his life, it was still unpredictable. One night he set his pants on fire after dropping ash on them from a cigarette. Another time a beautiful woman came in and started cutting her face with a razor. He learned afterwards that she killed herself

.

Cigarettes and beer were necessities for him at this time of his life. Food, by contrast, was something of a luxury. There were times he was so hungry he would have eaten the leg off a table. Drink took his mind off food in the same way as it took his mind off everything else.

He often said he didn't write during this period of his life but in later years some magazines from the time surfaced which show that he did. Sometimes he went without food in order to be able to afford the stamps he used to send his work to editors.

The next story he had published was in a magazine called *Portfolio*. He was proud of it, so proud that one night when he got drunk he showed it to some of the people he was drinking with. They stood outside the bar going, 'Gee, Hank, you use beautiful words.'

When a wind got up it blew the pages out of his hands and down the street. They ran after them. They were all over the road. A window washer put his muddy boot on one of the pages, shouting out delightedly, 'I have it!' All Bukowski could do was laugh.

'Let it go,' he said, 'Let them all go.'

He realized it was a mistake to mix his two worlds, one of the many mistakes he'd made when he got drunk. He'd had a momentary taste of grandeur but afterwards, he thought, they viewed him differently. He couldn't be totally spontaneous with them or they with him. A line had been drawn in the sand, a division created.

The *Portfolio* story had him in good company as two of the other contributors were Jean-Paul Sartre and Henry Miller. Caresse Crosby was the editor.

She wrote to Bukowski and said, 'Who are you?'

Bukowski wrote back, 'I do not know who I am.'

He was playing the role of the existentialist hero. It was like something Dostoevsky might have said, or Kafka, or Sartre. He was starting to cast himself in the guise of his literary heroes.

Even though he was living like a hobo he still read prestigious literary magazines like *Harpers* and *Atlantic Monthly*. He was aghast at what passed for quality fiction in them.

The writers they published, he thought, had all the staleness of those who'd never sucked on the pap of life, who became established figures by refusing to take chances. Bukowski believed writing was like everything else: a con game where people couldn't tell the difference between good and bad because they were so terrified of saying anything different to everybody else.

Editors told him to tone down his style but he found if he did that the life-blood went out of it. (He also found out that was what the editors wanted). He decided to keep doing what felt right, regardless of whether it found favor with the people he submitted it to. If you wrote the way people told you to, it was time to call it a day.

Sometimes he felt like doing just that because most of the poems and stories he sent out tended to come back to him. He didn't know what his problem was. Or what the editors' problems were. One thing was sure, though. It was unlikely he'd break through. He imagined he'd continue to drink heavily and be unpublished until one day he was found dead in a rooming-house somewhere, surrounded by wine bottles.

He reached his nadir in a tar paper shack in Atlanta that had neither light nor heat. Here he lived for a month on nothing but bread and candy bars. The rent was $1.25 a week. This gives us some inkling of the conditions. He stole an apple from a fruit stand one day when he couldn't afford to pay for it but he was caught and he had to give it back.

He wrote begging letters to editors, asking them to send him even a small amount of money to help him keep body and soul together. It was the first and last time he would subject himself to such humiliation. No matter how many times Bukowski was on 'the row', he had dignity in that regard, preferring to sink or swim on his own steam. It was out of character for him, but nonetheless a learning experience. It confirmed him in his basic belief about the selfishness of people.

Bukowski reached the end of his tether in a tar shack in Atlanta

One of the letters was to Caresse Crosby, who'd published him in *Portfolio*. He was surprised she wrote back to him because none of the other people he approached had done so. It was a very cold day. He tore the envelope open expecting great things from her. She said it was good to hear from him. *Portfolio* was now finished, she said, and at the present time she was living in a castle in Italy, having decided to devote her life to the poor. Bukowski shook the letter to see if there was any money in it but there wasn't. He was freezing and starving. Was he not one of the poor?

He also wrote to his father asking him for something to help him out, but all he got back was a letter from him saying that Bukowski actually owed *him* money. He went on to say it was time he stopped being a bum and got a decent job rather than frittering his life away in the sewer. The hectoring that had been driving him crazy in Longwood Avenue was now continuing - even at this geographical remove. He had to read the letter a few times to take in what he was seeing in front of his eyes. He couldn't even afford paper to write his poems on at this point of his life. He was composing them on the edges of newspapers with pencil stubs. He was in Knut Hamsun territory, just one step away from destitution, and he was expected to listen to the same old tune from his old man. He tore the letter up.

Days passed by, confirming him in his belief that nothing good lay over the horizon for him. He'd continue to starve and to be rebuffed by editors. Talent wasn't enough. Rejection slips would be as inevitable as the next sunrise, the next sunset. Readers didn't want truth. All they wanted was confirmation of their prejudices, their lazy presumptions. Preferably from the already established.

Life was a trap. He'd always known that. People's freedom, he said once, stopped when they reached the age of four. That was when they were slotted into their first system, a system that drained all the life-blood out of them. School threw down the first gauntlet. Jobs followed. Each stage progressively made you weaker until eventually there was nothing left to fight for. You could break the stranglehold by walking away but if you did that you were probably just going from one form of hell to another. In Atlanta, Bukowski felt that he was actually *in* hell. His future was going to be nothing more than 'suicide mornings and park bench nights.'

He went home soon afterwards. He feared he might be going from the frying pan into the fire but he didn't think he had any other option.

His mother was glad to see him but his father was as gruff as ever. Bukowski was hardly in the door when he started bleating on about the war that had just ended and how wonderful an army the Americans had that proved it could defeat Hitler. It was an army he'd been in himself, which made him doubly proud of it.

His conscription had something else to recommend it as well, he pointed out. 'If it hadn't been for the war,' he said to Bukowski, 'I wouldn't have met your mother and you wouldn't have been born.' Bukowski replied, 'You make that sound like a good thing.' There was a time he would have been beaten for a comment like that, or made sleep in the garage. No longer. They were like mirror-images of one another now, both equally adept at sarcasm. Bukowski had learned it from a good teacher.

Bukowski beefed up his bohemian side at this point of his life. One day he had himself photographed hanging onto the edge of a train as if this was a habit of his, jumping trains like Jack Kerouac or Jack London. Another photograph taken of him around this time tells a truer story. It has him spruced up in a white suit looking like a dandy as he stands outside his home. This was in the middle of a period he often referred to as his 'ten year drunk.' His future friend and biographer Neeli Cherkovski believed he liked his home – and his parents - much more than he pretended. 'Those rough tough types,' he said, 'often turn out to be Mama's boys.'

Bukowski would hardly have agreed with that estimation. Tensions continued with his father, escalating when he claimed authorship of a further story of Bukowski's that was published in *Portfolio* in 1947. It carried the byline Henry Bukowski, which was his father's name as well. The deceit was easy. Bukowski was disgusted by this latest piece of fraud. It reminded him of the invisible job his father manufactured some years before when he was out of work but still 'drove' to work. He left home in disgust, changing his writing name from Henry to Charles afterwards so it wouldn't happen again.

He rented a cheap apartment in the area. His aimless life continued. One night in 1948 when he was in the red light district of Alvarado Street he walked into a bar and spotted the woman who would form a huge part of his life for the next fourteen years: Jane Cooney Baker.

She was sitting at the counter. She was, he would write later, 'almost beautiful, almost young.' She had a protruding stomach. He described her as 'a dirty blonde.' The first thing that struck him about her was her legs. Bukowski was always a leg man. He loved looking at women when they hiked their skirt up around their waist to show more of them, or when they were getting into cars and exposed their thighs as they sat into the seat. Her shoes had heels like daggers on them. She struck him as someone who'd been 'roughed over by life.'

He asked her what she did for a living. 'I drink,' she replied. She sounded like his kind of person. 'You have beautiful eyes,' she said to him. He felt it was a corny comment but he was still glad she said it. Compliments had been thin on the ground for him up to now. Maybe his luck was about to turn.

They spent the evening getting drunk. As they were walking out the door together, the barman said to Bukowski, 'If anyone can tame her, you can.' He accepted the vote of confidence. They bought some bourbon and took it back to his place. When they got there they settled down for a long night's drinking. Jane sat down on his sofa, crossing the long legs that caught his attention in the bar. He looked hard at her. 'I'm going to fuck you,' he said. She took up her glass. 'Drink from the bottle,' he said. 'No,' she said, 'I don't like to be told what to do.' She took it up and made as if to throw it at him. 'If you throw that,' he said, 'Make sure you hit me with it and knock me out. Otherwise it's coming back at you.' She put the bottle down. They went to bed.

**This is the only known photograph of
Jane Cooney Baker.   It was taken when she was at school in
New Mexico. (Roswell High School)**

Soon afterwards they started living together. He heard rumors that she was a hooker but he doubted it — mainly because she was always broke. But he was under no illusions that she had sex with many other men after drink — or even *for* it.

She was lit up by a kind of decadent radiance for him. She seemed to have had a history. She looked like a woman who'd been someone once. She was ten years older than him. He wondered what kind of life she'd led. He tried to get her to talk about her past but she clammed up whenever he asked her about it. He suspected she was blocking something. Was there more to her than met the eye? He noticed she slept with a rosary under her pillow. What was all that about? She didn't strike him as the religious type. It didn't seem to sit with her lifestyle.

They paid a week's rent in advance at the first place they stayed but they didn't even last that long there. Within a few days a fight broke out between them. Furniture went flying in all directions. The landlady was shocked at the noise. She came up to their room and told them they'd have to move. They didn't seem unduly bothered. The following morning they were evicted. 'I thought you were decent people,' the landlady said as she sent them packing. 'We are,' Jane replied, 'You just never got to know it.' A few weeks later they went back to the same place looking to rent it again. The landlady was aghast. They were so drunk they hadn't even remembered being thrown out of it.

Together they rolled from apartment to apartment posing as husband and wife. Jane's beer belly was taken for that of a pregnant woman. It made the charade of marriage easy to negotiate. Landladies were sympathetic to them, thinking they had 'a little 'un' on the way.

One night Jane opened up to Bukowski about her past. She told him she'd grown up in Roswell, New Mexico. Her father was an army doctor. He died when she was a child so her mother had to go out to work. She didn't have the time to devote to Jane so she put her into an orphanage. Jane didn't take well to this. She was a free spirit and she bridled against the confinement. Whenever it got too much for her she broke out. In time she developed a reputation for going off the rails.

After leaving school she became pregnant by a man called Craig Baker. She had two children by him. He was a heavy drinker and after a while he got her in on it too. When his business collapsed they moved in with her mother. This wasn't a good move. They argued more often than not and the relationship broke down. A divorce followed. Now he hit the bottle even harder. One night when he was drinking especially heavily he was involved in a bad car accident and died as a result. Jane blamed herself. She thought the failure of the marriage had made him self-destructive. Ironically, she now started to become self-destructive herself. She stopped caring about her appearance and started to drink as much as he had. As a result, her children drifted away from her. This upset her more than anything. She moved to California and became a 'loose' woman.

Bukowski sympathized with her plight but he wasn't a sentimentalist. 'That was then,' he told her, 'and this is now.' She expected more empathy than that from him. They continued to argue and to drink. Jane gave as good as she got in such arguments. Sometimes their fights landed them in jail. Each of them bailed the other one out on different occasions. In bars they behaved audaciously. She dared him to do outrageous things like break windows by throwing bottles at them. When he was in the mood for devilment he acceded to her wishes. Getting thrown out of bars was simply another thrill. Drinking at home was just as good.

They accumulated many bottles in the places they stayed. Sometimes they drove out at the dead of night to get rid of them in case they proved to be an embarrassment when their room was being serviced. They threw the bottles into dumps into ditches, into garbage disposal units. Sometimes they just flung them out the window of the car and watched them shattering into pieces. Then they went home to sleep off their 'excitement.'

Jane was wild in bed. That completed the concept of an ideal woman for Bukowski, especially since he was sex-starved when he met her. More importantly, she was the first woman who ever looked at him without being aware of his complexion problems. 'What do you think of my face?' he asked her one night. 'If you mean the acne,' she said, 'I don't see it.' That impressed him.

They promised one another they'd launch a crusade against the world. She got through to him at a deep emotional level and also became the template for many of his literary creations. She would become Betty in *Post Office*, Laura in *Factotum,* Wanda in *Barfly.*

One of the jobs he got when he was with her was in a hotel but, like most of his jobs, it didn't last long. He was sacked for allegedly imprisoning the assistant manager in the men's room. He had no recollection of the incident. After that he got a job at a bicycle company. He was usually late for work because Jane liked to have sex in the mornings. 'What's the problem?' his boss said to him one day when he came in late. 'I'm on my honeymoon,' Bukowski told him. 'Then go back to it,' the boss suggested. He did.

He got another job picking cotton. It entailed a dawn rise. That meant he had to set a clock for one of the first times in his life. It wasn't easy because the spring on the one they had was broken. When he re-adjusted it, the minute hand went crazy. One day he arrived at the farm in the middle of the night. He didn't know what time it was. He thought it was strange that there was nobody else there. He was just coming off a binge and imagined it was about 8 a.m.

Jane enjoyed his eccentricity but they still fought, usually about stupid things. One of their arguments involved a transistor radio Jane owned. She played it so much it drove Bukowski crazy. He tried everything he could to make her stop but she wouldn't. One day, in desperation, he hurled it through the window. It landed on the grass outside and to his amazement, continued to play. Jane got a great kick out of that. 'You see?' she said, 'It likes me. It doesn't like you so it's defying you.' A few days later he threw it out the window again but it still continued to play. No matter how many windows he flung it through in the following weeks, he couldn't break it. Eventually he gave up. He called it 'a magic radio, a radio with guts.'

Each time he broke a window he'd take it off its hinges and bring it down town to be repaired. When the man was working on it, Jane would bring the radio back up to their room and turn it up loud to annoy him. Bukowski eventually had to accept it was there to stay.

Bukowski and Jane lived in their own world. Blithely oblivious to the behavior of everyone around them. One night as they sat in a hotel room drinking, Bukowski started talking about his writing. He told Jane he was an undiscovered genius. She said, 'No, Hank, you're just an asshole.' He threw his head back laughing. He never cared what she thought of him.

The phone rang then. He yelled into it, 'I'm a genius and no one knows it!' It was the desk clerk. He told Bukowski he was keeping all the other guests awake, that he'd been warned before and he wasn't going to get another warning. Then Jane took the receiver. 'I'm a genius too,' she roared, 'and I'm the only whore who knows it!' The two of them started chortling and the clerk hung up. Bukowski said to Jane, 'The cops will be here soon.' She said, 'I know.' They decided to take action. They put the chain on the door. Then they barricaded the sofa against it.

The police arrived soon afterwards. They heard footsteps coming up the stairs. 'This is the L.A. Police Department,' said a voice, 'Open up.' They didn't move, staying quieter than they'd ever stayed before. They didn't say anything until they felt sure they were gone. Then they crept over to the window and looked out. Everything looked still. The squad car was facing the other way and that made them feel safe. Then it drove off. Success. They knew they had at least one more night to spend in the hotel.

They sat sipping their wine. They looked out the window at two neon signs across the way. One said, 'Jesus Saves.'

The other was a large red bird that flapped its wings seven times. After the seventh flap a sign came up saying, 'Signal Gasoline.' They watched it for ages, counting the flaps until the sign lit up the sky. For years afterwards Bukowski looked back on nights like this with fondness, immortalizing them in his poems and stories. To quote Charles Dickens, 'It was the best of times, it was the worst of times.'

Jane didn't work much. She got occasional jobs but they didn't last long. Bukowski didn't mind supporting her. He had a protective attitude to her. She was his 'raven with a broken wing.' Whenever she wanted a bath in the evenings he used to heat up the tub for her. Sometimes she slept with other men, which led to ferocious rows between them. Anyone willing to ply her with drink for a given evening - when Bukowski couldn't afford to - seemed fair game.

Jane drifted into a part of him that he'd once been too inhibited to disclose to anyone. He laid bare his insecurities to her, his neuroses and his fears. There was no game-playing in the relationship, no striking of poses. They were just two people looking for a good time on lean resources. It was like two negatives making a positive. They had nothing so they had nothing to lose. Loving her was easier than anything Bukowski had ever done before. He slotted into her life like a hand into a glove and she reciprocated. All she asked of him was that he allow her to drink without giving out to her — an irony considering his past. He imagined he'd leave her at the starting-gates in this department but it ended up being the other way round. He'd finally met his match when it came to bending the elbow. And it was a woman. Where was his machismo now?

Drink afforded him what he called a 'necessary release.' It also released his muse. The writers he knew didn't understand that when they told him booze would kill him young. He felt this wasn't true, that the absence of it would kill him quicker. Without it he would have died from apathy. It was the beer that wrote the books. He was merely the funnel through which it operated.

From the time he met Jane he drank with more dedication than somebody pursuing a career ambition. It wasn't so much binges as a concerted policy. The consistency of his intake would have killed lesser men before they got to thirty.

He drank to maintain his sanity in the face of jobs he abhorred. Drink also helped him cope with the depression that hit him when he thought he wasn't going to be able to make it with his writing. The majority of poets around him, he claimed, were 'sucking on their own tits and crying for mama.' Their work was full of the kind of suffering that destroyed poetry, turning it into a self-serving set of angst-ridden diatribes. The neuroses of these writers, for Bukowski, came from the fact that their mothers fed them on the right breast instead of the left one.

Their contrived agony made him sick to the core of himself. He knew you couldn't put a rope around pain. That made it synthetic. He thought a lot of their suffering was fabricated. He could never write that way himself. (How could he after working in a slaughterhouse?) If this was the sort of thing that was being successful he was out of the game.

He knew poets who started off magazines publishing their friends. Then the friends published *them.* One hand washed the other. It was a literary form of incest. Nobody bought the magazines without having a vested interest in doing so. It was no surprise to him that so many of them folded up due to lack of contributors. The only way they'd have lasted, he said, was if the editors had very large families.

Even worse were those sad souls who deemed themselves so superior to the literary magazines that they didn't even bother sending their poems to them. They were happy to read them to fellow losers at workshops. A mutual congratulation society took root.

Such glad-handing went on everywhere. Even the great Hemingway succumbed to it. Hadn't he used Sherwood Anderson and Gertrude Stein to get to the top? Not to mention Scott Fitzgerald, who quipped after he fell out with him, 'Ernest was always willing to lend a helping hand to the man above him on the ladder.'

The main problem with writers, he believed, was that they had an insane believe in their worth. Such belief was usually in inverse proportion to their talent. They sucked on flattery like oxygen, needing the 'brotherhood' of literary gatherings to buttress it. None of this would have helped Bukowski at the typer. He had to work alone. 'The worst thing for a writer,' he declared, 'is to know another writer. And worse than that, to know a *number* of other writers. They're like flies on the same turd.'

Poets who pursued academic careers were even worse. They became emasculated, feminized, stiffed. They took the safe road. Pretty soon they started writing poetry that could have been produced by a computer. On the odd occasion that they got graphic they had to use a big word for it: existential. They were Eliot's Hollow Men: they'd measured out their lives in coffee spoons.

Bukowski didn't really like Eliot. He preferred Ezra Pound. One of his favorite books at this time was Ezra Pound's *Cantos*. Jane got to hate it. When he walked in with it one day she said,

'Don't say it's those damn *Cantos* again.' He said, 'Jane, we can't fuck *all* the time.'

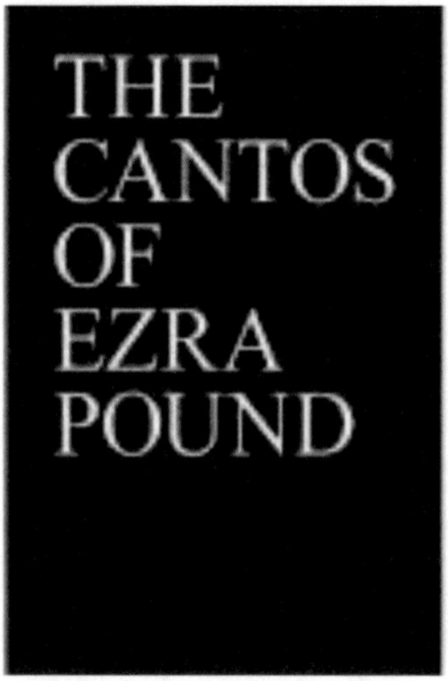

THE
CANTOS
OF
EZRA
POUND

Reading gave him peace just like writing did, or listening to classical music. Or drinking. To sit on a barstool and look at the ceiling was as pleasing to him as travelling the world might be to someone else. In this sense he was a simple man. In a bar he could dream like the waiter from Hemingway's 'A Clean, Well-Lighted Place,' without having to worry about his father grabbing him by the scruff of the neck and telling him to mow the grass.

That isn't to say he was blissfully happy at this time of his life. In his dark moods he thought about ending it all. In one of his stories he wrote about an attempt to gas himself to death failing because he woke up with a headache. 'The automatic pilot on the stove wasn't working,' he wrote, 'or that little flame would have blasted me right out of my precious little season in hell.' Another time he was so tempted to stab himself to death with a butcher knife. He had to grab on to the mattress of his bed with both hands to avert disaster.

One day when he was feeling suicidal he went for a walk. On a newspaper stand he saw a headline saying, 'Milton Berle's Cousin Hit on Head by Falling Rock.'

He started laughing. How could he kill himself after seeing a headline like that? Its farcical nature put him into a good mood. He stole the paper and brought it back to Jane. She enjoyed it as much as he had. The pair of them laughed until they were almost sick. They decided to get drunk to celebrate their good mood. (Any excuse would do). 'Milton Berle's cousin saved my life,' Bukowski said afterwards.

In 1952 he became a mail carrier. He'd been one briefly in 1950 when the Christmas rush provided short-term employment to pay for some outstanding bills – and some equally important liquid intakes. Now, eighteen months later, it became a full-time job. Bukowski hated most of his jobs but at least this one kept him moving and away from routine.

It also threw him into contact with a cross-section of people and the writer in him liked that. Some of them became the models for future characters in his books.

He was often treated aggressively by the people he delivered to, especially the poor ones who made up the lion's share of those living in his catchment area.

'He was a representative of the government,' his future friend Taylor Hackford said, 'Can you imagine that? Bukowski as a representative of the government?' It meant he was 'the enemy' to them, usually coming with bad news. Some people stopped him on the street looking for their letters in advance.

Often he got bitten by dogs. If he saw a 'Beware of Dog' sign on a property, the first thought he had was: 'How do I get in and out of here without having myself bitten?' It was even worse if a letter had to be signed for. That gave an aggressive dog all the time in the world to nip at his heels – or worse. He put many of these anecdotes into his first novel, *Post Office*.

He held this job for the next three years, an eternity by his standards. Jane spent most of her time waiting for him to come home. She still slept with other men on occasion. This usually happened after they had a row, or if he was out too long, but they always made up afterwards.

In David Stephen Calonne's biography of Bukowski he says the FBI had a record of the pair of them actually getting married that year. If this is true it's a startling revelation.

Also startling is Jane's birth date. This is listed on an FBI record as 1918. That would mean she was just two years older than Bukowski, not a decade older as he always said. Did he really marry her? It's difficult to know. The FBI miss-spelled her name as 'Coonye' on their records. This was obviously a typographical error.

The FBI file which suggests Bukowski married Jane

Bukowski could have pretended he was married to her to make renting (or job-hunting) easier. He might have wanted to make himself look 'respectable' for his post office bosses. Cohabitation in the fifties wasn't as prevalent as it is today. It looked better on a job application form to say you were married to a woman rather than living with her.

In a poem called 'The Birds' Bukowski wrote in one line, 'my 2nd wife left me,' meaning Barbara Frye. In a letter he wrote to E.V. Griffith of that year he says the material in the poem is factual rather than fictional. But if he really did marry Jane, why did he not mention it to people in his later years when there would have been no reason to lie about it?

If it was indeed a charade, he would have enjoyed pulling the wool over the eyes of the FBI, just as he'd pulled the wool over the eyes of the army psychiatrist by pretending he'd wanted to go to war. They had a dossier on him ever since that night in the forties when his Nazi leanings and the draft-dodging suspicion against him brought him to their attention, not to mention a spate of anti-establishment writings they found in his apartment - along with the copy of *Mein Kampf*.

He grew to despise his job as a mail carrier. The only way he could survive it was by taking unpaid leave every now and then. He'd go to bed for days on end, coming out only to eat or go to the bathroom. The therapeutic benefit of this, he said, was phenomenal. To lie there and just look at the ceiling was a much under-rated pleasure. Not many people realized this. They didn't realize the necessity of taking time-outs, of seeking pauses between highs — or lows.

After such breaks he appreciated everything around him that much more: the heat-soaked streets, the rain, even the traffic. His elation only disappeared when somebody crossed his path. That was when this misanthrope realized he was back in the real world.

He could never understand sociable people, could never understand the 'Friday night mentality' where those of limited intelligence deluded themselves into thinking what they were saying to each other in the bars was interesting. It wasn't. What made it seem interesting was the drink. This is what they should have been saluting, not one another.

'Most people are dumb,' he said, 'they don't know how to talk and they don't know how to think. They don't even know how to eat. They go to restaurants because someone tells them it's time to eat, not because they're hungry.'

The life he lived with Jane was light years away from all of this. If we wish to be cynical we could call it a relationship of mutual convenience rather than love. Bukowski himself confessed, 'I was all she could get and she was all I could get.' Each of them also gave the other a license to over-imbibe in alcohol, just like two obese people in a relationship might give one another a license to over-eat.

They were similar in many ways but different in a crucial one: Bukowski drank because there was nothing else to do whereas Jane did was because it was the *only* thing to do.

Alcohol may have been killing his body but he always insisted it saved his soul. 'When you work for a $1.75 an hour,' he said, 'you need to do something at night to keep yourself sane. You need a fistfight, you need a bitch, you need whiskey. Otherwise you couldn't face it all again the next day. I'm all for alcohol. It's the thing.'

They lived a life of normal abnormality. One day he was sitting at the window of a hotel room trying to work off a hangover. Suddenly he saw a man falling through the air in front of him. He'd thrown himself from an upstairs floor. Bukowski leaped from his chair. He called out to Jane. 'You're not going to believe what I just saw,' he said. 'What are you talking about?' she called back. She had a hangover too. She was in the bathroom throwing up. She came out. 'What is it?' she said. 'Somebody from the building just committed suicide,' he told her. She didn't believe him. 'Come here and look out,' he said.

She went over to the window. She looked down and saw the body splayed out on the ground. 'Aaaaargh!' she cried. She started to get sick again. Bukowski said, 'I told you so, baby.' What made the situation weird for him – apart from its obvious weirdness - was the fact that the man was neatly dressed. He even had a necktie on. He seemed to fall in slow motion, Bukowski thought, as if he was suspended in the air for a moment as he passed the window.

On another day it could have been Bukowski who jumped, or even Jane. They looked like candidates for it. Shortly afterwards they were evicted from their apartment on South Westlake Avenue in 1954 for drinking, fighting and foul language. The 'Notice to quit' was addressed to 'Mr. and Mrs. Bukowski.' It wasn't unusual for this to happen to them. T had been going on since the first premises they shared. Maybe the eviction even saved them some overdue rent. They packed their bags and moved on to the next battle zone.

This kind of routine had to come to an end sometime and it did. Fate took a hand in 1955 when Bukowski collapsed with a perforated ulcer. He could only have burned the candle at both ends for so long. Hardly the type to sign himself into a drying-out clinic, it took something like this to stop him in his tracks.

The problem came to a head one day when he felt his legs going from under him at the post office. He went home sick but felt just as bad there. He hated ringing doctors but this was different. He thought he was dying. When the doctor got to his apartment he only had to take one look at him to know he needed to be in hospital. He called for an ambulance.

Bukowski had been getting pains for some time now and ignoring them. 'I'm weak and I get sick easy,' he wrote to Whit Burnett, 'and I'm nervous all the time.' Up to now he'd been treating his 'short circuits' by using the Bukowski 'cure' of whiskey but on this occasion it hadn't worked. As he waited for the ambulance he started vomiting blood. 'Blood that comes from deep inside you isn't the bright red color that spurts from a cut on the finger,' he said, 'It's so purple it's almost black.' It gave off a foul odor. When the ambulance arrived he swallowed it for fear the driver would see it.

He was carted off to hospital. Here he hovered between life and death for the next few days. The ward he as in was situated next to the operating theatre. Many of the patients were beyond help. Each day he'd see the dead bodies being carried out and the sheets being changed as the staff made room for a new patient. 'We were too far gone to speak to one another,' he said. The only sounds to be heard were wheezing and coughing.

One day he felt blood rising up into his mouth. He couldn't make it to the bathroom so he vomited it onto the floor. The nurse on duty was livid.

'Why did you do that?' she screamed.

'I'm sorry,' Bukowski meekly.

She slapped him across the face then, which caused him to emit the immortal line, 'Florence Nightingale, I love you.' (In reality she was more like Nurse Rached from a film he would see years later, *One Flew Over the Cuckoo's Nest*).

He was given multiple transfusions of blood but the doctors didn't think he'd pull through so a priest was sent for. He wanted to give Bukowski the Last Rites but he refused them. The priest grew angry. 'Why do you not want them?' he asked Bukowski. He replied, 'I've lost my faith.' The priest wouldn't accept that. He said, 'Once a Catholic, always a Catholic.' Bukowski replied, 'Bullshit.'

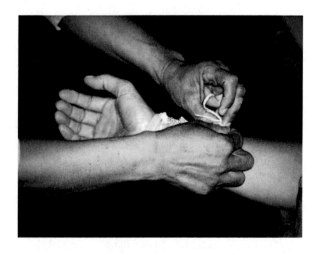

His father became his unlikely lifesaver. When Bukowski's blood credit ran out, somebody from his family had to prove they'd been a donor for him to qualify for another transfusion. His father turned out to be that person.

It was the last transfusion that caused him to turn the corner. He sat up after it and started to feel better.

His father came in to visit him, puffed up with pride over what he'd done. Bukowski told him he'd like to see Jane so he said he'd bring her in to him in a few days.

On the day in question, instead of bringing her directly to the hospital he brought her to a bar instead. Jane couldn't be in a bar long without getting roaring drunk and this day was no exception. By the time they were ready to go to the hospital she was hardly able to stand. When they got to Bukowski's ward she fell against his bed.

'How are you, loverboy?' she asked him.

His father snarled, 'I told you she was no good.'

Bukowski said, 'You did this on purpose. You're jealous I have her in my life. You got her drunk to humiliate me – and her.'

His father started nagging him about his life.

Bukowski exploded. 'One more word out of you,' he seethed, 'and I'll yank this needle out of my arm. I'll climb out of my deathbed and whip your ass.' For once the older man remained silent.

Lying in the hospital gave him all the time in the world to reflect on the frenzy his life had been up to this. His writing had got him nowhere and his drinking had all but landed him in the grave. Was there a message in that? Some miracle – or freak - had saved him.

His father wouldn't give him the time of day and yet he'd provided the life-saving blood. The irony was choice. But maybe he'd have been better off to die.

Who would have missed him? He could almost see the obituary: 'Charles Bukowski, three-time loser, breathed his last in the charity ward of an L.A. Hospital.' That meant one less drunk on the planet. Jane would be distraught but maybe not for too long. Sooner or later she'd pick up another slacker who'd give her another excuse to get wasted. If she needed one.

What did his future amount to? More rejection by editors, more crippling jobs, more problems with his liver.

He still continued to think of life as a series of traps. You were trapped by being born to horrible parents. Then school, jobs, women. Routine was a trap. Your mind was another one. You had to fight it, fight all the dead things it put before you. You had to burn with a raw fury or learn how to be a digit, to take orders like the rest until one day they put you in a nursing home with a bedpan and you sat them looking at the walls, zombified.

It was hardly Walt Disney.

He left the hospital feeling, as he put it, '900 years older.' Jane had expected him to tell her when he was getting out but he rang a cab instead.

He felt almost surreal crossing the city, as if he had died and come back to life. His apartment was on the second floor of the block he was staying in. He stumbled from the cab and made his way to the stairs. As he climbed them, his dog ran over to him, nearly knocking him over in his excitement.

He walked down the long hall to his room and turned the key in the door.

Jane was sitting on the couch smoking a cigarette.

She looked up at him.

'Why didn't you tell me you were getting out?' she said. 'What's there to tell?' he replied. And then he asked, perhaps inevitably, 'Where's the beer?'

The doctors told him he'd die if he took even one more drink. Some accounts of his post-hospital experiences say he took one that day; others that he waited a week or a month. Whatever the time scale was, he drank his first beer slowly, feeling nervous as he did so.

He even put some milk in it. When it didn't kill him he had another and then another, the third one without milk.

'And I still didn't die.'

So it was true, he concluded. Doctors lied to you. They were as full of shit as everyone else in the world.

Over the next few weeks he got stronger. As his body improved, so did his mental state.

He decided he was going to change his life, to drink a little less. It wasn't exactly a Pauline conversion but it was probably as close to one as this man could come. He knew he wasn't able to give up drink but he thought he might be able to cut down on it.

He resigned from his job at the post office and started writing with more zeal than usual.

He even bought himself a typewriter. Writing, he claimed, kept walls from falling and losers from giving in.

'It stalks death,' he said, 'It's the ultimate psychiatrist. It laughs at itself. It's the last expectation, the last explanation.'

Up until this point the lion's share of his work had been in prose form but now he started writing poetry. It wasn't too much of a transition because his poems had the unadorned style of prose and also a strong narrative element. The stories, likewise, had poetic elements.

Bukowski never liked delineations between different genres. It came out well or it didn't, that was all that was important to him. He didn't set any store by theory, or trying to put a shape on what he was doing. If you did that you killed it. That was what he thought was wrong with Hemingway. He tried too hard and it showed. The simplicity, or what passed for it, had been worked at. His art didn't conceal art.

Now that he was drinking less, he wondered how he was going to spend the time he'd previously been spending in bars. Jane suggested the racetrack as a way of filling the gap. It sounded like a good idea to him and he pricked his ears up when she said it.

For the next thirty-odd years it would do precisely that, in greater or lesser degrees. It became his home from home and his well of inspiration. It was to him what the bullring was to

Hemingway. The fact that beer was served there made it even sweeter for him.

On his first day he picked no less than three winners. He was immediately hooked.

'Beginner's luck!' he grinned.

He went back the following day like a man on a mission and won again. This time it wasn't beginner's luck. He'd been bitten by another bug than writing.

The track had a kind of carnival atmosphere for them. Racing was the last thing on Jane's mind, whatever about Bukowski's. She made fun of him even when he won. He enjoyed her 'couldn't give a shit' attitude to everything. She insisted on staying seated, for instance, when the National Anthem was being played, unlike everyone else. This fed into his anti-establishment attitudes.

Jane was a more visible protestor than Bukowski, a more natural rebel. Left to himself he probably would have stood like the rest, if only to deflect attention from himself.

Some elements of the track bothered him. He hated the half hour wait between races, for instance. It was a half hour in which he was in danger of being approached by people he knew and he always had a horror of that. He staved them off by burying his head in the racing pages.

He studied form with the same intensity as he did everything else in life. He usually waited until just minutes before the race to place his bet. That was when he got the best odds.

He didn't bet large amounts. That was unusual for a man who gambled wildly in almost every other aspect of his life. He was also more successful than most gamblers, maybe for that reason. His practical side came out at the track. He had an elaborate system of betting which one would have wanted a degree in mathematics to understand.

When he wasn't watching the races he spent his time looking at the other punters. Inside his head he found himself wondering what

81

kind of people they were, why they were there. When he got home he'd usually type up such thoughts in stories and poems. Many of them concerned losers. He felt like a loser himself. He liked the idea of a 'long shot' winning a race. Maybe he could do that in life too.

He drove to the track almost every day.

'If I don't go for a few days,' he said, 'I feel like a flower that hasn't been watered. I don't know if it's a monster, a God, a wrath or a snail. I can't explain it. If I could I wouldn't go.'

Asked once if he'd ever contemplated writing a novel about it he said, 'It would be too boring. Someone loses the rent money and goes home and strangles his mother.' (That doesn't sound too boring).

It was like a metaphor of life for him. In it he witnessed the joy and cruelty he also witnessed everywhere else. He saw the con, the 'fixed game' as he called it, the prohibitive tax, the pathetic sights of poor people ripping up their slips of paper in disgust, the whole mad frenzy and the crushing of hope.

The winners of the day, he thought, were merely postponing their eventual misery, maybe even making it more painful by having such illusions waved before their faces. This applied to himself too. It was all an illusion, but a pleasant one.

There were days he would have preferred to do anything but spend his time there. But still he went. It was as good a way as any to kill the day, to soak up the empty hours when his brain was recovering from the previous night's binge.

Watching 'the ponies' he could get himself up for the next night's one. It gave him raw material looking at the way they moved, the way they overtook one another, the way they fell, throwing their jockeys. He watched the expression on their faces, seeing in them a microcosm of all the joys and fears of everyone everywhere.

The track was where he wound down and then wound up. He watched the human animal at work and play. He got on winning streaks and losing streaks and accepted both with near-indifference. He knew there was no way anybody could beat the system but it was still fun trying, pitting his wits against a stacked deck. He had the dream of the win but also the realism of knowing no gambler ever won much in the long term. Somewhere between these two extremes he became just another gambler shelling out his wad at the toteboard.

He drove to the track in a car that cost him $35. It was falling apart. One night as he was going home with Jane the lights failed to go on. The only way to activate them was to hit a bump on the road. It didn't work the first time so he looked for a second bump, hitting that one harder. It produced the desired effect. To save gas he turned the engine off on the hills, freewheeling down them like a child at a funfair.

When he got home he tried to write about the events of the day. Losing inspired him more than winning. 'It's suffering that creates art,' he declared, 'Don't let them tell you any different.' If he won he wrote bad poetry or none at all but if he lost the words came flooding out. 'I can write an immortal poem if I've lost anything over $100,' he bragged.

What was important was to stamp the events with his personality rather than write in someone else's voice. At the age of 35, he claimed, nothing he read interested him. He needed to create a new way of seeing things, to take writing out of the hands of those who'd never lived, the people with 'carbon copy souls.' Such people were little more than 'the dull whispers of nowhere.'

The so-called literary heavyweights left him cold. He didn't want to be a 'significant' writer, just someone who related to the common man.

He didn't want to be the kind of writer who wrote for magazines like *Harpers*. Such magazines, he said, published stories beginning with sentences like 'Amanda carefully adjusted her Easter bonnet before heading down the tree-lined avenue towards the promenade.' What chance had he got with his down-and-dirty realism when that was the norm? On the other hand, how could such no-talent 'literature' threaten him? If he was to break through, he needed an editor who understood what he was trying to do, someone like Whit Burnett.

Hemingway said there were many great writers who went before him and that made his task of emulating them more challenging. Bukowski had his heroes too. People like Fante and Jeffers nudged him in the right direction. But he could never be awed by anyone. He was too much his own man for that.

The masses were asses, he said. A herd mentality was an ignorant mentality. If you saw two lines and one had fifty people in it and the other five, you should go for the latter. Almost by definition it would get you where you wanted to go more quickly.

Bukowski took this line of thinking a step further when he went from, 'Crowds are bad' to 'People *period* are bad.' The further away from the human race you could get, he said, the better off you would be. 'I hate people's hairdos,' he advised, 'I hate their dogs, I hate their flowers, I hate their cars. I hate the way they walk, I hate the way they talk.'

He was the classic sociopath. Even when someone brushed up against his elbow in a crowd it was enough to unnerve him. It was as if the very fact of being a member of the human race meant you inherited some contagious disease. People prattled, they rubbed off one another's prejudices, they saw nothing but the empirical. Genius had always turned its back on such beings, had always gone its own way. Maybe you got burned that way too, but at least you had a measure of choice in the matter.

That was what life was all about: getting burned. You got burned every day you woke up, every time you went to the corner store, every time you opened a can of mustard. There was no escaping it. All you could do was write about it, which helped. But even this was escapism.

He never thought he chose writing as a career. Maybe it chose him. He usually hated looking at his typewriter until he started working on it. It bothered him until he became so immersed in what he was doing that he didn't see it anymore. It became like an invisible tool. He'd go 'Hiya, baby,' to it as if it was a human thing, something he had to relate to like a person.

He always said he would have preferred 'Pimp' on his passport than writer. 'Writer' was a dirty word. Most writers cheated. Many got the 'fat head'. And then there were the ones who suffered from an excess of fake sensitivity.

He never wore the raiment of the writer, preferring people to see him simply as a man who sat at a window. 'Don't mouth up your books,' he said, 'It takes the air out of the tires.' Writing was like breathing, or sex. It came from some mad part of his head. He minted music out of the bones of his experiences. The talkers, like the academics, removed themselves from life. They were to be avoided on that account.

85

Writing had to grab him by the scruff of the neck for it to speak to him. He didn't like the idea of an author sitting behind his lines or officiating over them. The poem had to write the writer rather than vice versa.

E.E. Cummings once said he preferred the company of ice cream salesmen to that of poets. Bukowski put it this way: 'I've found more gut-life in old newsboys, in janitors, in the kid waiting at the all-night taco stand.' He preferred plumbers to poets. You could do without a poet but you couldn't do without a plumber. The only plumbers he didn't like were the ones who pulled poems out of their back pockets after fixing his sink. That was always a worry.

Academics were even more contemptible. He despised their cozy self-indulgence. 'If you're given a choice between a professor of English or a dishwasher,' he said, 'Take the dishwasher.' He saw them as so many eunuchs in the harem. They licked their lips at the periphery of life, wringing texts out to dry to satisfy moribund preconceptions. (The only academic honor Bukowski ever received was a certificate for completing a drink driving course after a motoring offence. He remained quite proud of this certificate to the end of his life). His hatred of academics was mutual. They frowned on him not only because of his subject matter but also because of his lifestyle – and his lack of a third level education. They looked down on him for things like the fact that he couldn't pronounce 'Dostoevsky' – even though he could write like him.

His typewriter was like a meat grinder to him. He churned out poem after poem on it, story after story. He was able to write up to 10 stories a week or 100 poems. The inspiration wasn't always there but the writing was always crisp and heartfelt. He became a writing machine in the same way as a shark was a killing machine.

He declared war on anything that could be construed as gentle in his writing. On the odd occasion that he permitted this it was

86

like a concession. Like Hemingway he cut himself off from feeling to survive life's casual cruelties. His humanity was hard won. It wrestled with itself like a luxury he couldn't afford.

He wrote drunk and edited sober – if at all. He splayed pages across the floor at the dead of night and walked over them to his bed. The next morning he tried to put his frantic ramblings into something approaching a unified construct. He'd look at what he'd written and go, 'Did I do that?' A lot of the time he had no recollection of the writing process at all.

He never wrote in the daytime. 'That,' he said, 'would be like running through a shopping mall in the nude.' Night-time was when the magic happened. Then you could sleep it off the next day. In *Women* he put it humorously: 'I'm just an alcoholic who became a writer so I could stay in bed until noon'.

Was he a writer who drank or a drinker who wrote? It hardly mattered because the two activities were almost synonymous for him. They were the two *sine qua nons* of his life.

He continued to agonize over his future as the relationship with Jane waxed and waned. He got a job in a furniture store and they lived a semi-normal life for a while but then the drinking got out of control and he found her with another man. To get revenge he slept with another woman. It was childish but necessary. The sparks flew again. They never looked like going the distance but neither was there an air of finality to their partings.

At least until Barbara Frye came into his life.

Slow Quicksand

I had no god. I liked to fuck. Nature didn't interest me. I never voted. I liked wars. Outer space bored me. Baseball bored me. History bored me. (Bukowski)

Barbara Frye was the editor of a magazine based in Texas. It was called *Harlequin.* Bukowski sent some of his work there in the mid-fifties. He'd submitted it more in hope than expectation but her reaction to it was ecstatic and she started publishing it. The pair of them then became pen pals. As the volume of her letters increased, a penny dropped for him. She was reaching out to him not only as an editor but a woman.

In one of them she wrote, 'No man will marry me. I can't turn my neck from shoulder to shoulder.' She'd been born with two vertebrae missing from her neck, making her look as if she was permanently hunching her shoulders.

He wrote back, 'For Christ's sake, I'll marry you!' He didn't really mean it. He was drunk at the time. But she took him seriously. He was shocked when he realized this but he didn't renege on his offer.

He didn't meet her until the day before they were married. He got the train down to Texas with just 35 cents in his pocket. When he saw her he didn't think she looked too bad. The neck problem wasn't obvious.

It wasn't long before they fell into bed together. He was surprised to learn she was as wild as Jane between the sheets. 'Does my neck bother you?' she asked him. 'It's not your neck I'm looking at,' he said.

After the honeymoon came the wedding. The newlyweds then visited her home town of Wheeler. The locals were good old boys who looked askance at Bukowski. He was as strange to them as they were to him.

He learned that her family had a lot of money.

'Not only did she live in the town,' he declared, 'She owned it.' This was a slight exaggeration but she came from wealthy stock. She was the daughter of a man who owned a series of oil wells. Bukowski wasn't as impressed by the money as some other people might have been.

'Baby,' he said, 'this will spoil everything.' Money was nice but he thought too much of it would cramp his style.

He needn't have worried: he'd hardly see a dollar of it.

Because of the shortness of his daughter's 'engagement' to Bukowski, Frye's father was understandably suspicious of his motives in bringing her to the altar. When he met him he asked him what he did for a living. 'Nothing,' Bukowski replied. He'd never tried to make an impression on anyone and he wasn't going to start now.

Being married to the editor of a literary magazine gave him the opportunity to settle scores with some people who'd rejected his work in the past. These were people Frye knew who were poets as well as editors. Bukowski was now able to turn the tables on them as he vetted the MSS they submitted to *Harlequin*.

His motive wasn't purely vengeful as he didn't like most of the work he saw anyway but it was definitely a factor in the equation. Frye didn't argue with him, regarding his opinion on such matters as superior to hers.

Sometimes she even over-ruled her own decisions to publish material he thought poor or reject poems she originally liked. One such over-rule resulted in the threat of legal action from an unhappy subscriber. In contrast to this she put Bukowski all over *Harlequin*. It was a welcome experience for him after having had so many of his poems sent back to him in the past.

89

Things started to go downhill for him when Frye told him she thought he should get a job. He found this difficult to understand considering there was all that money lying around.

He thought it was a better idea to spend his days at the racetrack and then come home and make love to her. Wouldn't that be more fun?

She didn't agree, which made her boring to be with for Bukowski. He also found her pretentious. She read *Time* magazine and put on a false voice when talking to people she was trying to impress. He believed the only people who did that were those who were ill at ease with themselves.

Bukowski wasn't mercenary but he felt frustrated about the fact that all Frye's money was so near and yet so far. It meant nothing to her because it was so accessible. For Bukowski she was proof of the old adage that only the poor could be truly happy. They, at least, believed money could solve their problems. The rich, on the contrary, knew it couldn't.

'Being rich,' he said, sounding like Ernest Hemingway, 'she was spoiled in that special way rich people are spoiled without knowing it.'

To keep her off his back he got a job stacking shelves in a drugstore. Then he worked as a shipping clerk for a while. He walked out of this job one day, telling Frye he got fired so she wouldn't give out to him.

She was attending art classes now. She suggested he go with her.

'It would be a nice career for you,' she suggested. 'Sure,' said Bukowski, ''then we could sit around all day showing each other pictures of apples and oranges.'

He would have preferred to slaughter pigs for a living. But when he went he turned out to have a talent for it – much better than hers, in fact. That bothered her.

His drinking started to bother her now as well. They argued a lot. It wasn't like with Jane where both of them were content to roll with the punches, where the abuse tossed back and forth was often in fun. Frye wanted Bukowski to change the way he lived but there was no way he could do that.

He was still frustrated that she wasn't getting any of her father's money while they were living so poorly. Any time he brought the subject up she didn't seem to be interested in pursuing it. 'She had this idea that she wanted to make it on her own,' Bukowski said, 'That was fine for her but what about me?' This wasn't in the plan for him.

Another bone of contention was the fact that she wanted to have children and he didn't. They differed on almost everything they talked about. The fantasy marriage of two outcasts was turning into the mismatch of the century. He wasn't the man she expected from the letters and neither was she the woman she expected. 'We both drew a bum hand,' he said.

Frye now got pregnant but miscarried the child. She became even more angry with Bukowski when that happened, accusing him of having 'bad sperm.' He took the accusation in his stride as the relationship went down the tubes.

He once described marriage as a kind of 'slow quicksand.' This it certainly was with Frye, a woman who changed from Cinderella to Lady Macbeth in his eyes, substituting poetry with a desire to climb up some vague career ladder. Far from what he'd originally envisaged, he found her to be a small-minded social climber whose interest in the arts was merely cosmetic.

The *folie a deux* stumbled on for two years. 'After that she decided I was a bastard,' Bukowski said philosophically. She served him with divorce papers one day. He was surprised but not too much. He felt these were superfluous as he was never the kind of man to hold onto a woman against her will. His philosophy of life, like his philosophy of love, was 'Easy come easy go.'

To 'celebrate' getting the divorce papers he took her to bed. It seemed right. The first time they made love they knew nothing about one another and the last time they knew too much. He compared the sex to the last sting of a dying wasp.

So the relationship was over. Had it ever started? Did a man have the right to expect happiness with a woman he'd only met a day before marrying her?

Frye now started dating a Turkish man. He wore a purple stickpin in his tie. That was all Bukowski knew about him but it was enough. She would be better off with such a man than he. After she was gone he wrote a poem about their marriage called 'The Day I Kicked Away a Bankroll.' It was a two-fingered salute to the life of easy affluence she pretended to offer and then withdrew.

The reason she left him, she claimed, was because he was always fighting an inner war with himself. What she didn't realize was that such a war kept him alive. It stopped him descending into the 'air-conditioned hell' Henry Miller wrote about.

Frye broke with the Turk after a while and went to Alaska to lick her wounds. There she married a Japanese fisherman. She became Barbara Hayakawa and had two daughters. She was happy with him but one of her daughters was troubled. One night she became hysterical and burned down their house. Uninterested in re-building it, Barbara moved again, this time to India. Here she became involved in a religious cult.

After the divorce was finalized Bukowski moved back to his comfort zone, getting himself an apartment in a rundown area of East Hollywood called Mariposa Avenue. This was where all the derelicts hung out, the no-hopers and the has-beens, the Z-list actors who'd fallen on hard times. He was happier here than in the nullity of everything Frye represented.

Police sirens blared along the streets every other night. There were knife attacks, brawls on the street, hookers parading themselves freely. 'It was just my kind of place,' Bukowski said. When he got there he parked his Plymouth outside No.1623 and walked up the stairs to Room 303. There was no air conditioning. Cockroaches scurried across the floor. He would spend the next six years of his life there.

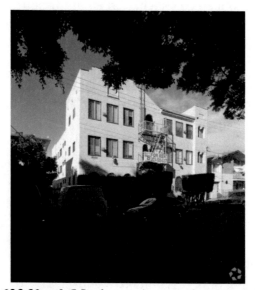

1623 North Mariposa Avenue is one of the iconic addresses associated with Bukowski

In the absence of Frye, Jane tried to get back with him. By now her drinking was showing in her features. She wasn't aggressive to him but in a way he missed that. The life was gone out of her for Bukowski. It was as if somebody had turned off a light switch. When he met her in the street he was shocked. He looked at her now as the rest of the world did, in the cold light of day. His own drinking blotted out that light for years but now it was blinding. Trying to talk to her he felt both embarrassed and angry, embarrassed because he had nothing to offer her anymore and angry because he knew she was destroying herself. He could see it better than most because he'd been with her so long.

'I saw you with that other woman,' she said, meaning Frye, 'I don't think she's your type.'

'It's over now,' Bukowski told her.

They arranged to meet for a kind of date, a throwback to the good old days – or the bad old days. 'I went back to my whore,' he said, 'who had once been such a cruel and beautiful woman, who was no longer beautiful but who had, magically, become a warm and real person. But she couldn't stop drinking.' When he asked her questions about what she'd been doing since they broke up she didn't answer them. Had she found another man? Or were even these a thing of the past? He dated her a few times afterwards but there was nothing there. They were dancing to a tune that had finished long ago. Drink had been the scotch tape that held them together. Now that it wasn't a feature of their being together anymore they became awkward with one another.

She wanted him to move back in with her but he knew if he gave in to her she'd bring him back to the bad places he'd been, the places he'd only recently got out of. The fact that they were still civil with each other nearly made things worse. A vicious argument would have been more comfortable to him than this bland vacuum.

He found himself becoming more affectionate to her than he'd ever been before and that was strange for him too. How could you be affectionate to someone with whom you'd always been in a love-hate relationship? It didn't gell for Bukowski. He wanted fire or ice, not civility. It had to be all or nothing for him, the dark colors rather than the neutral ones. The ultimate insult would be to have treated her like a girlfriend. She could never be that. She was, after all, his whore.

He knew he couldn't go back to her. The time with Frye had made him more practical. He also had something of a literary career going now. Jane wasn't interested in that. She'd never been. She just wanted a drinking partner. Where had the old Hank gone, she wondered. Had he lost his nerve?

He tried to explain his new position to her. He'd jumped off the Titanic onto a raft but there wasn't room for the two of them on it. If she climbed on, both of them would drown.

He went back to his old job at the post office to buy himself some thinking time. He busied himself in the routines he hated but which now served some kind of purpose for him.

Some seminal events were around the corner for him now. If Bukowski thought life with Barbara Frye was bad, worse was to come. In the next two years he would lose not only Jane but both of his parents as well. Within this relatively short span of time three people who'd once been the mainstays of his life were removed from it.

His mother contracted cancer. It was advanced before he heard about it. His father rang to tell him.

'She's in a nursing home,' he said. Bukowski didn't ask him why he wasn't informed sooner.

He hadn't been seeing her much of her since he came out of hospital. Because she'd taken his father's side so much in childhood he couldn't work up the enthusiasm to visit her. The last time he'd seen her was the previous Christmas Eve when his father brought her to visit himself and Frye. His father had spent the whole evening giving out to him about the fact that he'd never got anywhere in life. Eventually Bukowski yelled, 'Get your ass out of here!' His mother said, 'You can't talk to your father like that.' She was still at it. Then he told her to leave too.

He visited her a few times in the nursing home, usually when he had drink taken.

They had little to speak about when she was well and that didn't change now.

'Why do you write these terrible stories?' she asked him.

It was the same question she'd been asking since he was living at home full time. Nothing had changed.

On one of the visits she made a comment that would have made all the difference if it was made twenty years earlier.

'You're right about your father,' she said, 'He's a terrible man.' So she'd finally admitted it.

She told him they hadn't been getting on for years, that he'd even put her into a mental hospital at one stage.

She left him once but had to come back when she ran out of money. Bukowski thought it was a pity she hadn't seen through him when it mattered. What good was the truth to him – or her – now?

The last time he saw her was the day before Christmas Eve of that year. He arrived at the nursing home with a rosary beads for her — an unusual gesture from this supremely irreligious man — but the door of her room was locked. There was a wreath on it.

A nurse came over to him. She said, 'I'm afraid she died.' He tried to feel something but he couldn't. Too much damage had been done by now.

She was a woman who'd meant little to him in life and now she meant little to him in death. She hadn't been there when it counted. For him that was all that mattered.

96

His father failed to grieve as well. She wasn't long in the ground before he started dating another woman. Then he became engaged to be married to her. But it wasn't to be. Less than two years later he himself would be in his grave. The man who'd 'bastardized' Bukowski upon this 'sad earth,' as he once put it, had died at last.

The circumstances of his death were strange. He suffered a massive coronary one morning while pouring a glass of water for himself. Bukowski would allude to this in various poems in the years to come. His death seemed as absurd to him as everything else about the man. He collapsed before he even had time to turn off the tap. He lay dead on the floor for hours before anyone knew about it.

He was discovered by his fiancée. She'd called to see him because they were about to go out together that day. She got no answer after knocking on the door but she heard the sound of running water so she knew there was something wrong. A neighbor helped her break in. When she got inside she found him on the ground in a pool of water. The glass was still clenched in his hand. Bukowski thought he'd got out of life easily. He was spared the pain of his wife's lingering death.

Bukowski felt more relief than grief at the funeral. Afterwards he brought his body back to the house. He lay in an open coffin as neighbors called to pay their respects. A few of them remarked on Bukowski's facial resemblance to him, something he didn't want to hear. He put on his father's suit and flapped his arms about the place. He felt like 'a scarecrow in the wind.' This was his way of dancing on his father's grave.

He did all this in front of his fiancée. She was crying but he was unsympathetic about that. By consorting with his father she became as culpable as him. He was insensitive to her feelings. He would later write a short story in which his father practically rapes this woman. He wanted to make the funeral into a farce more than a tragedy. Towards the end of the evening he smoked his father's last Pall Mall. He felt as if he was expelling him from himself as he exhaled.

When the neighbors asked if they could have some of his possessions as keepsakes he gave them away without a thought. They took everything, he said, leaving him only 'the garden hose, the bed, the refrigerator and a roll of toilet paper.' It was like a kind of expiation for him. Ridding the house of objects associated with him also ridded it of his memory. That was the theory. In reality he would find it virtually impossible to shake off the influence his father exerted on him for the rest of his life.

This was a man who'd done nothing for him but try to break his spirit. He'd hit him while he was down, again and again, until one day he stood up to him and it stopped. Maybe the miracle was that he hadn't murdered him. Or that they hadn't murdered each other. All he could feel was a vague emptiness. There was nothing he needed to have said to him if he met him one last time, no pact of forgiveness he wanted to make. All his death meant was that there was one less malcontent on the planet, one less enemy for him to worry about.

He'd made a God of social status. That unlikely chimera disappeared from him early in life but it was manifest in his every thought and action. He was a glutton, a loser, a sociopath, a petty-minded liar. How could Bukowski mourn a man who hadn't even one redeeming virtue?

His death didn't bother him as much as the fact that he'd never really lived, his mind eaten up by resentment over his disempowerment. It was the same disempowerment Bukowski himself experienced in the assortment of crucifying jobs he had to take on to make ends meet. The difference was that Bukowski knew such jobs represented nothing worthwhile whereas his father bought into the conceit that they could lead to better things. Because of this tunnel vision he stood no chance.

Bukowski knew he'd inherited a lot of character traits from him. That was another reason his physical resemblance to him bothered him so much. He had a coldness in him that reminded him of his old man, a crustiness of manner. But whereas his father had little emotion to begin with, Bukowski's were merely buried.

He didn't leave a will but the mortgage on his house was paid up so Bukowski inherited that. Jane advised him to move back into it. 'It's the only chance you'll ever get to own a house,' she said, in a rare instance of practical thinking. But he wasn't interested. The neighbors, the street, the house itself - everything reminded him too much of his old man. He couldn't wait to get out of it, to get as far as he could from it all as soon as he could.

He received $15,000 from the sale of the house. That meant he had 'real' money in his pocket for the first time in his life. He drank some of this but invested some as well. Many people will be surprised to learn Bukowski ever invested a penny in his life but he had a pragmatic side to him amidst all the madness. (A future girlfriend, Pamela Brandes, claimed he was always scrupulous about paying his bills on time).

The money was welcome to him because he was only earning a subsistence wage at the post office at the time. Many of the magazines he wrote for paid either a pittance or nothing at all. Editors often preferred to send their contributors copies of the magazines in question in lieu of payment. He knew he'd need to be publishing books in order to make some real money.

Two people who helped him up the literary ladder more than anyone in his early years were Jon and Louise Webb. They were a married couple who ran a publishing company from their home in New Orleans. It was called Loujon Press, taking its name from their combined Christian names. They operated on a shoestring but produced high quality books. Bukowski spent many drunken nights with them in New Orleans. Roaches crawled up and down the walls as Bukowski poured out his heart to them about everything that engaged him.

They also published *The Outsider* magazine, another outlet for Bukowski. Webb had a colorful history. He'd been a police reporter in his early days but then went off the rails, becoming involved in an armed robbery. This resulted in him serving time in jail. He edited the prison newspaper when he was 'inside.' All of this impressed Bukowski no end.

The Outsider was only one of his outlets at this time. From the late fifties onwards he became 'king of the littles', his work appearing in practically every literary journal you'd care to mention *Quicksilver, Knight, Epos, Matrix, Pix, Nomad, Coffin, Coastlines* and a host of others. Developments in the printing trade made the cost of publishing such pamphlets cheaper than it had ever been. Many of them were stapled publications printed on hand-cranked machines. They were distributed in limited numbers for a nominal price.

Bukowski was 40 when his first book came out. (Al Berlinski)

By now Bukowski computed that he'd earned the grand sum of $47 from twenty years of writing. The self-styled Muhammad Ali of the printed word, he bellowed out, 'I'm the greatest!' at regular intervals but he was still only making peanuts for his labors.

He was nearly always drunk when he wrote. With a beer in his hand and the lines flowing out of him he owned the world. Sober he was more subdued but his sober life was his non-life. When he was drunk he slammed the words out like bullets from a gun. He still loved the sound the typewriter made, his finger digging hard into the keys like an act of violence.

His first book of poetry came out in 1960. Its publication was delayed for a number of reasons, making him wonder if it would ever reach the shelves. He became so frustrated by the delays at one stage that he wrote a snorter of a letter to the publisher, E.V. Griffith. He expressed the fear that he'd been taken for a ride in trusting Griffith. Such a letter makes us realize just how anxious he was to become published in book form.

A week later he had the book in his hands. This gave rise to a groveling letter of apology to Griffith. Unlike so many others, this man had come through for him. He revived Bukowski's faith in humanity.

The book was called *Flower, Fist and Bestial Wail*. It was thirty pages long. 'Never was a baby born in more pain,' he said. Only 200 copies were printed but it always held a special place in his heart.

It felt good to finally hold a book with his name on it in his hands. Publication in 'the littles' was nice but it was uncertain. Though he appeared in many periodicals, a lot of his writing at this time either went missing or was sent back to him.

One editor responded to a poem he submitted to him with an irate, 'What the fuck is this shit?' scrawled across the top of it. Bukowski wasn't disheartened by his reaction. He just said, 'How do I know it's not from some seventeen year old kid with acne using his father's discarded mimeo machine in his garage?'

Many writers stopped writing because they weren't being published but rejection seemed to spur Bukowski on. No matter how many of his poems came back he continued to 'make love to the ribbon.' He forced it to release itself to him like a drink's subtle magic.

He kept in touch with what other writers were doing but wasn't threatened by any of them, even the most famous ones. He felt he was head and shoulders over most of them, regardless of their status in society's eyes.

He saw Norman Mailer as a poser who strove too much after effect. Allen Ginsberg played his entrails across the applause of the crowd. William Faulkner was loved because he wasn't understood, which made people think they were missing something. Hemingway had his moments but he fudged his own dictates in the last reel. Was it all bulls and balls with 'Papa,' as Vladimir Nabokov alleged?

Hemingway also lacked humor for Bukowski. It's not clear if he read his lampoon of Sherwood Anderson, *The Torrents of Spring*, or the wry passages in books like *Green Hills of Africa* and *Death in the Afternoon*. Many of Hemingway's stories are also amusing, though not laugh-out-loud funny like Bukowski's ones. Maybe that was the difference. With Hemingway you had to search for the jokes. Some of them were between the lines and that wasn't Bukowski's idea of comedy. With him it had to be obvious. He didn't like 'clever' humor. That was for pseudo-intellectuals. Slapstick was more to his taste.

He spent so much time denouncing Hemingway in his life, one had to suspect a certain degree of insecurity in his attitude. This was no doubt fueled by the number of critics who accused him of copying Hemingway's style. Mailer was another oft-quoted influence. Asked what he thought of Mailer, Bukowski shot back,

'I don't think of Mailer.' But he did. It was only when he became relaxed about his own position in the literary pantheon that he stopped taking cheap shots at these figures.

Sometimes one got the feeling that any literary figure who became successful automatically fell from grace in his eyes. If Hemingway had remained as obscure a figure as Fante he might have continued to sing his praises. Likewise for Mailer and Miller — two writers who, on the surface, were saying the kinds of things Bukowski was saying. Once he became outstripped by these people a resentment seemed to set in.

In January 1961 he wrote in a letter to Jon Webb that it was only when a man got to the point of putting a gun in his mouth that he could see the whole world in his head. This was a grim foretaste of how Hemingway would kill himself six months later.

He was still seeing Jane off and on but the spark they had could never be ignited. She was living in a seedy hotel now - the Phillips on Vermont Avenue - and drinking more than ever. She was also out of a job. She'd been working as a waitress in a café up until recently but it closed down. The woman who owned the hotel allowed her to clean up some of the rooms for a few dollars a day. She put it towards the rent.

Bukowski met her on the street one day. They shot the breeze and then went for a drink. They brought some whiskey back to his place and drank themselves senseless.

The next morning he rang in sick to his job. A short time later a nurse employed by the post office came by to make sure he was telling the truth. He was in bed with Jane at the time. She hid under the covers until he got rid of the nurse. They made love afterwards but it was mechanical, the sex of two alcoholics looking for a follow-up thrill.

He spent Christmas with her that year. They bought a tree and put it standing in the main room. They decorated it with trinkets but they hadn't put it up properly and it wobbled. When Bukowski lay down to sleep on the floor it fell on top of him, the lights burning his flesh.

A few days later he went round to see Jane in her hotel room. It was early in the morning but she was already drunk. There were bottles of whiskey everywhere. He tried to take some of them from her but she wouldn't let him. They were precious to her, her viaticum for the journey of life.

Shortly afterwards he visited her again. When he got up to her room the door was open but she wasn't there. He walked over to her bed. He saw blood on her pillow. He went downstairs to the desk. The woman who owned the hotel told him she was in the county hospital.

He made his way to it. When he got there he was informed she was in a coma. He went into her ward and sat by her bed. A few minutes later she opened her eyes. She looked as bad as he'd ever seen her. 'I wiped away her guts as they ran out of her mouth,' he wrote in a poem. She said something to him that he'd never forget: 'I knew it would be you'. Then she lapsed back into unconsciousness.

She'd visited him in the same hospital in 1955 when he lay between life and death. Now the roles were reversed. He sat looking at her, willing her to open her eyes again, but she didn't. She died two days later. She was only 51. The news devastated Bukowski. A curtain had been pulled over a decade. His broken-winged raven had made her last flight and a part of him died with her.

He went back to her hotel room like a murderer might return to the scene of a crime. He was shocked by its grottiness, a grottiness he'd been a part of until so recently. He looked at her furniture, her clothes, her shoes. There were whiskey bottles everywhere – on cabinets, on shelves, even under the bed. It was her legacy.

He wrote about this in one of his most moving poems, 'The tragedy of the leaves.' His woman is gone and her empty bottles surround him 'like bled corpses.' It ends with him returning to a dark rooming-house where his landlady, a woman with 'fat, sweaty arms' screams at him for the rent he owes her, the world having failed them both.

There would be no more bunking down in tacky hotel rooms, no more nights of wild sex and drinking, no more falling in and out of one another's arms as they laughed at the lousy hand life dealt them. It may not have been love in the conventional sense but it beat what so often passed for it in the lives of the more well-heeled.

His precious gemstone was gone up to that big gin-mill in the sky. He believed he accelerated her demise by not going back to her. The thought merged with his grief and made it worse. She was the best friend he ever had or ever could have. And he'd thrown her away.

Seeing her in her coffin gave him a shock no doctor could. This was what happened to drinkers, he thought, the ones who didn't get warnings in the form of bleeding ulcers. She died in the way he should have died himself. It was a death everything pointed to, the inevitable spin-off of the years of excess. For a decade they'd been united on a journey to nowhere. Such a journey was now over for one of them. How long would the other one last?

She was buried in an unmarked grave at the San Fernando Mission. A wind was blowing. There were only a few people at the funeral: Bukowski, the priest, her son, the mentally retarded sister of the woman who owned the hotel and the people employed by the funeral home.

Bukowski bought a wreath of flowers to honor hers memory. It had stilts on it. The men who carried her casket from the hearse leant it up against a tree and it wavered in the breeze. The stilts didn't work properly. When the casket was being lowered it fell forward onto the ground. To Bukowski this seemed somehow appropriate. 'Everything failed her in life,' he said, 'Even the damn wreath wouldn't stand straight.'

Some prayers were said over the grave. Afterwards a row broke out with the priest about whether she was Catholic or not. That seemed appropriate too. Her son left the cemetery then. Bukowski was left standing with the sister of the woman who owned the hotel.

He met Jane's son later at the hotel. He said to Bukowski, 'How could you let her die in a place like this?' Bukowski replied, 'Why did you desert her?' Each of them was trying to blame the other for what happened but maybe neither of them needed to. Jane had been on her own path almost since the day she was born, her future already mapped out from the deprivations of her early years.

Her son was supposed to pay for the funeral but Bukowski knew that was never going to happen. 'He was half way back to New Mexico,' he said, 'before she was cold in her grave.' Bukowski got stuck with the bill instead.' It wasn't too expensive,' he said, 'not too much more than the cost of a good night's drinking.'

He went back to Jane's room the following day. He took a yellow bathrobe from her wardrobe to remind him of her – as if he needed anything to do that. He also took a few goldfish she owned. There was nobody else to look after them.

He went through the motions of his days, watched people busying themselves with their lives as if nothing had happened. How could life ever be the same for him now? Never again would he hear her insane laughter, never again be privy to her treasurable irreverence. Her death hit him a hundred times harder than the deaths of his parents. He felt as if he was sleepwalking, as if he was speaking to people through a fishbowl.

She was gone and he was still around. Why was he spared in 1955 and not her now? There was no logic in it. It was a lottery.

He tried to cope with it the way he coped with every crisis in his life, by getting drunk. Afterwards he went to the track. He met a girl there that he knew from the post office. He tried to have sex with her but he couldn't. He felt Jane was watching him.

Then he went to a strip show and got thrown out. It wasn't the normal way to grieve but was there any normal way? A few days later one of her goldfish died. It had tried to jump out of the tank to catch a fly. Or had it committed suicide? Bukowski had these crazy kinds of thoughts.

Death sharpened his mind about his future. The lure of suicide loomed large before him again, the sweet angel of escape. He kept a kitchen knife taped to the back of his door and thought of plunging it into himself. It would have reunited him with her. This wasn't Bukowski being melodramatic or fishing for sympathy. It was simply the way he saw his life. He was forever walking that gangplank. Not falling off was the surprise more often than not. Not even Milton Berle's cousin could help him now.

All of his relationships so far had been doomed to failure but they'd never been cut off with this finality. He had more pity than love for Jane in her last years but he still liked to think she was there for him if he ever needed her. She was meant to be a port where he could drop anchor anytime he fell off the wagon. Now that wasn't possible anymore. There would be no soft landing for him now if he fell off it.

He used his writing to try and get over her. The stories he wrote at this time were strange even by his standards. One of them concerned a man who murdered a blanket that fell in love with him.

He didn't believe in writing a story, he told his friend Ann Bauman, unless it 'crawled out of the walls.' Everything was crawling out of the walls for him now that Janes was gone. Some days he fantasized about being with her wherever she was. He wrote to Bauman, 'I do not think I will see many more days.' In the letter he enclosed one of Jane's bobby pins for her to use in her hair. He said he was waiting for death 'like a plumed falcon' for his 'caged blood.'

Three small books of his came out in 1962: *Poems and Drawings* from Epos Press, *Longshot Pomes for Broke Players* from Seven Poets Press and *Run with the Hunted* from Midwest Press. The latter was published by R.R. Cuscaden. Cuscaden wrote the first serious essay on Bukowski's work: 'Poet in a Ruined Landscape.'

The third issue of *The Outsider* was devoted to him in 1962. The Webbs dubbed him their 'Outsider of the Year', an award that touched him. It helped take away some of his grief over Jane. It was the first award he'd ever won. (To his death he never received a literary award in his own country, an astonishing omission). The honor was tongue-in-cheek on Webb's part. Neither was it continued. There would never be any other 'Outsider of the Year' besides Bukowski.

At the post office his problems worsened. The work was draining and the people almost as bad. He tried to keep his mind somewhere else to get through it. In the evenings he drank solidly, either at home or in the bars. Or both. If he had one too many he tended to become involved in fights. He didn't go looking for them but they often found him. He tried not to rise to the bait but sometimes it was impossible avoid doing so. He usually forgot what the fights were about the next morning. He often woke up in the drunk tank.

Some mornings he coughed up blood. He was also suffering from hemorrhoids at this time. Any visitor to his apartment was guaranteed to see many tubes of Preparation H lying around. He was prone to other problems too. He rarely put on shoes, for instance, walking across the floor in his bare feet and often stepping on broken glass from the bottles he'd drunk from the night before and left strewn all over the floor. He spent a lot of his time picking shards out of his feet to stop them getting infected.

Sometimes he flung bottles at the wall when he was angry, or just for something to do. People from the adjoining apartment would bang on the other side of it telling him to be quiet. He usually roared back abuse at them. One night he threw a barbell at the wall, creating a huge hole in it. 'I thought it was a good idea,' he said, 'but my landlord didn't.'

Towards the end of the year he was arrested for being drunk and disorderly. Because he was a repeat offender he thought he might get a prison sentence. If one was imposed it would have meant the end of his job. In the event he got off with a fine — probably because the jails were full with Christmas revelers. He was always sailing close to the wind in this respect. Some months later he was sentenced to three days in jail for being drunk or disorderly. The alternative was to pay a $30 fine. He chose the latter option: 'I figured it would be easier to part with my money than my mind.'

It Catches My Heart in its Hands, his first major poetry collection, was published by Jon Webb in 1963. Webb said to Bukowski as he handed him the first copy, 'You're a bastard but

I'm publishing you anyhow.' He added in more serious vein, 'You've ruined poetry for me because after reading you I can't read anyone else.' Bukowski replied, 'I have the same problem.'

Copyright of the Poetry Collection of the University Library, University at Buffalo, the State University of New York

The book gives us a more imagistic Bukowski than we see in the later collections. There are tributes to legends like Marilyn Monroe (who died the previous year) and the composer Borodin as well as various lyrical verses without much biographical content - except for 'my father.' He hadn't fully developed his style yet, which makes the book even more precious. 'Don't ever get the idea I'm a poet', he says in 'a 340 dollar horse and a 100 dollar whore,' but he sounds very like one.

Some of the images are surreal. They're coarse in texture but they radiate an inner truth. The book contains his best work from the mid-fifties to the early sixties. It was hand-printed in the Webb's sweatshop behind a mansion in the French Quarter of New

111

Orleans. They labored over its production with such devotion that Bukowski was speechless. It was the first book to be produced by Loujon Press and they were determined to make it special, using expensive paper that absorbed the ink beautifully without any offsetting. It was printed in Dickensian fashion in a room where rats and rain played havoc with the printing press. In a way this increased the romantic nature of the endeavor. Webb used a machete to guillotine the paper.

Bukowski was euphoric about the book coming out, even more so than with *Flower, Fist and Bestial Wail.* He even offered Webb money to help promote it.

Seeing it gave him renewed energy for his writing. A lot of this was still coming back from the magazines he submitted it to. When that happened it made him feel like 'a lamp-post with a dog pissing on it.' But he kept going, kept 'laying the word down raw.' Every new poem he wrote was a kick in the teeth for those who said he was a no-hoper.

Even if he didn't feel inspired he still wrote, keeping his hand in during the fallow patches like an athlete in training. He felt the bad poems created the good ones. They were the grunge he had to get out of his system to make way for the better work. The genie didn't always come out of the bottle. Sometimes you had to wrestle with it, to graft out a lyric until it began to sing. It was like jiggling a key in a lock until it clicked.

He worked alone, avoiding writers' groups like the plague. Too many people, he still felt, got their names in lights because they were well connected. Many of them lived with their mothers. Some let their wives pay the bills. They got themselves published in badly-produced magazines and it went to their heads. They did readings for nine or ten people and passed the hat around. Their friends attended, along with their families, paying their $2 for a magazine they stuffed on a shelf after they went home and never took down again.

Bukowski liked to think he had something more muscular about his style. Everything that took place in his life went into his poems: the DTs, the suicidal feelings, the stinking poverty, the cold sun that hit him as he crept from a park bench in search of his next mucky inspiration. No matter how bleak life became, he couldn't get rid of the curiosity to see another sunrise. Drunk or sober, he would create a kind of Black Mass out of the diseased mosaic of his days.

Notes from the Underground

Christ wasn't the only bastard who was nailed to the cross. (Bukowski)

Bukowski met Frances Elizabeth Dean, the woman who would become the mother of his only child, in the same way as he'd met Barbara Frye: through his work. She'd been taken with a poem of his which had a line she loved near the end: 'I would have screamed, but they have places for people who scream.' She was so impressed by it she went down to a bookstore and ordered copies of his other books of poetry. She liked them too, so much so that she wrote to him to tell him so. (She was living in Massachusetts at the time).

Bukowski wrote back, 'Buy my books. My publishers are starving.' She kept the letter. It had his address on it but she didn't write back to him for a year. By then she'd moved to California. Bukowski was glad to hear from her. He was feeling depressed at the time. She'd put her phone number on the letter. He rang her and said, 'You have to get over here. I need you.'

She took a taxi to his apartment. He was drunk when she arrived, which threw her. She went in and they started talking. Bukowski learned that she wrote poetry herself, that she was a divorced woman with four daughters.

Her marriage hadn't been happy, she told him, and she'd been glad to get out of it. She opened up so much to him he ended up telling her about Jane and all the other experiences that had formed him: the rooming-houses, the poverty, almost dying in hospital in 1955. The sun was coming up when their conversation ended.

Afterwards they met every now and then. She moved into an apartment near him and came over to him for meals. She didn't have much money but repaid him by cleaning his apartment.

'I didn't think you'd be like this,' she said to him one day.

'Like what?' he said.

'You're sensitive,' she said. He seemed surprised at her surprise. 'You mean you didn't know that?' he said. It was as if he was unaware of his tough guy image. (As time went on she witnessed his darker side, especially when he was drunk).

Frances was the first 'gentle' woman Bukowski became involved with. After the cynicism of Jane and the coldness of Barbara it was something of a shock for him. She exuded an almost Pollyanna-like attitude to life. He didn't know if was ready for her philanthropy, her unremitting love of her fellow man.

At times he felt her placidity was too easily won. He thought she hadn't suffered enough in life. How could someone just see the good side of people and not the snakes in the grass? She mustn't have been blooded yet.

There were nights when her do-goodery became unbearable to him, when he incited arguments merely for the sake of them. It was as if he was trying to uproot her from her stability, or make fun of her protest marches. 'The only movement I'm interested in,' he said, 'is a bowel movement.' Then there would be the times when he realized he'd gone too far, when he'd beat himself up for pushing her buttons.

He was annoyed by her intellectualization of literature, her rent-a-cause personality. His only cause, he told her, was himself. When she expressed outrage over people killed in a war he couldn't empathize. He didn't know them, he pointed out. A dog howling in the street in front of him elicited more of a reaction because he could see it happening.

Ideals, he pointed out, were abstract by definition. When he praised Nazism for fun at high school it was to knock the self-righteous off their pedestals. It was too easy to castigate Hitler. It was too obvious as well.

Bukowski admired anyone who said the opposite of the common wisdom. Such people were usually regarded as misguided souls. Too many people equated the normal with the moral.

Pressed on the question of his attitude to the distribution of wealth in the world, he joked that he thought capitalist when he won at the track but spouted on about Karl Marx when he lost. If he became rich, he said, he wouldn't worry about the lettuce pickers of Salinas. He wasn't Steinbeck. The only movement he was concerned with was a bowel movement.

He didn't see himself as left wing or right wing. The people in the middle left him cold as well – even if he was one of them. All you could do to keep your sanity was to stay outside the whole machinery altogether. Only that way could you keep a clear mind. He liked Zsa Zsa Gabor's remark, 'I was married to a capitalist and a communist. Neither of them would take out the bins.'

He told the Italian author Fernanda Pivano once that he was a conventional animal. 'I don't want to blow up a bridge,' he said, 'or change the government.' Neither did he stay awake worrying about nuclear war or saving the whale: 'I'm indifferent to the destruction of the human race. If they wiped out all humanity, nothing would be lost at all.' Of infinitely more importance to him was what kind of odds he's get on the ten horse the following Tuesday.

He didn't like being defined as a counter-cultural figure. He saw this as a label designed to stifle him. He never saw himself as pro- or anti- anything. Striking poses limited a person. It led to preconceptions about how they might 'go' on a particular issue. He fought hard against being stereotyped, usually making fun of anyone who tried it on him. Asked about gay rights, he said, 'What about rights for the rest of us? The gays have a parade. Why don't the straights get a parade?' Gays came out of the closet, he maintained, but pushed the straights back into another one.

He never wanted to hoist a flag for anything. The American flag was already tarnished for him.

He refused to associate his writing with any message. The anti-nuke brigade bored him and so did those hippies who chanted 'Hey, hey, LBJ, how many kids did you kill today?' In a few years, he knew, a lot of these bleeding hearts would be civil servants like himself. Either that or making large donations to the war effort from their stock market jobs. The fact that he never having begged for help when he was 'on the bum' fed into his idea that success was a function of effort, a notion the nanny state couldn't countenance.

He didn't want to be anyone's hero. Everyone had to look for their own answers. You couldn't find them in religion or art or politics. Witness his reaction to the assassination of John F. Kennedy. It meant little to him. 'I don't mourn him any more than

I mourn Caesar,' he said, 'You have to kill a lot of people to get to the top.' He believed Kennedy was created as an idol by people who needed such a figure to make their own lives feel better. This, to him, was to devolve responsibility.

Bukowski didn't mourn the death of John F. Kennedy

He thought Lee Harvey Oswald did the world a favor by killing him. Now people had to look inside themselves for answers. A martyr was mown down in his prime, they said, but all Bukowski could see was the death of a man who'd lived off the fat of the land. If they were looking for martyrs, he could provide them with one closer to home: 'I see men assassinated around me every day. I walk through rooms of the dead, streets of the dead, cities of the dead. How can I be concerned with one man when almost all men are taken from cribs as babies and almost immediately thrown into the masher?'

He saw his father in the same light – or darkness. He was bothered by that man's capitalist philosophy for two reasons: first because of its intense greed and secondly because he failed to achieve it.

These viewpoints may appear to be contradictory but such a contradiction was in his father as well. He believed in the American Dream with a passion. The fact that he couldn't attain it was due to his own failure of purpose. As a result he took out his frustrations on his wife and son. Bukowski always claimed he became a hobo because of his father. He filled him with a revulsion of the idea of owning property or becoming rich.

He liked expressing contentious ideas like these to people. He thought it shook them out of their complacency. Sometimes he said ridiculous things to wind people up. The pose of uncertainty he took on practically every social issue seems to have been a reaction to his father's dogmatism. He would never be as sure about anything as Henry Senior was about everything.

When people asked him about black rights he said, 'What about white rights?' When they asked him about women's rights he said, 'What about men's rights?' When were protestors going to march down Pennsylvania Avenue campaigning for post office clerks? Or starving poets?

His attitude to the *status quo* was what we might refer to as 'passive aggressive' rather than outright rebellion against the system. Revolution, he said, was just the substitution of one form of evil for another. When you were outside the system it was easy to criticize it but power had a strange way of making people compromise on their principles. When the smoke of rebellion cleared, new corruptions replaced the old ones.

He kept his head down and did his work even though he abhorred it, feeling there was no other way out. He seemed to abide by the 'render to Caesar the things that are Caesar's' *diktat*. You had to grin and bear it until your day of salvation came — if it ever did.

The secret of survival, he felt, was to play the system. This wasn't compromise in his eyes: it was giving an inch to take a mile. You had to straddle that middle course to stop yourself going under. The people at the top held the aces but you could bring your own deck to the party.

While Frances went to her protest marches, Bukowski stayed home and cracked open a beer. As he said to Fay, the character based on her in his book *Post Office*, 'I know you want to save the world but can't you start in the kitchen?'

He knew she was a good woman but her sense of triumphalism got to him. Sometimes when she pontificated he pretended to be asleep so he wouldn't have to talk to her. Equally annoying was her belief that the world was a fine place. Jane knew it was a sewer. It wasn't just a case of seeing the glass half full or half empty. It was a dirty glass.

The relationship with Frances changed when she became pregnant. He was surprised at this because she was 41 at the time, an age at which he though she was unlikely to conceive. He hadn't been using condoms because he didn't like them. The 'wise guy' who thought she was too old to get pregnant was wrong. '44 years of cleverness,' he said cruelly, 'went bang just like that. Think of all the young bodies I bypassed.'

He asked her if she wanted to marry him but she refused. 'I've been stung by that institution once,' she said, 'and that's once more than enough.' He could identify with that. So had he.

Those who knew Bukowski by reputation rather than personally thought he'd bale out of the relationship when she got pregnant but that wasn't his style. He liked to see things through.

He worried about the pregnancy because of Frances' age. He became more concerned about her than usual during the nine months. He could never have been called a New Man but he joined her in trips she made to the hospital and was concerned any time she told him she had a pain. Frances was surprised by his attentiveness to her and so was he.

Their apartment was too cramped for three people so they decided to move. They left Mariposa Avenue, where he'd been since 1958, and relocated to a roomier apartment on De Longpre Avenue. One iconic Bukowski address gave way to another one. The rental agreement was signed as Mr. and Mrs. Charles Bukowski even though they weren't married.

Despite his worries, this was one of the few times in Bukowski's life when everything went according to plan for him.

Nine months later Frances gave birth to a 9lb baby. It was a girl. They called her Marina. Bukowski could hardly believe it had happened.

'I became a father when most men my age are becoming grandfathers,' he said, 'I did everything late.'

His soft side came out when she was born. After all the tantrums and the violence, 'Whitman's wild child,' as Neeli Cherkovski called him, was tamed by a baby.

She was the 'sweet honey of my hot brain.' She coaxed him into submission with her innocence much more easily than twenty hoodlums in a back alley waving switchblades. He would never buy into the Spock psychobabble but he had a togetherness with her born of their mutual need.

She brought out sides to him he hardly knew existed, renewing his faith in the gentleness of humanity, something that had probably always been there buried inside him but unable to come out because of the horrific circumstances of his childhood.

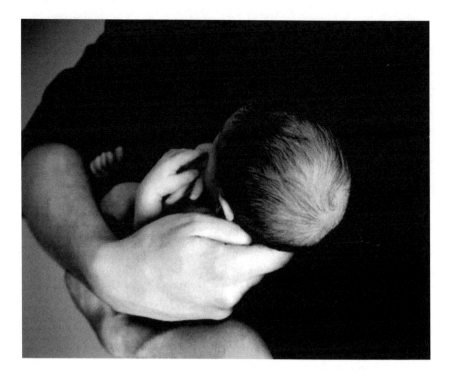

Marina Bukowski. Even the sound of it was music to his ears. She molded him to her wishes and made him young again - or rather brought him back to a childhood he never had. She was his sanity, his reality check. Why couldn't his relationships with adult females be this simple? Frances, he said, was 'just some crawling phantom in the night' - but she gave him Marina.

He couldn't argue with a child. With Marina he tried to avoid the mistakes that had been made in his own childhood. He wouldn't make her mow the lawn on Saturday, wouldn't be gluttonous in front of her, wouldn't try to make her mix with the rich set in high school. There would be no prerequisites to their relationship. He'd just try to be there for her as much as any grizzled old lush could, doing the things any father did. (He didn't make too pretty a picture as he bathed her in a tub in his back porch one day. 'Ooh!' said a young girl passing by to her friend, 'I just saw a disgusting old man in his shorts!')

He often said that there was no glory in either marriage or fatherhood. They were just states you got into because you had to. Seeing Marina in front of him, however, made him re-think that. As he sat at his desk spitting out his demons she crawled onto his lap and smiled her beatific smile at him.

He played peekaboo with her. He watched her developing her features, her personality. She was blithely oblivious to his problems and that diminished them for him. Even the post office became bearable because of her. He wrote to a friend, 'I drink myself sick and play horses and love my child and work like a coward on a job that has destroyed me for eleven years.'

In *Post Office* he claimed that he once held a knife against his throat intent on ending it all but then Marina said she wanted him to take her to the zoo and he put it down. This is reminiscent of Richard Brautigan, another alcoholic writer from the sixties. Brautigan said to his daughter Ianthe one morning, 'I would have killed myself last night but I didn't want you to find the body.'

Ianthe was only nine when Brautigan first told her he wanted to commit suicide. Sixteen years later he carried through his threat by shooting himself. Her love couldn't save him but Marina's saved Bukowski. He showed her the reserves of tenderness that attracted Frances to him originally, sometimes even surprising himself. He'd been too hurt in youth to allow his feelings show but he laid that ghost to rest now. There was no need to play the Hard Man after she was born. 'I got fed up spitting blood out of the side or my mouth,' he said, 'to show how tough I was.'

The relationship with Frances continued to deteriorate as the one with Marina grew. He didn't hate her the way he grew to hate Barbara Frye but they were totally incompatible. His drinking also continued to drive a wedge between them and made the concept of 'shared parenting' difficult. (The first word Marina learned was 'liquor.')

The post office – 'that place with 4000 and me sweating' – became harder than ever for him to handle now. He was on the 'graveyard detail.' He preferred that because it meant he could go to the track during the day. There were up to ten times more blacks on it but that didn't bother Bukowski. He didn't care what color a person's skin was as long as he liked them. 'It's hard being black,' he said, 'but it's hard being white too. It's even hard being alive.'

The post office building where Bukowski spent ten years

He was popular among his black co-workers. He didn't look down on them. Instead he joked with them. He said to one of them that he knew better than the others, 'I'm going to get me a black girlfriend because I know that would annoy you.'

They liked the fact that he didn't patronize them. To show their appreciation they protected him when he came to work drunk, hiding him from his bosses. It would have been instant dismissal if he was discovered in this condition.

Drunk or sober, the work continued to be loathsome. It was a relief to be off the streets in a white collar job but sometimes he thought the cure was worse than the disease. His head sang with pain as the drudgery of putting envelopes into slots for hours on end wore him down. Supervisors patrolled the aisles watching all the drones at their desks. 'We were like galley slaves,' Bukowski remarked, 'like people working on paddy fields.'

Anyone who slackened off even for a moment was picked out. There was no talking allowed. They only got two ten minute breaks in an eight-hour shift. If they were eleven or twelve minutes away from their desk, it was noted. Bukowski became a clock-watcher, waiting desperately for those precious ten minutes when he could go outside to have a smoke, but that only made the minutes drag more.

When he came home in the mornings he was grumpy. The fact that the apartment was cramped didn't help his mood and neither did a crying child. He'd usually be trying to sleep when Marina woke up. Like most children with their father she'd want him to play with her but he was usually too tired for that. More often than not he'd tell her he was going to lie down and he'd play with her when he woke. When that happened he had to try and adjust his body clock to the 'normal' one. He'd try and play with her but his heart wasn't in it. He'd usually want to write at this time. If he didn't play with her she might throw a tantrum. Her crying drove him crazy. He was tied between 'getting the word down' and being a good father.

He forgot the sleepless nights and the claims on his energy when he looked at her pleading eyes. She was the glue that held Frances and him together, even if it was only a tenuous one. There wasn't much else going on between them now.

125

Many nights when he was trying to write he was interrupted by a visit from his landlord and landlady. Francis and Grace Crotty were a hard-drinking couple who lived together but – no more than Bukowski and Frances – weren't married. They liked Bukowski from the off and wanted to see as much of him as possible. Whenever they'd see him working they'd say to him, 'Stop that silly typing, you son of a bitch. Come on down to our place and have a drink.' (They lived in the same building). Bukowski didn't want to upset them by saying no. The rent was cheap and he couldn't afford to jeopardize that.

When he got down to their room they'd start singing songs. They liked the lively numbers from popular musicals like *Oklahoma* and *Guys and Dolls*. If Bukowski was drunk enough he joined in. The nights often dragged on interminably but he didn't have the resistance to walk away. The Crottys provided free cigarettes and the free booze and this was like the food of life to him. He usually only went back to his room when Frances called with Marina to kiss him goodnight. This was more often than not a hint from Frances for him to come back with them. Sometimes he was glad of the excuse to get away. The following day Mrs. Crotty would knock on his door with food for him – everything from tomatoes to pears and apples. Sometimes she'd even bring a full meal or a chicken.

Frances didn't like the fact that he was so involved with the Crottys. In time it became another source of tension between them. One night when then he got back to the apartment after being with them he told Frances he'd had a toothache all evening and that it was quite painful. She wasn't in good form and didn't appear too interested.

She said she'd look for an aspirin for him but she either forgot or couldn't find one, which made Bukowski lose his temper. 'Forget it!' he said gruffly to her, 'Forget the whole goddamned thing.' She started to cry and then went to bed. A few minutes later she was asleep. At times like this, left alone in the middle of the night, he felt closer to the Crottys than he did to her.

Sometimes he did the day shift in the post office. It suited him in some ways but not in others. Desk work was easier on his body than some of the laboring jobs he'd taken up in the past but it was killing his mind.

He went AWOL often, sending in sick certs when he was hungover. He lay in bed waiting for time to pass, waiting for his body to heal itself or not, the alcohol both disease and cure as the minutes ticked towards his next red-eye shift. Now and then a nurse was sent out to him to see if he was malingering, like the time the nurse called when he was in bed with Jane and she had to hide under the covers.

The supervisor called once as well. He told him he was docking him two day's pay. Bukowski replied, 'Could you not make it a week?'

He was dying from doing 'the other man's thing.' He felt owned, beaten. He was like an accident waiting to happen, his misery underscored by the banality of his job. In the canteen he ate alone. If somebody joined him he tended to be abrupt with them. He didn't believe in talking for the sake of talk, especially if people wanted to discuss something like a ball game or what had been on television the night before. He had a profound antipathy to anything mundane like that.

If the supervisors stayed off his back and he managed to save enough of his salary to make ends meet, that was a good week for him. His needs were basic apart from the drink. The other life he lived was in his head.

His mind exploded with a million ideas for stories and poems. Writing was like playing hookey from reality for him. It was the place he ran to each evening so he could be a robot again the next day. He was like two people: the devoted father and the demented wage slave.

He loved playing with Marina but sometimes even she became too much for him. At times he felt he was losing his mind. When Mrs. Crotty said she wanted to put up new curtains in his apartment he said, 'You can't. There are dead bodies in here.'

Frances and himself had been going in different directions for a long time now. If they were emotionally attached to one another their oppositeness mightn't have been as much a problem as it was. She enjoyed having people around and he ran a mile from any company.

'She liked sewing circle poets,' he complained, 'People untouched by the grime of life.' They argued about this and about everything else.

Money was another problem. She hated it when any extra expense arose, like a problem he might have to have fixed on his car. It was running on its reputation now. The only good thing about it was the fact that he could use it as an excuse to stop meeting people. 'I can't,' became a familiar response to people who invited him out to meet them, 'The car wouldn't make it.'

Frances brought Marina on a trip to Washington now. That was where her other daughters lived. Bukowski was happy to be left on his own. He found himself hoping she'd stay away for good. For some reason she didn't seem inclined to do that, no matter how bad things got between them. She didn't like the heat but she wouldn't get out of the kitchen.

They had some fierce arguments. 'I can't take you anymore,' she said to him one day. 'I can't take me anymore either,' he replied.

He knew she'd have been more suited to a different type of man, someone less complicated than him. Why didn't she seek out such a man? She left her husband but she wouldn't leave him. Was it because of Marina? Maybe she didn't even know the reason herself. She seemed stuck in mud, trapped in her situation.

One day he came home from the post office and said to her, 'You'll have to leave.' He expected another fight but she just nodded. She accepted what he said with such resignation he felt she must have been expecting it.

In the end, he said, it was her poetry friends and church groups that did him in. He couldn't take all these people discussing peace marches and civil rights into the small hours as he tried to sleep in the next room. 'If they only had the decency to wait until I was at work,' he said.

In a poem she wrote years later, Frances thanked him for telling her to leave. 'He did both of us a favor,' she said to friends, more or less admitting she needed to be pushed. Bukowski also knew it was best for both of them that she go. The worst part was the fact that she'd be bringing Marina with her. He hadn't enough money to raise her on his own. Neither could he make a case for him being a better father than she was a mother.

She moved into an apartment a few blocks away. Bukowski paid the rent. He tried to look on the bright side. He could see Marina when he wanted.

After she was gone the emptiness set in. He looked for something to fill the void left by the departure of Marina. His writing always came to his rescue when he was feeling low before but it didn't now. His manuscripts lay strewn all over the apartment. They sat looking at him like parts of his soul that he'd flushed out of himself.

He felt hemorrhaged. How could such a little thing affect him so much? He wrote to a friend that if he was standing on a cliff with Marina and someone said, 'One of you will have to jump,' he wouldn't hesitate. He'd never felt like that about anyone before, not even Jane.

Frances brought her to see him every other day. He watched her playing on the ground in front of him and his heart melted. He wondered what she'd make of him when she grew up, this strange old man who couldn't hold onto his women, who crawled into a job he despised every day and then came home and tapped out a mountain of pages nobody wanted to see. Would she tell him he was a lunatic when she reached adulthood? Would he even live that long? Would the job – or the booze - kill him sooner?

He continued to turn up at work and go through the motions. Every day was like a week, every week like a month. He felt like Sisyphus, the character from Greek mythology, condemned to roll a boulder up a hill every day but never managing to reach the top with it. He couldn't believe he'd been in the same job, in the same building, for as many years as he'd been. Only drink saved him from going insane.

When he thought about it, there wasn't much difference between the bar stool and the post office seat. One destroyed his body and the other his mind. He was like an actor who waited on tables in the afternoon so that he could tread the boards at night.

None of the other people at the post office seemed to suffer like he did. He regarded his superiors as men who had nothing in their lives but the task in hand. Dead men, dead before death itself arrived, dead like his father, clocking in and clocking out like the automatons they were, in love with petty dreams that were commensurate with their own tunnel vision. He tolerated them only because they held the reins of power. Their pay checks were like a stranglehold on him. You couldn't bite the hand that fed. Well, not too much anyway. They knew he wasn't afraid of them in the same way as the bullies at school did when he was a child, which gave him a kind of subtle power with them.

He became threatening to them if he expressed any kind of an original thought. His kindness to the black workers was another bone of contention. This didn't go down well with the 'top brass.' There was a hierarchical structure that had to be adhered to. The blacks were supposed to be like menials, not equals.

Bukowski's friendship with his black colleagues at the post office didn't go down well with the officials. (Al Berlinski)

His writing posed another kind of problem for them. This was coming to their notice more and more as his profile in the literary magazines grew. His anti-establishment slant was like a red rag to a bull to them. Post office drones weren't supposed to have a life outside work. There was a job to be done, that was all that could be said. He was expected to do it without question and without deviation of purpose. It was like Kafka's Joseph K transplanted to downtown L.A.

His physical problems were worsening now as well. He often came home from work feeling dizzy. He had pains in his arms that were so bad he could hardly lift them. Was he getting a heart attack? He didn't know. He seemed to have all the symptoms. He went to doctors to have himself checked out but they found nothing.

The authorities thought he was putting it on when he told them about the pains. They said they were probably psychosomatic. In some ways he thought they might be right. It reminded him of the time when his acne was at its worst as a young man. Acne vulgaris, he knew, was an outer manifestation of an inner turmoil. What his bosses didn't realize was that you couldn't see depression on the end of a stethoscope. You couldn't put it on a wall chart. How could one tabulate the residue of a thousand nights tossing and turning in a bed wondering if you'd live long enough to see the dawn?

Another problem with the job was having to mix with people. He'd just gotten rid of Frances' milk-and-watery friends but the post office people were worse. All he had in common with them was the fact that they were all stuck in the same rut. He let them know this in no uncertain terms any time one of them tried to get close to him. Ever since his schooldays he hadn't felt comfortable with 'the crowd.' Who could have predicted that in years to come Bukowski would stand in front of hundreds of people reading his poetry?

For now he preferred sitting alone in front of his typewriter. He could be himself with that. He didn't have to role-play with it. It was a placid concubine. If he bled his emotions onto its surface it repaid him with its beauty. And maybe even some dollars.

The people at the post office complained about the job but deep down he felt they were content in it. They had become institutionalized over time. Maybe every worker did. That was how the system perpetuated itself. Eventually everyone fell in love with his chains. They weren't only putting envelopes into boxes but their souls as well.

He felt a million miles away from them in the way he thought. They discussed the weather, their families, a possible raise in their salaries. Each night they went home to lives as dull as their jobs. They were only half-alive. Some of them, he thought, wouldn't have had the imagination to have a nervous breakdown. And yet they made *him* feel like the oddball.

The job was killing him physically and spiritually. What saved him – apart from drinking - was 'the word.' No matter how bad things became, he never stopped writing. He wrote a story every other day. He was never much for editing but he often struck gold at the first try. He kept telling the same stories in different ways. He felt like a painter splashing colors on a canvas of A4. Many of them centered on his life, or at least had parts of it present in some aspect of them. He re-wrote his past every night, twisting the spools of his life like an old movie that highlighted his favorite scenes.

The unfeeling parents. The lawn-mowing. The President Hoover story. The boils. The acne. An occasional kindly teacher. The beatings. The end of the beatings. Rooming-houses. Park benches. The war. His imprisonment for draft-dodging. Meeting Jane and becoming her soulmate. Drinking with her as if there was no tomorrow until the 1955 experience. The death of his parents and then her own death. Sex. The marriage with Barbara Frye. The child by Frances.

All these became the themes he developed and re-developed like interlocking tables or Chinese dolls, picking the words like apples off trees, seeking to make sense of them or not make sense of them, heaping image upon image as classical music blasted away on a broken-down stereo in the background.

He still sat at the window while he worked. Street noises were catalysts to his imagination just like the music was. 'I use it as background,' he said, 'the same way other people might turn on a television.' He hated television.

Some writers liked to work in silence but Bukowski was galvanized by noise. It stimulated his brain. People passing by the window often found their way into his work.

The long night's journey into day ended with a trudge back to work. He abhorred it but, as he said, 'I have no trade and I like to eat.' In another sense it was a necessary evil: the death of the soul that made the life of the page possible. It was the pact he made with the devil to keep going.

Another advantage it had was the fact that it stopped him drinking during the day. When Brendan Behan gave up his painting job he couldn't work off his hangovers with quite the same aplomb. Similarly, when he was in jail he didn't write. Bukowski needed breaks from his writing and he got these when he was in the post office. After work there was the racetrack to perform the same function. He never *didn't* write when he was in the post office.

Crucifix in a Deathhand was published in 1965. Most of it, he said, was written during a 'hot, lyrical' month in New Orleans. The book was only possible, he believed, because of the kindness of Jon Webb. He invited Bukowski down to New Orleans to oversee its production. He stayed with a friend of Webb's, Minnie Seagate, who ran a restaurant around the corner from him. She liked her drink so she got on well with Bukowski. On his first night down there he got drunk with her. The next morning he went around to Webb. 'Any new poems?' Webb asked him. 'No,' Bukowski replied, 'Just give me a beer.' 'No poems no beer,' Webb said. So Bukowski went off and wrote some. When he came back he got his beer.

He worked with Webb every morning for the next few weeks. They sat at a small table in the kitchen with roaches running up and down the wall in front of them. Every time Webb needed an extra poem, Bukowski had to go away and write one. Amazingly, he seemed to be able to do so without too much difficulty. There are many beautiful images in these poems. They're characterized by a tenderness we don't usually associate with Bukowski. 2000 copies of the book were printed, a huge increase from his previous collection.

1965 also saw the publication of *Cold Dogs in the Courtyard*, a poetry anthology that had Bukowski exploring his dark side. It ran to just 23 pages. Only 500 copies were printed but at least it was another title - from a man who once doubted he would write even one book.

The following year he was entered for the Pulitzer Prize. Frances referred to it as the 'Foolitzer' Prize. She showed her mercenary side when she said to Bukowski, 'I want nineteen weeks of child support payments in advance.' She wanted to bring Marina to camp with her. He could only laugh at her demand, a preposterous one to any way of thinking. He was having trouble even meeting a week's support on his salary and the 'Foolitzer,' he knew, definitely wouldn't be won by him. He wasn't far enough up the totem pole to be seriously considered even for a nomination. He was so anonymous, he said, he felt like 'a monk fornicating a goose in a coalmine.'

The authorities at the post office started to tighten the screws on him now. One of his bosses in particular had a grudge against him. He gave him all the dirty jobs as 'punishment.' For most of his shift, Bukowski sat inside a plexiglass cubicle about the size of a phone booth. To sort the mail he had to raise his hand up every few seconds and put it into a pigeonhole. 'We were pigeons ourselves,' he said, 'except we were in different kinds of holes.'

When postcodes were introduced, there was a test of knowledge of the areas the sorters had to cover. If they didn't answer the questions they were asked within a certain amount of time they could lose their jobs. It was called The Scheme. Bukowski dreaded it. It made a stressful job even more stressful. He left 'pools of sweat' under him on the floor whenever he took a break. Every six months there were different tests to evaluate the sorters' worthiness to do the job. These stressed him even further.

The fact that his attention was becoming more diverted into his writing made the work harder to do. Learning off all the postcodes was chewing his brain alive. He tried to be away from his desk as much as he could, still stretching out the allowed ten minute breaks to fifteen or twenty when his supervisor wasn't around. 'I spend more time in the crapper,' he said, 'than the janitor who cleans the place.'

One night his friend Neeli Cherkovski called around to his apartment. 'I'm on the cross,' Bukowski told him. Cherkovski advised him to walk away from the job and try to make his living writing poetry. Bukowski guffawed at this suggestion. The only way a poet made money, he maintained, was by teaching in a university. That wasn't a possibility for him because of his negative feelings about academics. It would have been 'the final murder of the soul.'

Cherkovski asked him what he was going to do. Bukowski told him there was another possibility. A man called John Martin had been on the phone to him and seemed to be interested in doing something with him. He was the owner of a company that supplied offices with furniture. The company had a printing press for running off stationery. He was interested in using this to publish creative literature.

He was due to call on Bukowski in a few days. He'd been reading him for some years. He'd actually written him a letter in 1965 telling him how much he admired his work in *The Outsider*. Maybe he'd be the person who could usher in his creative publishing idea. Cherkovski wished him luck on that score.

A few days later, true to his word, Martin arrived at Bukowski's door. He was an unassuming man with a shrill voice. The first thing he said to Bukowski was, 'I worship you.' Bukowski replied nonchalantly, 'That's all right.'

He offered Martin a beer but he refused it. He was teetotal. He asked Bukowski if he had any writing he could show him. Bukowski opened a closet. Inside it were MSS stacked four feet high. As soon as the door swung open, a blizzard of them tumbled out onto the floor. Martin's jaw dropped in shock. He went down on all fours and started sifting through them. He couldn't believe

136

what he was seeing. He thought Bukowski might have had enough poetry stockpiled for a collection or two but there seemed to be enough here to fill the Library of Congress. He read as much of it as he could on the spot, feeling as if he'd stumbled on a goldmine. Bukowski told him to take what he wanted.

He offered him $30 for one of his poems there and then. He said he'd like to make a broadside of it. 'I'll get back to you on the rest of them,' he promised. Bukowski said that would be fine. He was quietly optimistic about the encounter but he'd been stung so badly by unscrupulous editors in the past he didn't get his hopes up too high. It might come to something or it might not. Martin, meanwhile, went home with enough reading material to last him the rest of the year.

At this time Bukowski was also communicating with a Chicago-based poet called Douglas Blazek. Blazek edited a magazine called *Ole* – pronounced to rhyme with 'hole' rather than the Spanish 'Olé.' He accepted some of Bukowski's poems for the inaugural issue and afterwards became a friend. Bukowski referred to him as 'the kid with the mimeo machine in his kitchen in Illinois.'

Blazek worked in a factory. He was just as miserable there as Bukowski was in the post office. The pair of them compared notes on this. For Bukowski it was refreshing to touch base with a poet who wasn't living off the state, or some rich relative. In the evening both of them worked their magic on the page to get rid of the detritus of their work.

Bukowski liked the rough look of *Ole*. Rummaging through its pages he was reminded of being back in New Orleans with the Webbs, doing everything by hand. They were two small guys trying to survive against the odds.

Blazek revived Bukowski's interest in prose. He'd more or less stopped writing it after his 1955 debacle. He published two of his manuscripts as chapbooks the following year, *All the Assholes in the World and Mine* in 1955 and *Confessions of a Man Insane Enough to Live with Beasts.* The latter was his favorite title of all the great ones he came up with in the following years. 'It's a pity I had to waste it on a pamphlet,' he pined.

Blazek became a penpal of Bukowski's right through the sixties. He completed a trio made up of the Webbs and a Louisiana poet called William Corrington. These people became the touchstones upon which Bukowski unleashed his torments in subsequent years. He threw everything into the letters just as he did into his creative work. Sometimes it was hard to tell the difference.

Many of them were written while he was drunk. 'Bukowski's letters,' Jory Sherman wrote, 'reeked of cheap booze and the rancid sweat of whores.' They have his humor, his darkness, his bewildered attempt to make sense of his life.

A frequent theme is the fact that he's broken and weak, which makes one wonder where all the energy that's in them came from. They seemed to be his substitute for meeting people. You could leave a letter when you felt like it, he knew, and pick it up later when you were in better form. People were different. They didn't usually absent themselves when you wanted them to.

The letters were followed up by anti-climactic meetings with the people they were written to. Bukowski didn't like Corrington when he ran into him in 1965. He was fine from the safety of the postal system but he was threatened by him in the flesh. He found him too cocky. Neither was he impressed by the younger man's championing of Barry Goldwater, a politician he had little time for.

Corrington told Bukowski he'd had a novel accepted by a publisher. He was now revising his ideas about poetry, he said, and coming around to the idea that the novel was a superior genre. This was treachery in Bukowski's eyes. Corrington was turning his back on the thing that had kick-started their friendship. How could he let the novel leapfrog over poetry like that? For Bukowski there was no contest.

'He's left his wife for his mistress,' was the way he put it to Jon Webb. What was the big deal about novels, he wondered? Every second writer had one under the mattress, ready to be inflicted on some long-suffering editor. Did he do it for the money? Cash, he said, turned a man's head just like it did a whore's one.

Corrington's novel was called *Lines to the South.* Bukowski didn't like it. He gave it a poor review. He'd been enthusiastic about his previous work, *The Anatomy of Love and Other Poems,* but didn't think this measured up to it. Or was he just annoyed with him when he wrote the review? In subsequent letters to him the tone is decidedly more formal, with 'Mr. Corrington' being used as the form of address rather than the original 'Willie.'

Corrington fell further in Bukowski's estimation when he started to get seduced by campus values and became a university lecturer. 'I do not consider you my superior,' he wrote to him, 'even though I am a postal clerk and you are a Dr. of Literature.' He lost the plot entirely for Bukowski when he went to Hollywood, the last den of iniquity for him. He became the property of the establishment, he thought, sucking the life-blood out of literature by institutionalizing it.

Bukowski could never forgive Corrington for becoming a university writer. Universities, for him, were places poets went to die. He liked Flannery O'Connor's comment when she was asked if she thought universities stifled writers. 'It doesn't stifle half enough of them,' she replied.

The main reason he was annoyed with Corrington, however, was for something else entirely. The University of California had offered to publish Bukowski's letters in book form in a deal set up by John Martin. After it was set up, Bukowski wrote to Corrington asking him if he could send back all the ones he'd written to him. The money he got from the book, he said, would give him a year or two off from a job that was killing both his body and mind. He hadn't kept carbons of the letters as that wasn't his style. (If he had, all the poems he sent out to publishers over the years that went missing would have made an interesting collection).

Corrington, to his horror, refused. Something else Bukowski should have kept a carbon of was a letter he had from Corrington saying he'd send his letters back to him any time he wanted them. When Bukowski reminded him of this, Corrington said he hadn't remembered sending such a letter. Bukowski found it and returned it to Corrington without xeroxing it. Corrington denied getting it. He then wrote back to Bukowski, again refusing to return his letters. 'I plan to use them,' he said cynically, 'to put my son through college.' Bukowski was incandescent with rage. It was as if the letters were going to be his pension. Shortly before this, Corrington had asked Bukowski to return the letters he'd sent to *him* for a similar project to Bukowski's and he did so on the spot. Any other action would have been inconceivable to him. Now Corrington was digging his heels in. Why? It didn't seem to make sense.

Afterwards he approached Douglas Blazek with the same request. Having been scarred by Corrington's refusal he wrote to Blazek with some trepidation. He said refusing to return someone's letters was like a whore taking his wallet while he slept. The nervous tone suggested he thought Blazek would refuse his request but he didn't. This renewed Bukowski's his faith in him in a manner Corrington failed to.

When he met Blazek in 1967 they didn't get on. The meeting was as disappointing as the one with Corrington had been. The experience seemed to say to Bukowski: Stick with letter-writing and stay inside your door. (Which was his preference anyway).

His correspondence with Jory Sherman was equally anti-climactic. Sherman was the West Coast editor of *The Outsider* magazine. He was the man who first put Bukowski in touch with the Webbs. They also used to drink together. Their correspondence was lively for a time but it ended with Bukowski declaring to his sometime boozing buddy that there was never any real friendship between them.

This is an allegation Sherman hotly disputed in his memoir, *Friendship, Fame and Bestial Myth*. He relates enough anecdotes in this book to convince us that he was indeed a confidante of Bukowski in his pre-fame years. He also praises him highly in the course of it, both as man and writer, but there's an undertow of resentment running through the pages as well. Bukowski was obsessed with becoming famous, Sherman tells us, but once he reached his goal he spent most of his time reviling his new status.

Bukowski also had a mercurial relationship with the poet Al Winans. Winans was editor of the literary magazine *The Second Coming*, one of Bukowski's favorite outlets during the lean years. His correspondence with him ran intermittently through the 1970s and 1980s. Bukowski fell out with him after Winans wrote a poem about him which he deemed pejorative and also because he felt (wrongly, as it turned out) that Winans was storing up his letters to sell for profit.

Like Bukowski, Winans was a postal clerk by trade. He was also a big drinker. He got into trouble with the law after being arrested one St. Patrick's Day for jumping into an empty taxicab that had the keys in the ignition. He seized his opportunity and drove off in it. He was under the influence of drugs at the time.

Their relationship went through peaks and valleys, the best times being when Bukowski was submitting material to *The Second Coming*. The magazine went bust when a car accident virtually emptied Winans' bank account.

Winans took Bukowski's mood changes on the chin. He stayed friends with him after his career took off and also kept Bukowski in touch with literary gossip. To repay him, Bukowski propped up Winans' spirits anytime he felt dejected about what he was doing. He assured him *The Second Coming* was one of the best literary magazines around. Winans was also a strong supporter of

Bukowski's work, publishing as much of it as he could in good times and bad.

The relationship became strained when Bukowski refused to write a preface for Winans' poetry collection *North Beach Poems* and also for a Jack Micheline book. The refusal hurt Winans, especially in the light of Bukowski's previous praise both for his own work and Micheline's. He was effusive when it came to verbal praise, or praise in his letters. Such endorsements were different from putting something out for the world to see. Bukowski admired what John Dos Passos called 'the hot struggles of the poor' in the writings of Blazek and Micheline but when it came to issuing superlatives on book jackets he tended to cry off. If the person was dead, like Robinson Jeffers or Sherwood Anderson, he had no problem rhapsodizing about their talents but among the living he tended to see himself as 'the leader of the tribe.'

Harold Norse was another regular correspondent. Bukowski didn't generally like gay writers but he made an exception for Norse, a globetrotting poet with a wide orbit. Like Bukowski he was an underground figure who went on to reach a wider readership with time. Both of them had been published in *Ole* and *The Outsider* before bigger audiences presented themselves. In the mid-1960s a special edition of *Ole* was devoted to Norse with tributes from the likes of James Baldwin and William Burroughs. In his novel *Beat Hotel* Norse used the cut-up technique Burroughs would later fine-tune in his own work.

At one point Bukowski regarded Norse as the greatest poet living. He often read his work aloud to friends. His only problem with it was that it was too refined, lacking the madness of his own work. He told people he could never write as well as Norse but it's questionable whether he would have wanted to. Norse had what he called a 'holy' attitude to poetry, choosing every word with undue care. He manicured his nails, as it were, on the edge of his experiences. This could never be Bukowski's way. He preferred to dive in headlong and see what happened.

Norse sneered at Bukowski, adopting a superior attitude to him. If Bukowski insulted him when he was drunk he took it personally, not realizing it was probably the drink talking. (Bukowski liked to say, 'Before a man can meet the gods, he must learn to forgive the drunks.')

Their friendship seesawed with the passage of time. Norse became annoyed when Bukowski used one of his letters as the basis for a journalistic article. Bukowski later accused Norse of badmouthing him to John Martin, saying Martin was over-publishing him at the expense of more talented writers. Norse denied ever saying this but Bukowski had his doubts. He was familiar with people feeling Martin thought too much of him. He gave Norse a hard time over this. 'Bukowski puts you on a pedestal,' Norse spluttered, 'and then he knocks you off it. He can be so detestable you want to shove him up a camel's ass, but then the snotty charm of the bastard comes through.'

Bukowski also corresponded with a fourth poet, Gerald Locklin. Locklin was professor of English at Long Beach State University. He went from a position of being dismissive of Bukowski's talent to revering it. He knew all the clichés that went around the literary world about him but chose to ignore them. He knew Bukowski's hardboiled pose was getting better as he grew older. The reason some people praised the early work, he thought, was because they were jealous of his new-found fame and tried to find some way to debunk him. Saying he'd sold out – a common criticism - was a sly way of assuaging their frustration at not getting anywhere with their own work.

Locklin was respectful of Bukowski's books when he reviewed them periodically in the posh literary journals for which he wrote. He collected such reviews in his book *A Sure Bet*. This gives a very objective appraisal of both Bukowski's gifts and his shortcomings. He knew he had a soft center but chose not to exhibit it often, adhering to the 'a man's gotta do what a man's gotta do' credo with people until they occupied a place of trust in his heart. This didn't happen often. In the book he writes about the conspiracy of silence that surrounded Bukowski until he became famous. At this point the establishment realized he wasn't going to go away so it launched a full frontal assault against him. The people who despised him as a poor drunken bum now started to despise him as a rich drunken bum.

**Gerald Locklin, one of the few poets
Bukowski didn't fall out with at some point**

Locklin stayed friends with Bukowski the only way he knew how: by keeping out of his way. He knew where he lived but never called unannounced, knowing he only came out of his 'cave' when he wanted to. Bukowski was rude to people who inflicted themselves on him when he didn't want to see them. He

144

appreciated friends like Locklin who didn't abuse their privileges. 'I did not,' Locklin once said, 'show up on his doorstep with two six-packs and the conviction that I was doing him a favor.' As a result of this, the atmosphere between them was cordial if they met at readings or functions.

Frank Sinatra used to keep a sign on his front gate that said, 'You better have a damn good reason for ringing this bell.' Bukowski had a simpler one with the words, 'Go Away' on it. He thought Santa Claus had the right idea: Visit people once a year. Having said that, he suffered some 'door-knockers' because they kept him in touch with the literary scene. Others he saw because they published him. He was always ambitious in that direction. When people visited him they were always shocked by his living conditions – the bottles lined up on the floor, the ash trays overflowing with cigarette butts, the dishes piled high in the kitchen sink. ('A man who has a tidy kitchen,' he liked to say, 'is dead in the soul.')

His appearance shocked them too. If he was in the middle of a binge, or coming out of one, his clothes were usually unkempt, his beer belly thrust out over his shorts. At times like this he made Stanley Kowalski look tame. His eyes would be gone back in his head. Some people said he had the saddest eyes they ever saw. Others remarked that they looked '1000 years old.'

Bukowski was now about to begin a column called *Notes of a Dirty Old Man* for John Bryan's newspaper *Open City*. This radical paper sold for fifteen cents at vending machines on street corners. It was also circulated to various media outlets like recording studios and movie lots. A lot of copies were given away free as well and that widened the circulation even more. It consumed Bukowski's interest. Bryan gave him leverage to write about anything that took his fancy. Once he happened upon the title for the column, he claimed, it wrote itself.

The first article he did for Bryan was a review of A.E. Hotchner's biography of Ernest Hemingway in 1967. He used it to take pot shots at a man with whom he sometimes seemed to be obsessed. Like a lot of people, Bukowski preferred the tight-lipped style of the early Hemingway to the elder 'Papa.' His review of the book was more like a denunciation of him than anything else. He'd shot himself just six years before. Bukowski wasn't surprised. For him the decline in his talent was like a graph going dramatically downwards for years now. He hadn't even liked *The Old Man and the Sea*. 'Ernie bagged his last trophy,' he derided, 'himself.'

Ernest Hemingway
(Library of Congress)

The following week he began his *Notes of a Dirty Old Man* column. His first article was a kind of apologia for drunk drivers – a subject close to his heart. He was hitting the ground running.

Open City took Bukowski's name from the literary magazines and put it onto the streets. The people who read it loved his outrageous style, his outrageous attitudes.

'It was like pissing words for a living,' he said, 'Things came out that I didn't know were there. It was as if I was discovering them instead of inventing them.'

He always started with some zany title for the column. A phrase like 'Twelve monkeys flying under a dead moon' would come to him and he'd write it down. Then he'd compose a narrative around it. It was like the time when he was writing all those assignments at the College of Journalism as a young man, out-writing his classmates by a volume of about ten to one. Sky was the limit then and sky was the limit now. Logic went out the window.

The column didn't net him much cash but he loved its instantaneous nature. Short stories were disguised as opinion pieces and vice versa. He liked working towards a deadline. That got his juices flowing. 'A lot of times,' he said, 'if I didn't have the deadlines I wouldn't have written anything at all.'

After years of submitting work to the poetry magazines and waiting weeks (if not months) for something to appear, it was a buzz for him to write something at a weekend and see it all over town a few days later.

Bryan loved his style. He knew it would grab readers' attention. When he told Bukowski 'It's in!' each week after reading his copy, the words acted as a real adrenalin rush for him. After a while Bryan didn't even need to read what he wrote to say those two words. They were automatic.

Some readers weren't as impressed by the columns as others. A psychiatrist wrote to him once advising him that he needed help. A telephone operator sent him money to try and entice him to get of drink and eat good food. A man who called himself King Arthur offered to write his column with him to make it better.

He used the wide berth Bryan gave him to the hilt. It was the sixties, after all, the 'Everything goes' era. No longer did he have to worry about the way he phrased things. Calling himself 'dirty' instead of having someone else do it freed him up to say anything he liked in whatever way he liked. He was given a license to shock like an open check.

Sometimes he overdid it. One column he wrote made fun of Jon Webb, which resulted in Webb blanking him for a time.

His disloyalty towards Webb reached its nadir after he died. Bukowski wrote a story in which he tried to bed Louise after the funeral. These incidents evince the worst possible aspects of his character. Harold Norse said, 'He was a great writer but a horrible man. Everyone who knew him was a possible target for his wrath.' Bukowski didn't see it like that. He had a thick skin and expected other people to have too.

Most of the columns were biographical. He told his life story in instalments, interjecting asides on anything and everything: politics, literature, sex, work, poverty, health, death. Bryan lapped it up. He lived near Bukowski and the pair of them became good friends. He even babysat Marina for him now and again.

Other columns were written like short stories, the absence of capital letters reminding one of e.e. cummings. Images tumbled from his pen in vitriolic cascades. He left readers in little doubt that for him the American Dream was rotten to the core.

It was a style of writing that was unfettered, a kite let loose in the wind. It was freefall parachuting of the mind, undercut with the malevolent glee of a man who had nothing to lose because he'd decided not to play the game. He bit on negativity like a bone, twisting it this way and that.

The column also gave him the opportunity to indulge his misogynistic feelings. 'Women are basically stupid animals,' he wrote on one occasion. He got away with comments like these because he was Bukowski. There could be no other explanation.

Notes of a Dirty Old Man ran for two years in all. Bukowski's 'philosophy' in the column, according to Bryan, was, 'Life is a meaningless pile of shit. It goes nowhere but the grave. What's left is drinking, fucking and playing the ponies. Take whatever you can

lay your hands on. Save your own sweet ass. Fuck everybody else.'
It wasn't exactly a Sunday school sermon.

When Bryan asked Bukowski to edit a supplement for the paper it got into trouble.

He chose a racy Jack Micheline story about a young girl. When this was published, Bryan was arrested on obscenity charges. The case was eventually thrown out but the publicity it engendered resulted in the shutting down of the paper. The 'open' city wasn't as open as Bryan thought.

Bukowski didn't take any blame for the incident, instead turning on Bryan and calling his paper 'half-ass.'

His attitude smacked of defensiveness. Bryan was disappointed with him. He looked on his comments as ungrateful, a poor recompense for all the times he'd put himself out for him.

'I loaned Bukowski money,' he said, 'I worried about his crazy communist wife, I babysat his blue-veined daughter, I listened to him scream and curse at the world, I wiped up his treacly vomit, I trusted the crazy bastard with my life.'

His overall estimation of Bukowski was the same as that of Harold Norse: he was 'a great writer but a lousy human being.' Bukowski went on to write a damaging story about *Open City*, 'The Birth, Life and Death of an Underground Newspaper.'

Afterwards he turned his attentions to a 'sister' publication, the *Los Angeles Free Press*. His writing here was equally wild, equally unfettered.

He basically took up where he left off in *Open City*. By now people knew what to expect from him – anything. Heated expectation greeted his outlandish utterances. Anything was fair – or foul – game for his poison pen. Nobody was safe. He wrote in blood and sweat, if not tears. Readers were either disgusted or highly amused – or both. Like all cult figures, he polarized them. No matter how trivial the subject he imbued it with the indelible Bukowski stamp.

By now he'd become the property of the hippies, something he hardly embraced with open arms. He'd spent too many years in blue collar jobs to throw his lot in with the 'flower children.' He saw them as little more than smoked salmon socialists, the left luggage of a movement that might have originated with legitimate motives but eventually descended into self-parody. 'They won't realize how much shit they're swimming in,' he said, 'until the blow the dope out of their eyes.'

He was also turned off by their bumper sticker snippets.

'Make love not war.'

'Buck the system.'

'Don't trust anyone over thirty.'

Such epithets sounded cute until you examined them. What was wrong with people over thirty? Maybe it was the people who were under thirty that were the problem. As for war, how could we avoid it? Maybe there was more honesty in it than what passed for love. And were they really bucking the system by sitting round on beanbags smoking weed and going, 'Groovy, baby'? For Bukowski, marijuana took the edge off an experience instead of adding to it.

While the hippies 'dug' Bukowski's style of writing, they found it difficult to reconcile it with his old-fashioned job in the post office. He even dressed like a 'square.' (Harold Norse said he wore 'the kind of clothes ex-convicts wore after being released from prison.')

Bukowski didn't want to go to San Francisco with flowers in his hair. Still less did the image of a trendified Jesus clone with a florid shirt and jewelry dripping down to his navel appeal to him. He refused to compare mythologies with the hipsters who proliferated at the fashionable coffeehouses. He had no intentions of breaking bread with the tribalistic baby boomers still wet from their mother's milk as they yammered on about the evils of fascism from the bonnet of Dad's E-type Jag. He allowed such showmen their day in the sun. Meanwhile he plodded homeward from the post office every day in his 'square' mail sorter's shoes to commune with the page.

Even James Dean's frenetic 'You don't understand me!' from *Rebel Without a Cause* rankled with him. Was this suburban jerk-off supposed to typify angst? Try acne vulgaris on Longwood Avenue instead. Or a father who incinerated mice. Dean grew up in an era when the winds of change were blowing. Bukowski's formative years were the Roaring Twenties — with most of the roaring being done by his parents. The 'swinging' sixties had also passed him by. The only thing that swung for Bukowski in that decade was his beer arm.

151

His lack of 'cool' signaled a new kind of hip for the Beats. They looked on him with a mixture of awe and incredulity, reactions he took with a grain of salt. For this grinder, street cred also meant work cred.

He found it difficult to respect anyone who didn't hold down a job. That was one of the things he admired about people like Neal Cassady.

He only met Cassady once. He was out of his mind with speed at the time. He showed Bukowski another kind of speed when he brought him on a ride in his car. Bukowski thought his end was near as Cassady screeched round the corners, apparently intent on crashing his vehicle at any one of them.

They survived that journey but a few weeks later Cassady was dead — 'deliberately, perhaps' according to Bukowski. He gave him this dubious tribute: 'He was almost as crazy as I am.' His main problem, he felt, was the fact that he lived under the shadow of Jack Kerouac.

Another writer Bukowski corresponded with at this time was William Wantling. He'd been a Marine stationed in Korea but succumbed to drink and drugs after being demobbed, spending some years in prison afterwards. He wrote to Bukowski from there. Caryl Chessman was in the same jail as he was. He became a cause of Wantling's for a while. He was of interest to Bukowski too, as he was of many writers who opposed capital punishment, even Brendan Behan.

Bukowski's problems at work reached a head now. His *Notes of a Dirty Old Man* columns had been a thorn in the side of the post office officials for some time.

They didn't think it looked good for someone who wrote like that to be sorting mail for the government. They called him into a room for what was euphemistically called a 'consultation.' A representative from Washington was even called in to officiate.

As soon as Bukowski was sitting down, the representative said to him, 'We don't know what to do with you.'

He showed him a drawing of a penis on legs which had been used to illustrate a story Bukowski wrote about a man who'd had anal sex with another man by mistake. (He was too drunk to realize it wasn't a woman).

He asked him if he'd written the story. He said he had but that he wasn't responsible for the illustration.

Aspersions were cast upon the nature of the material.

Said Bukowski, 'Are we to consider the postal officials as the new critics of literature?' The representative replied that certain moral standards were expected of public officials.

'What do you mean by morality?' Bukowski asked.

The man said the civil service was the wrong place to be working when he was documenting his sexual adventures.

Why?' asked Bukowski. He accused them all of threatening his freedom of expression 'in a manner that might interest the American Civil Liberties Union.' They backed off at this and he returned to his desk. The Frozen Man had the last word.

He never saw what he was doing as obscene. The only obscene thing for him was poor writing. His basic thesis was that there was nothing you couldn't write literature about. Nobody had the right to say what was or wasn't poetic — least of all the 'clean fingernail' brigade.

Was he really a 'dirty old man'? When he wrote for the pornography magazines he gave them more than the usual bump-and-grind gratuitousness. He always tried to graft a storyline onto the boudoir frolics. 'The sex stories pay the rent,' he said, 'That's all I can say about them. Sex sells.' But he never tried to market sex as a fantasy, portraying it more as a natural bodily function. Neither did he try to be erotic like a D.H. Lawrence or an Anais Nin. He preferred to steer away from the ineffectuality he saw in such writers. Hard living meant hard loving. He spared us the patina of respectability that was often put over the subject.

He hated most of the writing he read about sex. When it wasn't cliché-ridden it spent its time hitting the reader over the head with some message about Personal Fulfilment. He didn't see sex either as taboo or Holy Grail. It was just there, like the Golden Gate Bridge or the Statue of Liberty. It was tragic because it generally lasted longer than love and funny because people's need for it often got them into ridiculous situations. 'I used sex to draw the reader in,' he said, 'Then I write what I really want around it.'

Bukowski went into hospital in March 1966 to have some hemorrhoids removed. It was a painful time but he managed to see the funny side of it: A 'good clean heart attack,' he suggested, would have been more honorable. He wrote about the experience in *All the Assholes in the World and Mine.* Books had a way of taking the harm out of things.

The money they brought in was also nice. His sick pay had run out by now. His medical insurance didn't cover his medical bills. Every dollar was precious.

His next book, *The Most Beautiful Woman in Town,* was published by City Lights in 1967. It featured many of the stories he'd written for obscure magazines over the years, delivered in his inimitable style. They had a throwaway style, bringing one into the thick of the action as soon as they began. The characters were one-dimensional and the plots wafer-thin but few writers explored the seedy underbelly of L.A. with the outspokenness of this man. .

He had the knack of making the ridiculous sound plausible. Witness the story 'Six Inches' where he deals with the male phobia of emasculation in a literal rather than metaphorical manner. Other stories like 'The Fuck Machine' leave one in little doubt about their content. '3 Women' is gloriously decadent in its depiction of a *menage-a-trois* set against the backdrop of boozing and poverty...and bad clocks. 'The Birth, Life and Death of an Underground Newspaper' concerned his work in *Open City* and the problems it entailed with the post office officials. 'Life and Death in the Charity Ward' dealt with his near-death experiences in 1955.

The most controversial story in the collection was 'The Fiend.' This featured a man fantasizing about raping a child. To many readers it seemed like an endorsement of pedophilia. It's Bukowski's most objectionable printed work and it caused a lot of outrage when it was published. John Martin had refused it but it appeared in the sex magazine *Hustler*. Bukowski couldn't see what all the fuss was about and that enraged people even further. Poetic license was fine but sometimes he blurred the boundaries. This was one such case, especially when he said the story was based on a real incident of him seeing a child playing in a neighbor's yard one day and becoming aroused by her. He was asked in an interview if he could ever conceive of himself as raping a child. He said he couldn't but the reason he gave caused even more outrage: fear of doing time. (In later interviews he changed his tone and said the story was total fiction and the subject matter horrendous)

Also published that year was *Tales of Ordinary Madness*, a collection of stories that originally appeared in magazines like *Knight, Pix, Nola Express* and *Open City.* Much of the material is autobiographical. Some of it is delightfully decadent. He raises banal facts to the level of hilarity by the sheer force of the writing. This isn't so much ordinary madness as extraordinary sanity. An uneasy mix of narrative and manifesto, it has Bukowski embracing all his pet themes: booze, jail, the track, politics, poetry. There were also some more unusual elements in it, like clogged toilets, cliché-ridden pests and surreal blankets. The sex scenes, as one might have expected, make *Last Tango in Paris* look like *Mary Poppins*. We can read them either as the demented ramblings of an iconoclast or inspirational nuggets from a prophet. More bemused by his lot than tortured by it, Bukowski takes some solace from the fact that no matter how badly off he is, he can still detect shit in others — and maybe even pull a chick or two.

He transmutes his suffering into the stuff of high farce, refusing to become solemn about it. It's like Kafka written by Mickey Spillane, a loopy onslaught on inner city slimeballs. Rotgut beer and raw sex keeps the tubes flowing. The latterday Proust finds himself confronting a beautifully profane existence.

Note of a Dirty Old Man, a further compilation of all his *Open City* columns, was also published by City Lights Books that year. If it didn't cause quite as much consternation as the columns, that was only because Bukowski was already a legend of the underground by now.

His comments on sex, as one might have expected, were too hilarious to offend. 'It's interesting but not important,' he wrote, 'It's not even as important as excretion. A man can go seventy years without a piece of ass but he can die in a week without a bowel movement.' He wrote about sex as a 'stage play laugh where you have to cry about it a bit between acts.' Boccaccio was his role model in that respect. He didn't think he could write as well as him because he didn't have his detachment. The man-woman thing, he conceded, 'even confuses the great Bukowski.'

The collection contains such contentious aphorisms as: 'There's nothing as boring as the truth,' 'The well-balanced individual is insane' and 'Almost everybody is born a genius and buried an idiot.' Hospitals, he added, were 'places where they attempted to kill you without explaining why.'

Bukowski applied for a grant from the Humanities Foundation that year but it was refused. He knew he was producing better material than the other recipients of this grant and he also knew decisions were made about it for the wrong reasons. There was probably as much politics in the literary world as there was in the political one. The providers of such grants tended to mete out their funds to the 'safe' writers.

Poetry, he said, was 'dying on the vine like a whore on the end stool on a Monday night.' Part of the reason was that it was too 'poetic.' Bukowski always wore his learning lightly. He wanted to bring poetry to those who'd never read it before, to 'de-poeticize' it, as it were. He preferred 'pomes to 'poems.' Poems had overtones of sterility. Poems, on the other hand, were drawn from real life – from the gutter, the dockyard, the boxcar.'

In 1968 John Martin brought out a broadside of Bukowski's called *At Terror Street and Agony Way*. It contained poems he'd brought round to his friend John Thomas one night. It's a book that nearly didn't make it because Thomas accidentally put them out with the garbage one night. Both of them thought they were gone forever. Luckily for posterity they were dictated onto one of his tapes and thus preserved.

A mixture of rumination and quietly-evoked angst, the book copperfastened Bukowski's reputation. The fact that it was published by Martin was a slight embarrassment to him. He apologized to Jon Webb for not offering it to him but he couldn't afford to live on Webb's lean rations anymore. Martin was his first taste of real money and he had to go with that. At 89 pages it was his lengthiest work to date. Martin ran off 800 softback copies and 75 hardback ones.

The first serious study of Bukowski's work appeared in 1969. Written by Hugh Fox and published by Abyss Press, it had a print run of only 300 copies. The style was arresting. Fox obviously knew his Bukowski but there was too much padding in it. Fox also drew too much on quotations from his work, making the book look more like a reader's guide than anything else. He made his point about Bukowski being the lonely hobo fascinated by decay in the book's first quarter and then insisted on making it again and again in a myriad of only slightly varying ways. Bukowski also came across as something of a moaner in the book but it was an interesting read all the same, even if only to remind us how deeply surreal the early poems were.

Bukowski now launched the magazine *Laugh Literary and Man the Humping Guns*. His co-editor was Neeli Cherkovski. Their ambition was to raise the hackles of the establishment. It was published by the aptly-named Hatchetman Press. They wrote some of the material themselves under fictitious names. They felt their worst was better than some of the other contributors' best.

From his days reading submissions to *Harlequin*, he knew just how terrible poetry could be when it wanted. Neither did he wish to spare the blushes of the people who created it. Not content merely to return unsuitable manuscripts, sometimes he poured beer on them before returning them to their authors. At other times he dipped them in eggs. Some he even set alight. Or else he sent rejection slips with four-lettered words plastered all over them. Some submissions he even threw up over. One he 'baked.' He'd worked so hard to get accepted himself he could never countenance sloppy prose from others. This made him almost as harsh an editor as some of those who trashed his own work in the past. Maybe the ruthless editing was his revenge on such a breed. The poacher had become a gamekeeper.

Sometimes he got drawn into correspondences with authors he rejected. This usually ended in bitterness. He learned that you couldn't be a gentleman editor, couldn't let bad writers down gently. The boil had to be lanced cleanly and without any apologies. That only brought the crazies round to his door.

Laugh Literary had only one subscriber. He bitched about an article they printed and they told him to get lost so now they had no subscribers at all. The magazine closed down after three issues. The last one featured a story about Bukowski knocking Ernest

Hemingway down in a fight. The cover showed him with Cherkovksi and an 85-year-old window-washer who happened to be walking by when the photograph was taken. He was wearing baggy trousers held up by suspenders.

The magazine served as a conduit through which he could denounce his pet hates (like Robert Creeley) and publish authors who meant something to him, like Doug Blazek, Harold Norse and a wealthy Californian poet called Steve Richmond. Richmond idolized Bukowski and went on to write a memoir of him, *Spinning off Bukowski*. This was published by Sun Dog Press in 1994. After reading Bukowski, Richmond abandoned his plans to become a lawyer. He set up a bookshop instead. In 1966 he printed a poetry broadsheet featuring some of his work. The words 'Fuck Hate' were written on the cover. This led to a police enquiry into the 'obscene' nature of the material inside. Richmond was subsequently arrested and imprisoned. Litigation concerning the magazine's contents went on for years afterwards.

1969 was also notable for the German translation of *Notes of a Dirty Old Man*. This was engineered by Bukowski's German translator Carl Weissner. Weissner did for Bukowski in Europe what John Martin was doing in the States. (It was slightly easier there because of his German heritage). Bukowski liked Weissner. He helped him 'crawl back to the Fatherland.' Some of the warmest letters he ever wrote were to him.

Bukowski featured in a Penguin anthology of poetry that year alongside Norse and Philip Lamantia. Norse had been offered a volume of his own by Penguin editor Nikos Stangos but he nominated Bukowski and Lamantia as two writers he thought would look better in its pages. As well as clocking up impressive sales, the book gave Bukowski a platform to reach a wider readership. He was grateful to 'Prince Hal' (as he nicknamed Norse) for the gesture, expecting it to pave the way for bigger opportunities. *Notes from the Underground* came out in book form as well. As he approached his fiftieth year, the world was finally sitting up and taking notice of him. The eagle had landed.

John Martin read all of these outpourings with interest. Bukowski rang him occasionally at the dead of night. He told him the post office was killing him. Martin sympathized. They became friends from a distance. Martin was now hatching a plan for Bukowski.

Later in the year he cobbled together a collection of Bukowski's work from all the poems that had been piling up in the 'littles' over the years. It was called *The Days Run Away Like Wild Horses Over the Hills*. It contained some of his purest poetry even if he hadn't yet found the coarser voice that would be associated with him in time to come. Like *It Catches My Heart in its Hands,* in a sense it's more interesting for that. It allows him to exhibit a more eclectic mélange of imagery.

There's a plaintiveness hinting between the lines. What he gives us is the rhetoric of suggestibility rather than statement. Image is piled upon image in a quirkily fascinating confection. He dedicated it to Jane. It represents the culmination of a body of work stretching over most of his past. On the negative side, the versification is often abstruse. Neither is there much human interest here. If he'd continued writing in this vein, one doubts he would have found such a huge following in the future. There's no discernible style or theme. The mood ranges from idyllic to ominous.

Not long after its publication. Martin decided to approach Bukowski with a proposal. It was a gamble to end the decade on - and one to finally get him a life.

The Iceman Cometh

It was good to be old. It was reasonable that a man had to be at least 50 years old before he could write with anything like clarity. (Bukowski)

By now the post office authorities were getting ready to suspend Bukowski for his repeated absenteeism and what they saw as his subversive writing. If they did, he didn't know what his next move would be. How could a fifty year-old man get another job that was steady?

He wasn't making enough money from his writing. Apart from his living expenses and rent there was the child support and his expensive drinking habits. The track cost money too. What good was being a legend of the underground when you were starving? He had attained what Graham Greene once referred to as 'the exclusiveness of unsuccess.' Or as a character says to him in a novel he would write a few years down the road, 'You're the most unknown famous man I ever met.'

His co-workers revered him for standing up to the people above him because they didn't have the gumption to do that themselves. Bukowski carried an aura of danger about with him despite his quietness. The unspoken rule seemed to be: Don't mess with him or you'll get your fingers burned.

One day he was standing by an open window and an official came over to him.

'Why did you open that window?' he asked.

Bukowski replied, 'I didn't open it. I'm just standing here.'

The man went away. Maybe a year before he would have accused him of telling a lie. Maybe he *was* telling a lie. It was a small incident but a significant one. The post office workers weren't allowed even the smallest piece of freedom unless they

162

fought for it. Bukowski fought more visibly when he stood down the representative from Washington about his objectionable story in *Open City* but sometimes the little daily battles like this were just as significant. An 'open' city should have an open window.

Despite all this, he knew his days were numbered at the post office. If the authorities didn't get him, his body would. His back pain was getting worse and his knees rubbed raw from him scratching them.

His whole body seemed to be giving up the ghost. If anyone so much as touched him it sent 'reams of agony' through him. How long more could he last before it gave out for keeps?

His ideal would have been a part-time job to keep the wolf from the door but this wasn't feasible. He made the job part time by going missing but you couldn't keep doing that. Some weeks they even landed him with overtime. At Christmas things went crazy with the tsunami of mail coming in. That was another reason he hated Christmas so much.

He told a colleague he'd like to have been allowed to work just as many hours as would meet his needs and then bunk off. It would have meant less money but so what.

The colleague must have known him better than he knew himself. He said, 'It wouldn't work for you, Hank. You'd starve to death.'

One day John Martin called to his apartment again.

'I might be able to get you out of your job,' he said. Bukowski asked him what he meant.

'I have a proposal to put to you,' he said. Bukowski's ears peaked up.

'Go on,' he said, 'What is it?'

'I'm willing to offer you a monthly stipend if you do nothing but write,' Martin said. Bukowski wasn't sure he was hearing him correctly.

'What do you mean?' he asked him. 'Just what I'm saying,' Martin said, 'If you leave the post office and spend all your time writing, I'll pay you for it.'

It sounded too good to be true. Getting paid for writing was like getting paid for sex. His mind started to form a picture. This was something he'd dreamed about for ten years, maybe more. A life of doing just what he wanted and being answerable to nobody. Was he really hearing it? Was Martin pulling his leg?

'How much?' he asked. 'How much can you survive on?' Martin countered. Bukowski shrugged his shoulders. 'I don't know,' he said.

He made some space for Martin and himself at a coffee table and they started to do 'the math.' He said he'd need $15 a month for child support, $30 for rent and about $50 for food and extras. That worked out at $100 in round figures. Martin said he could afford it. He'd just sold a collection of D.H. Lawrence first editions to the University of California for $50,000. Lawrence was his favorite author.

To Bukowski it sounded like a fair deal. He started to think about it in earnest. Could it be this simple? After all the years of trying, had the mountain finally come to Muhammad?

. 'Is it yes or no?' Martin asked him. He could only give one answer. 'I'll do it,' he said. They shook hands.

Which of them could have known that they were shaking on an arrangement that would run day run into millions of dollars in almost a dozen countries? They were gambling on literature as Bukowski and Jane had once gambled on horses.

What Martin offered him wasn't so much a comfort zone as a breathing space. Bukowski was about to come out of the hole, to leave the cul-de-sac for the main highway.

'A miracle ran up my arm,' he said, 'like a crazy mouse.' After years of sending messages in bottles to uncertain destinations, one of them had finally become washed up on the shore. No longer would he have to die from doing 'the other man's thing.'

He wrote about his feelings in the poem 'the 12 hour night.' It was cowardice, he said, that kept him tied to his routines for so many years.

The day he took up Martin's offer was the day he decided to fight the fear, to snatch at life. It wasn't so much a thirst for adventure as panic. This was also the way he'd felt when he first left home. At that time he was running away from something rather than to it. Now he was running from something but also to something else.

There was another difference too. He had more to lose now. It wasn't like the old days where he could leave a job on Friday and be in another one the following Monday. No matter how terrible the jobs he used to work in were, at least they were available to him. They wouldn't be now. His 49-year-old bones were creaking. On the other hand, anyone pushing fifty owed it to himself to gamble on change.

It was a gamble for Martin too. $100 a month wasn't small potatoes in 1970. (He hadn't told his wife he was going to make the offer to Bukowski for this reason). There was the possibility Bukowski would drink the money. Why was he willing to risk that?

He took him on, he said, because he was read by 'so many whores, taxi drivers, sex freaks, circus barkers and Fuller Brush salesmen.' It was hardly the traditional market for poetry but at least it was versatile. He had a hunch the work would sell to such a large target readership.

To add to Bukowski's good mood, he even offered him the $100 in months where he wasn't able to produce work for one reason or another. He was effectively saying, 'I know you're good enough to make us both solvent.'

Walt Whitman

Martin admired Bukowski's pared-down style. His bardic tone reminded him of Walt Whitman. Whitman had also been regarded as a ne'er-do-well in his day but came to be seen as a luminary with the passage of time. Would the same happen with Bukowski? Martin felt it would. He thought he was a genius. He said he'd make it his business to transmit such genius to the world.

Bukowski once told Stephen Kessler he would probably have been 'dead or mad' if Martin hadn't come along when he did. He arrived at a time of his life when he was getting ready to give up the ghost. He thought it was probably good for him that he hadn't become successful when he was young. Most writers, he felt, made it too early and suffered the consequences, unable to last the pace. They were sprinters. He saw himself more as a marathon man.

He likened himself to a woman who always thought she was going to be a spinster but got married late in life. That made him more determined than ever to make a go of things. Financial hardship was the price of freedom but it was a price he was more than willing to pay. He'd never been well-off but now every cent would be earmarked.

Martin had big plans for him. He told him he believed he could write great books for his new company, which he was going to call Black Sparrow Press. He promised him he'd hand-deliver the books to their destinations if necessary, that he'd get them into libraries, that he'd move heaven and earth to make him a household name. His wife Barbara would design the covers.

Bukowski left the post office at the end of December. When he was going out the door for the last time he heard one of his co-workers saying, 'That old guy has some guts.' As he listened to him he thought, 'Maybe desperation would be a better word.'

He didn't feel sorry for the people he was leaving behind. His attitude was: Let the slaves remain in their cages. They weren't worth saving, he thought, because they didn't want to be saved. What they craved was the comfort of the familiar – the same parking space day in day out, the same meals in the canteen, the same mindless routines to engage their pulverized minds.

He was getting away from people he referred to as 'the yellow men with bad breath and big feet' – the supervisors who'd done their best to break his spirit over the years, not with a razor strop like his father but rather the viciousness of their tongues. He'd outlasted them and now it was time to look ahead. He was about to come down from off the cross.

He threw a party that night to celebrate. It went on until the next day, and then the next, and the next. In fact it didn't end until the last day of the year. On New Year's Eve he looked around him at the wall-to-wall bodies – some who seemed to believe they had live-in rights – and decided it was time to throw them out.

The move to Black Sparrow Press wasn't a rags-to-riches story for him. It was more like rags to more preferable rags. He was existing on subsistence rations for a long time after leaving the post office. Being jobless also meant he had no respite from his mind all day.

The job robbed him of writing time but the people he met there gave him ideas for his poems and stories. No matter how talented a writer was, he could do little if he never left his house. (Unless he was Marcel Proust). In the same way as going to the track fertilized his mind for the night's work at the typewriter, the activity of turning up at a preordained venue and participating in the ordinary events of any day - even if one had no respect for those events – was beneficial.

Left to mooch around his apartment without any routines he worried if his source of inspiration might dry up. It seemed to do that sometimes when he went on unpaid leave. Being off work also gave him too much time to drink. How was he going to deal with that? Or the fights drink always seemed to give rise to?

With or without the drink he knew he'd have to extend his repertoire now that he was marketing his wares for a living. To reach a larger readership he felt he'd have to go back to writing prose. He often said he preferred writing poetry because he could do it no matter what kind of mood he was in. Prose was different. He had to feel good for that. This was the opposite to the way most writers felt. Bukowski was opposite to most writers in almost everything.

For the first week after he left the post office he did nothing. That in itself made him feel elated. When did he ever have the luxury of goofing off before and still know he had a check coming in the mail? But if he goofed off for too long it could have been dangerous. He might have gone back to the 'old' Bukowski, the one from the Philadelphia days or the Jane days. 'The bird was out of the cage,' he said, 'but he was just sitting on a branch.'

He found himself getting cold sweats. He didn't know if they were from panic or the DTs. Would he survive on Martin's money? Would they take him back in the post office if his new life failed? He found himself becoming worked up about everything, even the parking arrangements in the apartment complex. Some of the other tenants kept blocking him as he went to drive out and he couldn't deal with it. One day he snapped. He went to the extreme of ordering a switchblade in the mail to intimidate them.

His car was starting to give up on him now. The gears were shot. He had to put it in reverse before it would go forward. This led to some tense situations. When he was stuck in traffic the drivers behind him thought he was going to reverse into them. One of the doors was also hanging off. The dashboard was held together with tape.

To get a cut on his rent he offered to do jobs around the apartment complex. He took out the garbage for a reduction of $10 a month. It was like Jane cleaning the rooms in the hotel she stayed in shortly before she died to save a few precious dollars. He was still a wage slave, albeit in a different guise.

He continued to drink with the Crottys to keep the rent down. Mrs. Crotty told him he was crazy to leave his job. 'Craziness keeps me going,' he replied.

He wasn't out-and-out crazy. He still had some money in a savings account from the sale of his father's house and $3000 in a pension fund from the post office. But money had a habit of 'walking' if you weren't adding to it. He knew he'd need to get going on his writing soon.

When Martin asked him if he had any novels in his back catalogue he told him he hadn't. He'd also resisted writing one. 'I seldom work with prose,' he wrote to Henry Miller once, 'mainly because if they turn it down I'm dead.' His point was that it took a lot longer to write a novel than a poem so the loss was greater if it was rejected. But he felt confident Martin would accept any novel he wrote if it was half way decent.

He decided to start one now. He seated himself at the window of his apartment facing the street. He placed a bottle of whiskey beside him and started slamming into the keys. Words crawled across the page like, as he put it, 'drunk spiders.' He chose the same time as he would have been going into work. This was a new kind of work. He was his own boss now. He would fight on his own battlefield. Fifty years of comic absurdity was about to be vomited out.

He set himself a target of ten pages a night but sometimes he overdid that. In the mornings he'd come downstairs and see up to twenty, or even more. A lot of the time he was so drunk he wouldn't have even remembered typing them. 'I kept ahead of the game,' he said. 'If I did eleven yesterday I'd only have to do nine today. If I did twelve I'd only have to do eight.' There was discipline amidst the chaos.

The novel was about his time in the post office. It was written in a staccato style. It mixed comedy and tragedy as he chronicled some of the seminal events of his past in a mad medley of words.

He didn't know how to finish it. The pages were all piled up in a drawer. Some days he was afraid to look at them. Then one day he came back from the track and the ending flashed into his mind. It was a sudden ending, which meant the book was going to be shorter than he expected. He typed up two or three more pages and that was it. He rang Martin and said, 'Come and get it.' Martin said, 'Come and get *what*?' He hadn't even known what he was working on.

The name he chose for the book was the only thing about it that wasn't original: *Post Office*. Martin speed-read it just as Bukowski speed-wrote it. You couldn't do anything else with a book so compulsive. 'The writing is so powerful,' he gushed, 'and you've done it so fast. 'That's where the power comes from,' Bukowski told him, 'I don't refine.'

Excited and all as Martin was by the novel, there were still parts of it he wanted to change. He told Bukowski he'd like to clean up the style, to tidy up the grammar, to get rid of all those dangling participles. (Bukowski wasn't sure what dangling participles were but he didn't like the sound of them). He even wanted to put a glossary at the back explaining certain terms Bukowski used that weren't in common usage. Bukowski objected. He liked the chaos, the mix of tenses. It made the book hop. You didn't know what was coming next. 'I lived a messy life so the writing has to be messy,' he argued. They reached a compromise. Some parts were taken out and more left in.

Post Office became a best-seller. It put Bukowski's name on the literary map for different types of readers than those who bought 'the littles.' He dedicated it to 'Nobody.' It contained in miniature many of the themes he would finesse in his later writings. It also introduced his alter ego Henry Chinaski to the world.

For the diehard Bukowski devotees who gobbled up everything he wrote from the chapbook days, *Post Office* was something of a compromise. It didn't so much show contempt for the idea of genre as a profound disregard for it, locating itself somewhere between *noir* ruminations and slapstick burlesque. It didn't fall into any category because it was written by a man who refused to consider what he was doing. A jagged diary of anecdotal mirth interspersed with bouts of agony, you never know what you'll find on a given page. If it's a Marxist document one would be entitled to enquire if that signified Karl or Groucho.

Structurally speaking it's all over the place. It's difficult to discuss it in the traditional terms of plot because Bukowski never really thought in those terms. In this sense it's an *un*book. (Bukowski would have liked Flann O'Brien's *At-Swim Two Birds,* a novel in which the characters rebel against the author.)

It's written in the style he admired in John Fante. As well as giving us a grueling account of his work life, it has the humor of his hellraising and his search for a ticket to Easy Street.

Most of the characters are easy to recognize. Betty is Jane, Francis is Barbara, Faye is Frances and Marina is herself. Anecdotal snippets are piled on top of one another as Bukowski negotiates his tenuous path through the mind-numbing boredom of the post office, getting himself in above his head with the women in his life before emerging relatively unscathed at the end, taking what life throws at him in as cavalier a fashion as he can muster.

The naturalness that was his signature tune is evident from the word go. He creates humor from what would have been dark tableaus in another writer's hands. That's probably what made the book such a huge success. Few white collar men with high sex drives - and a healthy sense of the absurd – could have failed to identify with it.

It was the first time Bukowski could write about his daily grind without recrimination, or the threat of a visit from one of his superiors. He'd broken free from them and could now cock a snook at them from the safety of the page.

Early on in the book Chinaski rapes a woman to whom he delivers a letter after she accuses him of being lecherous. Such a taunt he takes as a kind of come-on. Feminists saw this segment as demonstrating the classic male fantasy, i.e. that women who evince prudish sentiments are often just 'asking for it.' Bukowski didn't agree, saying something more perverse was afoot.

Elsewhere he drinks, has sex, goes to the races and uses every ruse imaginable to spend as much time away from his desk as he can. He carries his mail in the rain, gets threatened by dogs, tries to deal with the impatience of those awaiting letters and finally becomes a 'regular.'

Afterwards there's the marriage to Joyce — negotiated with the same passion with which one might buy a pack of cigarettes — and a brief sojourn in her home town in Texas. This was chosen by experts, he tells us, as 'the last town in the USA any enemy would attack with an atomic bomb. I could see why.'

Her father thinks he's after her money. This leads to a discussion of that four-lettered word called work. Suddenly the honeymoon is over.

Bukowski never had the work ethic and when his wife is a millionairess it makes the prospect even more ludicrous. He goes back to the post office and she becomes a clerk.

The marriage rumbles on for a while and then she sues for divorce, a decision he accepts with his customary nonchalance. ('All I'd lost was three or four million.')

Thereafter he has a brief dalliance with Betty but the magic is gone. Shortly afterwards she dies. There's a moving funeral scene and then it's back to the races, the bars and other women.

Chief among these is Fay. She's trivialized for her philanthropy. He mellows a little towards her when she gives birth to his beloved daughter ('Maybe she hadn't saved the world, but she'd made a major improvement') but the relationship collapses. Too many other things are wrong with it for it not to.

All of his relationships seem destined to do so sooner or later. It gets so he almost expects his women to walk. She leaves him for her love-ins and her hippie dippie coffeehouses. He doesn't miss her, this ageing poster child of the flower power era he so despises.

The final section of the book deals with his departure from the post office. It's a mixed blessing, relief combined with fear. What does the future hold for him? He feels the lure of suicide but his daughter gives him the will to go on.

The publication of *Post Office* was a watershed for him. It put him on a different echelon.

He couldn't believe he'd written it, that all those thoughts and images were inside him waiting to get out. Now that they had, he was curious to know what else he had in the tank.

'If I live to be fifty,' he said once, 'I'll be there.' Well he had. And he was.

A few months later he boarded his first ever plane, travelling to Washington State to do a poetry reading at Bellevue Community College.

174

Bukowski was never on a plane before the Washington reading

He was so nervous he threw up before it. He didn't like the idea of publicizing his work like this. Readings, he claimed 'reeked of self-love.' A jerky video of the event has survived. It presents us with a Bukowski who hadn't yet learned how to work a crowd. The atmosphere is subdued. Nothing more raucous than giggles are emitted by the audience, even when he gets feisty. He reads from a seated position, making little effort to create chemistry with them. Every now and then he sips wine from his flask, assuring his listeners that if he's happy they will be too. (Nobody is under any illusion the flask contains iced tea). They hang on his words as if he's a high priest come to visit. Everything is very civilized, with nary a heckler in sight. He's at the beginning of a journey that will be the most sensational one of his life.

The collaboration with Martin had started with a bang. Even this early he had a feeling it was going to reap dividends for both of them. Getting the monthly allowance took all the pressure off him to survive financially. 'That $100 was like $5 million to me,' he said. Martin also bought him a new typewriter now, 'One I could beat the shit outa.' He even sent him stamps to make it easier for him to mail him his poems.

Apart from Martin he wasn't making much money. The poetry magazines paid chickenfeed. Checks from the sex magazines were either late or non-existent. He had to scrimp to meet the cost of Marina's upkeep and his living expenses. This was long before he was able to command large fees for his reading. What he earned at Bellevue was harmless.

He also did a reading at the University of New Mexico that year but this didn't net him much either. After paying for the flight, the drinks in the airport, the taxi to the venue and more drinks at a party afterwards, he almost lost money on the deal. Getting laid a few times by co-eds 'sort of' made up for the poor money.

He now met Linda King, the woman with whom he would have the most explosive relationship of his life. Leaving the post office, apart from everything else, meant he had more time – and energy – for dating.

A Mormon from Utah, she had a colorful history. She was a divorced woman with two children. She'd had a nervous breakdown after getting married and underwent electro-convulsive therapy for it. She even heard voices.

Her marriage ended, she said, one day when she didn't feel like cooking breakfast for her husband. She expected him to say, 'Okay, let's eat out,' but instead he said, 'Let's get divorced.'

She felt he did her a favor by having that reaction. She was relieved to be away from him. She didn't chase him for money because she didn't want to annoy him. If she did, she thought he'd look for custody of her children by throwing the 'nervous breakdown' charge at her and accusing her of being an unfit mother.

She'd wanted to be an actress originally but he hadn't approved of that ambition. He encouraged her to take up sculpturing instead so she did that. She also painted and wrote poetry.

176

Bukowski was twenty years older than her. The first time they met was at a reading. As well as his poetry, Bukowski read his story 'Six Inches.' It was about a woman who shrank her man to that size so she could use him as a dildo. It drew a few laughs. When he was finished King went up to him and said, 'You don't seem to like women too much.' He replied, 'Baby, I love them.'

The next time they met was at another reading. This time she read as well. Like Bukowski, she was something of a performance artist. The difference between them was that he stayed relatively still during his readings - at least until the wine took its toll – but she liked to jump about the place. The poem she was reading on the night in question was based on her experiences under ECT. It gave her every opportunity for drama. Bukowski thought she was over-the-top but he liked the way she moved. He was watching her body more than listening to her words.

She staved him off that night. 'She's a tremendous flirt,' he said, 'She dances like a hot whore but she doesn't fuck.' The next time they met she offered to sculpt his head. It was her sister's idea. King had four sisters. She was the youngest of them. Bukowski said he'd be happy for her to do so.

She called to De Longpre Avenue the following day. When she arrived she heard him puking inside. 'I've come to take pictures for the sculpture,' she said from outside the door, 'Will I come back when you feel better?' 'No,' he said, 'I'm all right now.' Puking wasn't exactly unusual for him.

He let her in. She looked beautiful to him. He was shy with her. What was she looking for? He wondered. How could someone so beautiful be interested in someone so ugly?

They started dating. One of her friends said, 'What rock did you find him under?' It was like the beauty and the beast.

She was fascinated by his living conditions: the dirt, the grime, even an enema bag that was hanging from a shower pipe. 'He's got a dirty mind and a dirty house,' she thought. It was a contrast to the

177

blandness of the marriage she'd just gotten out of. He didn't have a television either. That was something else that made him attractive to her. Everyone she knew talked about what had been on TV the night before.

At this time he thought her name was Morona. One of her sisters had written a play called *Queen of the Morons* and she'd played a part in it. She couldn't think of a name for her character so she'd settled on Morona. She said to Bukowski, 'Most men think women are morons anyway, right?' He said, 'I guess so.'

They fell in love, as she put it, over the clay. She found him to be one of the most natural men she'd ever met. Everything was 'out there' with him – his likes, his dislikes, his sulks. He wasn't capable of hiding his feelings.

When she talked about her breakdown he was sympathetic. Anything unusual about people appealed to him. He didn't think she was nuts because she heard voices. He'd also heard voices too in his past. He'd seen visions too, usually when he was drunk.

She told him about life growing up on a ranch. The contrast between this and his own upbringing interested him. She told him about her strong connection to her sisters. Some of them wrote poetry as well.

Bukowski didn't like King's poetry very much. 'It rhymes,' he said in exasperation, 'That's gone out.' When she started writing poems that didn't rhyme, it freed her up. Then he got to like her work. He suggested she submit it to some of the underground magazines he was connected with and she did that. Occasionally it was accepted. Afterwards they worked on her poems together. He advised her to change the way she phrased things to make them sound better.

They went to the track one day. Here she saw another side to him, an unexpected one. For every race he seemed to have a different system of betting. His concentration was razor sharp. 'It has to be,' he told her, 'My finances are on the line.'

They went back to his place afterwards and made passionate love. Bukowski liked to kiss and King taught him how to do it better. 'He came from a different era to me,' she said, 'One where a woman wasn't expected to have special needs in that department.'

They started living together at De Longpre Avenue. King was glad when Bukowski suggested this as she'd been having difficulty trying to find a place for herself. 'Nobody wants to let to a divorcee with two kids and a dog,' she complained. They were in adjoining apartments but they might as well have been in the same one because they spent most of their time together. The only time they were apart was when Bukowski went down to Mrs. Crotty. (She was still summoning him for singing sessions). He made it out to be a duty when she invited him down but King thought he secretly enjoyed it. ('How could Bukowski ever refuse free beer?') Sometimes she suspected he had sex with Mrs. Crotty after her husband fell asleep.

He enjoyed doing the ordinary things with King – cooking, reading the papers on a Sunday morning, chilling out. She gave him shampoo for his hair one day and he became fascinated with how silky it felt afterwards. (Up until now he'd used soap to wash it). He liked seeing her putting on her make-up, seeing her hairpins on cabinets, her shoes in wardrobes. For a time he considered marrying her. He even wrote a 'dual' poetry book with her, *Me and You and Your Sometimes Love Poems.* This was too risqué to be published by Black Sparrow Press. King wrote in an incantatory style to match Bukowski's. Nothing was excluded in her work, not even oral sex. Jerry Kanstra described her as 'Bukowski with a cunt.'

As well as writing poems to – and with – one another, they also exchanged dozens of letters. King's ones were just as graphic as Bukowski's. Some of them made his sex stories in *Hustler* look tame by comparison. Others were mushy, as were his to her. He said things you wouldn't have expected to find him saying in a thousand years: 'I love this paper I'm writing on because it's going to you.' 'I feel like a 21 karat (sic) ring or a zoo at feeding time.' 'I'm fifty Christmas trees inside.' 'You've brought water to the desert, you've brought miracles where miracles had ceased.'

Being away from her, he wrote, made him feel as if he'd been murdered. He thought she was more beautiful than a movie star. He was fascinated by her hair and her eyes particularly. Many of the poems he wrote to her focus on these features.

King had a love/hate relationship to Bukowski. He brought out the best and worst in her – sometimes at the same time – and she in him. She drank a lot with him but she wasn't in the Jane Cooney Baker league.

She thought he was drinking himself to death. Alcohol also interfered with his performance in the bedroom. 'You're too drunk to do it at night,' she taunted when he didn't satisfy her, 'and too sick in the morning.' But she was fascinated by him – by his eccentricities, his edge of danger, the softness he kept so well concealed.

They launched their book at a party. After the speeches were finished, drama ensued. This was never far away from Bukowski when he was in a public place. He became enraged when he saw her dancing with different men. This she seemed to do almost without realizing it. 'How else am I going to enjoy myself?' she pleaded. He had two left feet when it came to moving around on a floor.

He picked up a bottle and held it by the neck. 'Okay,' he said to the men standing around him, 'Which of you guys is first?' They all backed off. Bukowski threw the bottle at the wall. It shattered into pieces. Exit Bukowski. He walked towards his car and sat in. He gunned the engine. King banged on the bonnet as he started to drive off. 'I hate you, you son of a bitch,' she screamed at him. The party was over.

Their arguments were legendary. 'Our tempers exploded like shooting geysers,' King said, 'and we'd roar down our emotional rollercoasters.' Each of them abused the other both physically and verbally in what came to resemble a sado-masochistic orgy of negative energy. What she was doing with this madman, she wondered. Being the youngest of five children, she thought maybe the family brains had run out before they got to her.

One night when Bukowski got drunk he sat on top of her and started pummeling her with his fists. She ended up with two black eyes. The next day he couldn't remember having done it.

'We split up twenty or thirty times in a year,' she said. In her heart of hearts she knew he wasn't the right man for her. He knew she wasn't the right woman for him either but no matter how bad things became between them they couldn't stop seeing one another. The fights between them were almost worth it for the making up afterwards. The energy they expended on such contretemps seemed to fuel them with an almost sexual excitement, particularly if drink was involved - which it usually was.

Bukowski generally behaved like an adolescent when he was with King, especially if they were at a party. He stubbed cigarette butts out in beer cans and continued to drink from them with the butts in them. He peed in wine bottles. He insulted people as soon as looking at them. Maybe he was trying to make up for all the fun he'd missed during his youth.

'You're going through your second childhood,' she taunted. 'I never had a first one,' he shot back without missing a beat.

One day in 1971 she riled him so much he broke her nose in a tantrum. Another night he accused her of being a lesbian for a joke. She threw him into a fireplace for that. Sometimes he became so obstreperous with drink she had to call the police. Bukowski got used to being hauled down to the station. Some of the policemen preferred to chat to him about his writing than to lock him up. Many of them were fans of *Open City*.

King had a lot of male admirers. Bukowski accused her of setting these off against one another in order to increase her desirability. Anytime she gave another man a peck on the cheek he became furious. 'We were from different generations,' she said, echoing her 'different era,' comment. He used terms like 'shackjob' to denote living together. That said it all for her about his anachronistic attitude to relationships. 'You missed the sixties,' she told him one night. He replied, 'I'm having the sixties in the seventies. I used to feel crowded with all the hippies everywhere but they're not around anymore. They're working on Wall Street now.'

The longer they spent together, the more they drank. Alcohol had never done much for King. Some of the time she drank merely because he encouraged her to.

She once accused him of turning her into an alcoholic. He disputed this, saying he never pushed a bottle at her. That was probably true but it was such a big part of his life she'd have needed the willpower of a monk to get through her time with him without imbibing.

Her father had also been an alcoholic. That made her doubly wary. She forbade Bukowski to drink when her children were around. Sometimes he agreed but if he was in a funk, as he tended to be a lot of the time, he did his own thing.

She never knew what to expect from him. Her feminist side was enraged by his sexist comments but she was bored by other men she dated, men who were too predictable, who lacked his edge. He was a challenge for her. His whiff of cordite turned her on. She wanted to tame him, to drive his chauvinistic traits out of him by seducing him. And yet she enjoyed part of that chauvinism. It was like what Marlene Dietrich said about women: 'We change our men and then we don't like what we've turned them into.'

She told him he was 'a dirty old man with a puritanical streak.' One of the reasons she levelled that charge at him was because he refused to 'go down' on her. That was something else he'd missed from the sixties. Under her tutelage he learned to correct it.

He called her his black widow spider, his praying mantis. She believed he cut himself off from the possibility of ever loving women because of the fear of being psychologically emasculated by them. 'Because your mother let you down,' she taunted, 'you think all women are potential traitors.'

Every time they fell out she took the sculpted head from him to let him know how angry she was. Then they'd make up again and she'd give it back to him.

It was like a shuttlecock going to and fro between them. He called her a slut and she called him a pig. They argued and made love and argued and drank and argued and laughed and partied. There was no logic to it.

In the middle of it all she accused him of using her as raw material for his work. He was constantly writing while he was with her. 'You have to keep sending it out,' he told her, 'Otherwise how can it get published?' She wondered how he could drink so much and still function as a writer. He had that enormous energy.

Both of them wanted different things from the relationship. King had done the '2.2 children thing' and needed a change. Bukowski was sex-starved but also in need of emotional nourishment. King, he said, gave him that like no other woman since Jane.

Whenever he talked to her about Jane she blew a fuse. 'I can't be involved in a relationship that has three people in it,' she complained, 'I can't live with dead bones and dead memories.'

Another woman in his life at this time was Liza Williams. She was a record company executive. Like Bukowski, she wrote for the *Los Angeles Free Press*. He asked her for her phone number one day when he was out walking with King. King could never forgive him for that.

'It's to do with work,' he said by way of an excuse.

She didn't believe him. 'I never saw a more blatant example of two-timing,' she said. He went on one of his break-ups with King shortly afterwards.

Williams wasn't as pretty as King. She was also a little older than her. She didn't have her 'grand flame' for Bukowski. He was thinking of King more often than not when he was with her. If he'd met her before King they might have made a go of it but not now. 'I never met a man who made love like you do,' Williams told him, but his heart wasn't in it.

He wrote to King to tell her he was dating Williams. 'It's just sex with her,' he said, 'It's spiritual with you.' He wasn't in love with her, he said, but he was afraid to leave her because she'd threatened to kill herself if he did. King wasn't interested in that kind of talk. She wrote back to him to say she wished them both well. They'd probably be compatible together, she suggested, because they shared a mutual interest in suicide.

Williams brought Bukowski to Catalina for a treat in 1972. It would be his first and last tourist holiday. 'I'm not the type to watch ducks on the pond,' he told her, 'and I don't go for

184

moonlight walks on the beach.' Nature meant little to him and she respected that. She let him do his own thing after they got there. When the sun shone he stayed in the shade. It made no difference to him if he was on Mars or Mariposa Avenue. He still had to do his writing. 'All I want is my beer and my typer,' he told her. She'd brought her electric one to keep him occupied. It was a nice gesture. As she lounged by the sea he stayed indoors hitting the keys.

Catalina, where Bukowski vacationed with Liza Williams

When the holiday was over she asked him if he'd enjoyed himself. 'It was fantastic,' he said, 'Just like home.' The highlight of the trip for him was watching the cowboy film *Jesse James* on television.

He hadn't seen it before. In his story 'No Neck and Bad as Hell' he casts Williams as a Vicky, someone who's so terrified by the scene where James is shot that she hides in the next room. Bukowski has to tell her when it's safe to come out.

Bukowski wrote King a letter while he was with Williams. In it he told her how much he missed her. He said he wanted to come back to her if she'd have him. She replied, 'I cannot respond to

185

love letters written on the belly of another woman. Send me another and I'll shit in it and send it to her at the *Free Press.*' King wasn't a woman to mince words.

Bukowski's head was in a muddle with all this drama. In his youth he'd been deprived of women and now he had two on the go. Sometimes he felt like walking away from both of them. He once said there was no sweeter experience in the world for him than closing the door of his apartment and facing its walls alone.

He loved silence. He often said he hated when the phone rang. Sometimes he jumped with fright whenever this happened. One time he left it off the hook for weeks at a time to stop it disturbing him. When the phone company informed him this violated one of their codes he took the back off it. He put some rags around the bell to stop it making a noise and then screwed it back on again. One day he even put it in the fridge.

When people rang his doorbell, as mentioned already, he rarely answered. If they rang twice he tended to holler something back at them. He found polite refusals generally resulted in anger. You had to ignore people totally to keep them at bay, he said, 'even if they throw stones at your window.'

It was the same with young poets who were anxious to make a name for themselves and sent him their work for appraisal. Usually it wasn't good. He didn't believe in leading them on so he would tell them frankly what he thought of it. This generally didn't go down well. 'what they wanted,' he said, 'was for me to tell them they were geniuses. We all believe we're geniuses but only some of us are.'

Bukowski took criticism well when he was starting out but he was unusual. Most people were more thin-skinned. The people who wrote to him asking for his view on their work and got a negative response always took it worse if he was polite to them. He found it better to ignore them. Ignoring people always worked. Eventually they forgot about you.

One of the main reasons he liked writing, he claimed, was because pages couldn't talk back. They didn't insinuate themselves on you when you were feeling bad. They didn't castigate you for writer's block. They kept their own counsel, being there for you when you were ready for them. Human beings, on, contrary, were selfish. They presented themselves uninvited at your door. They throttled you with verbal onslaughts.

People's conversation bothered Bukowski so much he sometimes found himself screaming at them to be quiet. One of the reasons he liked classical music so much was because it didn't have a human voice. (Opera did so he couldn't listen to it).

He agreed with Walter Pater that all art aspired to the condition of music. That was why he regarded *Finnegans Wake* — a book that has its main appeal in the sound rather than the sense — as James Joyce's finest novel. Most people see it as his most unreadable one but such things never bothered Bukowski. He always pardoned glitches in experimental work. Infinitely less bearable was the well-honed non-event. 'When people read me,' he said to Neeli Cherkovski, 'I want to think of them as not reading literature but actually participating in life.' When he made that statement, ironically, he himself was in the process of withdrawing from life. He told Sean Penn that no matter how low he felt, the presence of another person could never help.

He once wrote a poem about a man who lived in a hole in the ground. When people asked him why he just shrugged his shoulders. None of them considered the obvious answer: he was in the hole because he wanted to be in it. Anything was better than being with them.

If Bukowski was sitting alone in a restaurant he resented people coming up to him making small talk. Their assumption was that anybody unaccompanied would appreciate such a gesture. Bukowski didn't. If he was sober he would be reasonably polite but if he was in his cups it would be a case of, 'Do me a favor and disappear.'

His reclusiveness made Greta Garbo look sociable. 'The more I think of human beings,' he said, 'the less I think of them.' Will Rogers' dictum, 'I never met a man I didn't like,' made him want to puke. 'I have yet to meet a man I truly liked,' he asserted.

With women it was different. He bent the rules for them. He answered the door to them if they were pretty. If they sent him their poetry he wrote back to them about it. He liked the poetry more if they included a photograph of themselves with it – or a phone number. Some of his lovers came from situations like this. 'I preferred the photographs to the poem,' he said, 'but often neither was good.'

Many people sent him their work because they felt they were better than he was. If he could get into print, their thinking was, why couldn't they? These were the ones who thought it was easy, that Bukowski just woke up one day and found himself famous, like Lord Byron.

He always said he was no better a writer after he became famous than before. The only difference now was that his books sold better. He hadn't improved his style of writing. He just kept at it and now it was bearing fruit. He was like an old racehorse that suddenly started winning for no discernible reason.

One of the magazines he contributed to at this time was *The Wormwood Review*. The editor, Marvin Malone, became a friend of his. Bukowski was working on some paintings at this time and Malone liked these as well. He encouraged him to take more interest in them but he didn't get anywhere. One night Bukowski decided the colors on them were too bright. He dunked them in a bath of hot water to try and give them a fresh look but it didn't work. He ended up putting them in the garbage. When Malone saw him next he was shocked. 'Do you realize what you've done?' he screamed, 'You've thrown away $2000 worth of work!' Bukowski didn't seem too bothered.

His sketches were usually done in the style of James Thurber. Some of them were used to illustrate his books through the years, alongside Barbara Martin's cover designs. Others were just doodles. He often illustrated his letters with doodles as well. In time he fell out with Malone, accusing him of going for 'the comfortable poem.' How many others had gone down that route? It was hardly surprising. Lace dresses, fleecy clouds, the inevitable sell-out to a *Harpers/Atlantic Monthly* zeitgeist.

Success brought a lot of changes to Bukowski's life. Most of these bewildered him. How was it that a man with boils the size of apples was having two women fighting over him and others calling uninvited to his door from all corners of the globe? He felt neither Williams nor King would have looked the side of the road he was on when he was struggling. Success was an aphrodisiac. It brought strange creatures to his door.

Men called too, as mentioned, but they weren't as welcome. Most of them were excited simply to be meeting their hero. One prosperous-looking man told Bukowski he'd been with him 'in spirit' during his lean years. He replied, 'Your spirit wouldn't have been much use to me. Your money might have been.'

They told him they'd been with him in spirit during the lean years. When they said he saved their asses with his work he replied, 'The only ass I really tried to save was my own.'

John Martin was a big part of that salvation. They enjoyed a healthy publishing relationship but they lived separate lives. They didn't hang out together and that was probably why they never fell out. It was also better that Martin didn't like alcohol. Bukowski tended to turn on people he drank with sooner or later, which could have spelt disaster for their arrangement. If his women left him when they finally twigged that the man wasn't as good as the poems, this could also have been the case with Martin. He was safer with Bukowski from the distance of the page.

Even at this level he could almost see the steam rising from him. Imagine what it would have been like if Bukowski arrived at his doorstep after being turfed out of an apartment by one of his lady friends, or having to face him first thing in the morning when his mouth felt like the inside of an ash tray.

People often ask whether Bukowski would have become as famous as he did if it wasn't for Martin. It's an unanswerable question. Martin was a canny marketer of his merchandise. Bukowski was a good ball player but he needed somebody to run with the ball if he wanted to become more than an icon of the underground.

He always felt he'd do his best writing after the age of fifty. It was as if there was another person inside him that was gestating all those years but couldn't quite get out due to the residue of toxic elements in his life. One day he believed it would burst forth like a seasoned wine, in books the rest of his life had been a preparation for. Roughly speaking that's what happened – with Martin as the catalyst.

Bukowski allowed him a lot of control over his work. He was never precious about the deletion of passages in poems or even whole poems.

He realized many of them lacked structure. He wasn't the type of writer to crawl round his floor at 3 a.m. looking for a word that rhymed with 'orange.' But sometimes he got annoyed with Martin when he said he wanted to 'clean up' his work, as he tried to do with *Post Office*. Why would anyone want to clean up a 'dirty' old man?

He had another publisher besides Martin, of course: Lawrence Ferlinghetti of City Lights Books in San Francisco. Ferlinghetti was a rebel publisher who was right up Bukowski's street in terms of attitude. He would love to have discovered him. He campaigned against censorship for people like James Joyce and Henry Miller in the past, thriving on literature that sailed close to the wind of respectability.

He brought out Bukowski's *Erections, Ejaculations, Exhibitions and General Tales of Ordinary Madness* in 1972. It was a book that contained many of the stories that were published in the sex magazines.

Some of these were too strong for Black Sparrow, who preferred what Bukowski called 'the safe shit.' When John Martin didn't want something, Ferlinghetti was only too happy to bring up the rear.

'He took the droppings from the sparrow's nest,' was the way Bukowski put it.

Lawrence Ferlinghetti

Martin did, however, publish a poetry collection of his that year. It was called *Mockingbird Wish Me Luck.* He dedicated it to King 'for all the good reasons.' It was well up to the standard of his recent collections and occasionally exceeded it.

'The rat' gives us another mini-dose of memories, bringing in his father, sex and the war before concluding that nothing really has changed in his life in the past 35 years. 'WW 2' is written in a jerky format. It reminds us of everything from Bob Dylan to The Beats. The poem trades on his old war stories, or rather the much-quoted story about how he *avoided* the war. Nobody could trivialize jingoism like Bukowski. Here he has a rare old time sending up the draft procedure, how he crawled out from under that particular wire with a mixture of fabricated neurosis and very real apathy. 'A sound in the brush' is a more solemn anti-war

192

statement, a fairly standard polemic about a soldier dying for a 'Cause Unknown'.

A more personal note is struck in 'the dwarf', where Marina asks him what's wrong with a diminutive woman they see. He apologizes to the woman for Marina's attitude. The anecdote must have struck a chord with him, having been the butt of so many taunts in his youth about his ungainly appearance.

In 'a man's woman' he gives feminists every opportunity to debunk him as the classic male chauvinist pig. One wonders how much of this is him and how much a poet having fun with a persona. Perhaps half and half. The misogynistic streak is continued in 'tight pink dress'. In the penultimate poem of the collection he addresses Linda King by name, hinting that she may leave him one day, imploring her to do so with grace rather than ruthlessness.

On the eve of the book's publication he told Martin he thought it represented his best work to date. He was as excited as a sandboy as he waited for it to hit the shelves. Each title that came out, he said, felt like the first one. The years of waiting made his recent crop of titles all the sweeter.

South of No North, a collection of his stories, came out that year too. Dedicated to Ann Menebroker, it contained more tales that confirmed the libidinous author as the colossus of rough trade. 'Hospitals and jails and whores,' he wrote, 'these are the universities of life. I've got several degrees.'

'This Is What Killed Dylan Thomas' has him trawling his way through the world of poetry readings, vomiting before them, enjoying the attention of women and thinking back to the years of isolation when his only visitors were money-hungry landladies or the FBI.

'The Way the Dead Love' is another exploration of his back pages: the crushing labor, the blinding depression...and Milton Berle saving his bacon. In 'Remember Pearl Harbor?' he writes about the draft-dodging interrogation he endured in the forties. 'The Killers' borrows Hemingway's short story title but hardly his style. Hemingway himself appears in 'Class' and also in 'No Neck and Bad as Hell.' These are slight works that represent the slapdash element of Bukowski, the part of him that often tossed off stories without too much care. He's better when he's drawing on his own experience. In 'All the Assholes in the World and Mine' and 'Confessions of a Man Insane Enough to Live with Beasts' he pulls out all the stops to write about his 1955 hospitalization. In general it's a satisfying collection, an essential addition to the Bukowski myth.

Californication

No sexual relationship stands still. No sexual relationship is bound by common sense. No sexual relationship is by the will any more than passion is. (John Braine)

In his love life - for want of a better term - Bukowski was still oscillating between King and Williams now but his heart was with King. 'Valentino would have kept both of them' he claimed, 'but then that's probably why he died so young.'

He told Williams he didn't want her to care so much for him. 'Is it okay if I *almost* love you?' she asked. She told him she thought he was afraid of love, that he preferred whores to lovers. He didn't argue with her when she said things like that. Maybe he believed they were true. If he was born a woman, he always said, he would have been a prostitute.

When he finally broke with her she carried through on the suicide attempt she'd threatened, taking an overdose of tablets one night. Bukowski saved her life by putting his fingers down her throat. When he did so he dislodged her dental plate. This seemed to upset her more than the fact that she'd nearly died. 'I don't want you to see my teeth,' she moaned. Farce was never far from tragedy when Bukowski was around. 'She had these bad teeth,' he said, 'so I pulled them out. There was blood and vomit everywhere.'

When she recovered she attacked him. He felt he deserved every blow she rained down on him. 'She should never have put her trust in a slob like me,' he said. She was a beautiful woman both inside and outside. The problem was simply that he didn't love her. If she didn't kill him – she also threatened that – everything would be fine.

He went back to King after leaving her. She'd known he was thinking of doing so. That was part of the reason Williams had tried to kill herself. King was always in the background when she was with Bukowski. She could almost see her in his face.

He was glad to be back with King. By now they were like bad habits of each other. The arguments grew more fierce and so did the sex.

Like Williams, King also threatened to kill Bukowski. Afterwards – as seemed mandatory after he received a death threat from an angry girlfriend – they made love. Suddenly, *Who's Afraid of Virginia Woolf?* was beginning to look like *Little Red Riding Hood*.

Bukowski was short of cash at this time. Martin's money helped with the child support but after drink and general utilities there was never much left over.

His biggest money-spinner was poetry readings. That was the main reason he continued to do them. There was always a demand for them but he hated them. His eyes stung and his back ached but the money was too good to turn down. 'I did them to pay the rent,' he said, 'I'm a poetry whore.'

He was usually nervous before going on stage but once he got out there he relaxed.

'All I had to do,' he told his friend Barbet Schroeder, 'was take one look into those rows of people and then I felt totally superior to them and at ease and on my game.' Were they a threat to his integrity? 'Of course, but I still have enough left after them.' The compromise meant nothing to him: 'It's no more than a mosquito bite.'

In time he would earn more for a single reading than for a year in his job at the post office. He kept hiking up the fee to dissuade the organizers but they didn't seem to care. Some of the universities didn't ask him back if he was too raucous but in other venues his wildness swelled the numbers attending.

'I didn't much like the people who came to my readings,' he said, 'and I didn't like myself either.' The best part was chatting up the stewardesses on the flights to the venues, or wheedling more drinks from them than he was entitled to.

After the readings finished he busied himself getting drunk and trying to seduce the professors' wives. 'If this is what killed Dylan Thomas,' he grinned, 'I don't mind having some of it.'

He played a character called Charles Bukowski as he read. This was someone he usually became after about nine p.m. – or three bottles of wine. Being shy by nature, he needed the alcohol to give him the dutch courage to perform. He usually kept a bucket beside him.

'It's for puking into,' he explained to the people in attendance. Some of them thought he was joking...until he started to actually puke. He sometimes threw beer bottles at them to get them to join him in his drinking. This would give extra life to such nights when he became bored with the poems.

He even got an offer to do a reading in Canada. 'Do Eskimos really kiss with their noses?' he asked. Soon afterwards Raymond Carver invited him to do one in Santa Cruz. He wasn't a great admirer of Carver's work. 'What's all the fuss about?' he asked. But he decided to do it anyway.

He was drunk when Carver met him at the airport. He invited him back to his house for dinner. When he was there he started to paw Carver's wife. He'd forgotten his poems so a book of them had to be found somewhere. Otherwise he would have had nothing to read. When he got on stage he started to abuse the audience, drinking gin as if it was going out of fashion.

Linda King read that night as well. She got quite a good reception, which surprised Bukowski as he didn't think much of her work.

He felt a bit threatened by her popularity. One of her poems was called 'The Cock.' When she'd finished reading it, Bukowski chortled, 'She's muscling in on my territory!'

Afterwards there was a party at the home of one of Carver's students. Bukowski continued to misbehave there, getting drunker by the minute. He put his hands up the dresses of any woman he got near to. Some of them ran from the house in shock.

Eventually Carver – another alcoholic – started to drink too. 'I'm okay if I stick with beer,' Bukowski told him, 'but if I start on whiskey I'll probably start throwing people out the window.'

The pair of them started to talk about their lives. Bukowski told Carver he couldn't understand how so many women were throwing themselves at him considering he was 51 and 'as ugly as sin.' He told him about Linda King and how violent she was, how she'd probably claw his eyes out if she heard he saw him with any other woman at the reading.

The pair of them stayed up all night drinking. The following morning they had breakfast together. Carver couldn't eat his so Bukowski ate it for him. Both of them had ferocious hangovers. It was a miracle Carver managed to get Bukowski to the airport in one piece for the flight back to L.A.

Most of the readings Bukowski did in the seventies were raucous. He loved bantering with the audience. When the poems weren't going down well there was always that to fall back on. One night a man asked him what he thought of Sputnik. He roared back, 'Why don't you fuck your Jewish grandmother?'

He did one for City Lights in late 1972. There was a party afterwards and King attended it. Inevitably, another fight broke out between them.

She accused him of cheating on her. When he denied it, she bit his arm. She started pummeling him with punches then. When he tried to defend himself the two of them fell down a staircase together. At the bottom of it, they continued to tussle. 'If he wasn't so good in bed,' King told the people watching, 'I think I'd kill him.' Bukowski replied, 'I wish she would.'

He had a more dramatic encounter at another party he went to at this time. The conversation turned to war. He was giving out about the conflict in Vietnam when a man started bragging about how many people he'd killed there. He was a veteran. Bukowski told him it didn't take guts to kill anyone in a war because it was legal. They started arguing. Bukowski told the man he was annoying him and that he wanted him to leave the room. The man went away but shortly afterwards he came back. This time he was carrying a gun. He took it out. Everyone was terrified – except Bukowski.

'You don't like me, do you?' he said to Bukowski. Bukowski said, 'That's true.' The man put the gun to Bukowski's temple. 'Do you still not like me?' he asked him. Bukowski said, 'No.'

He then told Bukowski he was going to shoot him. 'Go ahead,' Bukowski advised, 'You'd be doing me a favor. I'm a depressive. I've been looking for a way to get out of life for years.' The man was flummoxed. Bukowski continued, 'If you pull the trigger you'll be solving my problem but creating one for yourself. You'll spend a lot of time in jail or whatever else is going on around here. Maybe they'll give you the chair, I don't know.'

The man dropped the gun. He started crying. Then he left the room. All the people who were standing around Bukowski came up to him. They congratulated him for his bravery. 'I wasn't being brave,' he said, 'I told him the truth. I wasn't frightened. I felt like I was in a movie.'

He thanked everyone for the help they'd given him in trying to disarm the man. Not! He heard later that he'd tried to hold up a drugstore and was arrested. Later they put him into a mental home. 'He was nuts,' Bukowski said, 'but so was I. It's strange when you get two nuts together. I was ready to go and he knew it. That's what made it interesting. He bit off more than he could chew when he put the gun to my temple. If I said "Don't do it," he might have pulled the trigger.'

Bukowski's profile had grown much bigger by now. In 1973 Taylor Hackford made a documentary about him. *Bukowski* was shown on the local Los Angeles television channel, KCET. A fly-on-the-wall film, it shows Bukowski going about L.A. on an average day. One scene has him reading his poetry in San Francisco. He helps himself to beers from a strategically positioned fridge on the stage. Another scene shows him going to the track and talking about 'women and pussy.' He describes himself generally as a man with 'hemorrhoids and a bad heart.'

Linda King and Liza Williams also appeared in it. Williams said she saw herself as his 'custodian.' She said she liked his primitive image. She talked about sitting around with him watching television and being aware of his 'hostility.' Bukowski doesn't look too hostile, however. He grins for most of the time, even when he's been threatening at the poetry reading. 'One more beer and I'll take all of you,' he says at one point, to howls of laughter.

The film won the Los Angeles Corporation for Public Broadcasting award but drew a lot of complaints from viewers because of the number of expletives used in it. Bukowski liked it but he wasn't too keen on the people he met after the reading. He described them as drunks in his *Free Press* column. Hackford reminded him that it was he who was drunk after the reading, no one else. Bukowski knew he was right but he refused to backtrack on what he said in the column. 'When I write,' he told Hackford, 'I'm the hero of my shit.'

The program was another step along the way of his growing recognition. It was premiered in a local cinema. Bukowski went to it with King and his friend Jory Sherman. He was intent on making the most of the night so he tanked up on bottles of whiskey beforehand. As he sat swilling the whiskey after the film started, a young usher came by his row. He said to Bukowski, 'That's not allowed in here.' Bukowski looked him up and down. 'Fuck off, kid,' he said. Nobody talked to Bukowski like that, especially during the showing of a film about him. He was mobbed on the way out.

William Wantling died in 1974. Bukowski's friendship with him had dwindled over the years. He thought he went soft, that he sold his talent down the river after he became an academic. After Wantling invited him to do a poetry reading at the Illinois University where he taught English, Bukowski wrote a nasty column about him. It denounced both his character and his work. He disguised his name slightly, referring to him as Howard Stantling, but everyone knew who he was writing about. Two weeks later Wantling died from a massive coronary. He was drinking heavily at the time and suffering from depression. Some of that was caused by Bukowski's article.

His widow, Ruth, was outraged with him. She'd been a friend of his just like William had. She didn't regard his article as the sole cause of her husband's death but she thought it tipped him over the edge. She visited Bukowski soon afterwards expecting him to comfort her, or at least express some remorse, but this wasn't his style.

'Why did she come to see me if she's in mourning?' he said to King, 'I'm not a shrink.' To shake her out of her grieving he started to hit on her, telling her he wanted to fuck her. She was shocked. Afterwards she described his behavior as 'emotional rape.' She said it was the ugliest experience of her life. Bukowski hated it when women cried but he should have made an exception in her case. As if this wasn't bad enough, he went on to write about her in his next book *Women*, intimating Wantling died because she wasn't giving him enough sex. His treatment of her was revolting. This was the side of Bukowski nobody really wanted to see.

He now received a $5000 grant from the National Endowment of the Arts. It was the first official acknowledgment of his talent. Martin's $50,000 from the sale of his D.H. Lawrence works had just run out but for the first time in its history, Black Sparrow had brought in more money than it spent. 'We were on our way,' he chirped.

Burning in Water, Drowning in Flame was also published that year. An anthology of some of Bukowski's best work, it has him developing the voice he would soon make his own. Touching on his wild drinking escapades and his erratic love life, it whets our appetite for future collections. It was divided into four main sections, the last one pleasing him most with the manner in which he dissects the weird times he had with King and Williams. Al Winans brought out the Bukowski edition of *The Second Coming Years* that year as well, which thrilled him beyond description. It retailed at $2 in a limited edition. Today copies fetch up to a hundred times that figure.

Factotum, Bukowski's second novel, appeared in 1975. It bore many resemblances to his first with its scattergun style. Short chapters document short jobs on the road as this hard-drinking drifter engages in some heart-breaking encounters with hoboes, employers and (perhaps most importantly) himself. As a record of a life lived on the fringe of society it's indispensable. He never wallows in self-pity no matter how horrible his circumstances become, preferring to milk his absurd scenarios for humor. Each time he gets kicked he dusts himself down and runs at life again. It's like Horatio Alger without the breaks.

Written in a style that's curiously restrained, we follow our anti-hero through a barrage of dead end jobs and dead end dreams. He drops in and out of society with as much speed as the next beer – or landlord - requires. 'I always started a job,' he writes, 'with the feeling that I'd soon quit or be fired, and this gave me a relaxed manner that was mistaken for intelligence or some secret power.'

He gets over twenty jobs in the book. He also crosses America four times in the course of it. This isn't rugged individualism, it's Dickensian toil without any prospect of promotion. He feels worse than the Knut Hamsun of *Hunger* or the George Orwell of *Down and Out in Paris and London.* 'Compared to me,' he would say often in later years about Hamsun, 'that guy didn't even get scratched.'

'The idea,' he decides at one point, 'is not to think. But how do you stop thinking? Why was I chosen to polish this rail? Why couldn't I be inside writing editorials about municipal corruption? Well, it could have been worse. I could be in China working a rice paddy.' He takes on jobs he's totally unsuited to, pulling any scam he can think of to be kept on. Any time he's let go he embarks on a new one. 'I filled out so many job forms,' he tells us, 'I memorized the right answers.' He feeds potential employers the bullshit they crave. Life isn't a matter of truth or justice. It's a question of doing it to him before he does it to you.

Jobs pass the dead hours of the day. Afterwards comes the magic of alcohol, or sex. These fulfil his bodily needs. The other half of him is thinking, fantasizing. Chinaski hangs in there, as

203

tough as old boots but with a smidgeon of humanity buried behind the patina of tough guy-ism. Thoughts of suicide hint now and again but he knows it would be too easy to cave in. He decides to kick against the pricks, to fight fire with fire. By the end of the book he seems spun out as he sits impotently before one of his beloved strippers.

Tina Derby was a stripper he knew in real life. She was married to a man called Brad. Brad ran a sex shop. Bukowski loved cruising their beat, passing all the neon-soaked strip joints of night-time L.A.

They lived in a bungalow next door to Bukowski. He liked visiting them or having them visit him. Tina was pretty and had a great figure. Their nights together were pretty wild. The Darbys enjoyed watching Bukowski getting drunk and behaving outrageously. One night when he was with them he started 'eating' a page of the *Free Press*. His reason? 'Everyone should eat their words now and again,' he pronounced. 'You know what, Hank?' Tina said, 'You're crazier than a bunch of monkeys.'

She often teased him by crawling all over him like a cat as he lay naked on her bed. Brad liked to photograph these sessions. So did a man called Claude Powell. Some of Powell's photographs appear in Jim Christy's biography of Bukowski, *The Buk Book*. The text covers his whole life but the photographs in it seem to have all been taken on the same night. We see a positively debauched-looking Bukowski here. He seems like he's in the throes of a binge - or just coming off one. The shots of him with Tina have a kind of posed lechery about them.

Linda King didn't approve of his friendship with the Darbys. She thought there was something degenerate about it. Bukowski had to laugh at that. 'Me degenerate? Come on. You know I'm a pillar of the community.'

Whenever King became annoyed with him she continued to confiscate the sculpture she'd done of him. 'My head is on the plate again,' he'd say, 'I feel like John the Baptist.' Was Salomé going to do another of her dances the next time she took it back? At this point the situation bore all the hallmarks of a child custody situation, the head going to and fro like a yo-yo. 'It's our baby,' he joked. When he trivialized her like that, King grew even more angry with him.

They couldn't be together and they couldn't be apart. When King bought a house in Utah, Bukowski moved in with her as a tenant. She witnessed the family side of him there. Marina sometimes came to visit from Santa Monica. Frances was living there now. 'He never raised his voice to her,' King said. She also witnessed his soft side with her own daughter, Carissa, especially when he read bedtime stories to her. Bukowski had a great rapport with children and loved it when they were sassy to him. 'You got me there!' he'd say if they gave him a smart answer, throwing his head back laughing. He enjoyed making them laugh too, his own childhood having been so bereft of humor.

He loved Marina's naturalness, what he called her 'ancient wisdom.' He didn't want her to attend school, believing education robbed children of their spontaneity. He played a Batman and

Robin game with her one day. 'You be Batman,' he said 'and I'll be Robin. When she asked him why he wanted to be Robin instead of Batman he said, 'Because he does nothing.'

A man phoned King one night and said he liked her poetry. He asked her if he could come around and talk to her about it. She was flattered by his attention and agreed. He arrived with a bottle of whiskey. Not long into the visit it transpired that it was Bukowski he admired, not King. He'd been using her to get to meet Bukowski.

The man was gay. When Bukowski realized this he threw him up against a wall and started hitting him. The pair of them fell through a window and shattered it. There was glass and blood everywhere. Then they fell down a flight of steps into a heap. King phoned the police. They arrived sometime later with guns drawn and hauled the two of them off to jail. 'I was only trying to help you,' Bukowski declared as he was led off.

Shortly afterwards she brought him camping with her. Her sister and children went as well. It bored him to tears being in the middle of nowhere. 'He was a shark out of water,' was the way King described him. One day he told them he was going off somewhere to write. He walked into a wood. Hours later he still hadn't returned and King became worried. She went looking for him. She finally found him in a panic shouting, 'I'm lost. I need help!' It wasn't the tough Bukowski she was accustomed to. In the country he was just another lost soul.

'How could you be lost?' she said, 'This area has a fence all around it.'

'I climbed it,' he said.

She shook her head in dismay. It could only have happened to Bukowski. He told her he wanted to go back to L.A. 'I know where everything is there. I need a racetrack. Even though I hate people, I want them now.' He wrote about the incident in *Women*, embellishing it to make it stand out more. (In the book he falls into a swamp and is almost stung to death by hornets).

King suspected he was seeing other women at this time. Any time he said he was going to visit his friend Steve Richmond, who lived nearby, she thought it was for this reason. One day she decided to call on Richmond to see if he was there. He wasn't. She asked Richmond if he knew where he was but he said he didn't. She didn't believe him. Men never told on one another, she thought. When Bukowski heard she'd visited Richmond he accused her of having sex with him. Anytime she was ever with a man without him being there too he presumed this would have happened. It was his paranoia kicking in.

Bukowski was paranoid about Linda King being unfaithful to him in the middle of his own infidelities. (Al Berlinski)

Bukowski started disappearing in the afternoons now, saying he was going to the grocery store. King put two and two together. One night he told her he was going out to get some material for his column and she decided to follow him. She remembered him saying he knew a woman in a place called Hillcrest Avenue so she drove there. When she got to Hillcrest she saw him walking down the street. He seemed to be getting ready to go into an apartment. He had a bottle of whiskey in one hand and some beers in the other. It looked like he was stocked up for the night.

She was driving her Volkswagen, a car she loved. It was able to 'climb mountains,' she maintained. She decided to see how it would fare on a curb. She drove towards him, climbing the curb with the car. When he saw it he hurled himself backwards. A moment later she had him pinned up against the wall. She said to herself: 'The sonofabitch wants something for his column? I'll give him something for his column.'

The liquor had fallen from his hands at this point but it wasn't broken. She got out of the car and started smashing it. 'You're sleeping with her, aren't you?' she yelled at him. Bukowski was speechless for once. He looked at her with his mouth open as she drove off.

A few minutes later she turned the car around and drove back. The sight that confronted her was unique: He was brushing up the broken glass with a broom. She didn't know whether to drive over him or not. 'We were just going to have a few drinks,' he said tamely. She wasn't buying it. She continued roaring. 'You think you can live with me and screw someone else?'

One bottle remained unbroken. She picked it up and threw it through the window of the apartment. A few seconds later a woman appeared in a skimpy robe. 'What's going on?' she cried. 'So you're the woman who's screwing my man,' King shouted at her, 'You're in your nightgown. That's so cozy.' The woman walked back into the apartment. King followed her, chasing her up the stairs. She pulled the robe off her. The woman – who was now naked - looked at Bukowski. 'Get her out of here,' she said to him, 'I'm calling the cops.'

Bukowski realized King wasn't going to cool down. There was only one thing for it. He told the woman he'd have to go with her. At this stage she didn't seem to care what he did. Bukowski got into the car with King and she drove him back to her house. She'd won.

She thought she'd solved the situation but a few weeks later Bukowski went off in his car again and again she followed him. When she got to Hillcrest Avenue and saw his car parked near the apartment he'd been at before. This time she didn't throw any bottles or try to run him down. She drove back to her house and wrote him a note. It said, 'I'll be gone for the summer. My sister bought a bar. I'm going to be her bartender. You can stay in the house while I'm gone as long as you water the plants. I'll expect you out of here when I get back in the fall.'

He was. He moved to an apartment in a place called Carlton Way.

He started seeing another woman now, a cocktail waitress called Pamela Brandes. (Some biographers refer to her as Pamela Miller). She worked for Pussycat Theaters, a chain of cinemas that showed sex films. She was Miss Pussycat Theaters in 1973. She met Bukowski one night after being out for a night's drinking with a friend of hers, Georgia Peckham-Krellner. They were in the bar where Janis Joplin was supposed to have supped her last brew. Krellner's 32nd birthday had been the day before and she was still celebrating it. She was drinking Southern Comfort.

Krellner liked to celebrate. A woman who was into drugs as well as drink, she'd just shed a lot of weight and was feeling good about life. She loved Bukowski's work. She thought he was 'the best fucking writer alive.' Brandes knew nothing about him except the fact that he was the 'dirty old man' of the 'Freep' (*The L.A. Free Press*) Krellner suggested they ring him. Brandes was reluctant at first but then she thought, 'Why not? It would be like a symbolic way of bringing Joplin back from the dead.

She rang the operator. When she said Bukowski's name she didn't even have to give an address. The number was given immediately. She couldn't believe it was that easy.

'I've got it!' she told Krellner. By now Krellner was almost too drunk to know what was going on. Brandes dialed Bukowski's number. He answered it with a bored 'Yeah?' She told him it was her friend's birthday and she was a big fan of his. She was wondering if they could call around to see him. 'Okay,' he said, still sounding bored. He told her to bring a six-pack. 'It might be difficult,' he said, 'because of the time.' (It was now after 2 a.m.). 'You'd be surprised what a little cleavage can do,' she assured him.

The cleavage didn't work but she didn't let that deter her. The pair of them set off for Carlton Way without the six-pack. After taking a few wrong turns, Brandes managed to locate his apartment. Krellner was singing an Eagles song to herself as they arrived. They got out of the car and rang his bell. He peeped out through the blinds. 'Who is it?' he growled. ''It's us,' Brandes chirped, 'the birthday girls.'

He let them in. He had a T-shirt on him that was too sizes too small for him. Brandes was shocked at his skin. It looked like 'a road map to hell was imprinted on his face.' She tried not to stare at him. He had a knife behind his back. He never answered the door without that because Carlton Way was such a rough area.

He looked at her body. 'You've got the cleavage but you don't have the six-pack,' he said. She apologized, telling him she'd tried her best to get it. She introduced him to Krellner. She said her own name was Cupcakes, a nickname from a previous boyfriend.

They sat down. Brandes was shocked to see he was living in such a dump. There were beer bottles everywhere. The ash trays were overflowing. He asked her what she'd like to drink. She said 'Champagne.' Amazingly, he managed to find some.

Krellner told him she'd read *Post Office*. 'Did all that shit really happen to you?' she asked. 'Unfortunately yes,' he replied. He started to flirt with her as his mood lightened. 'You've got the soul,' he said to Krellner, 'and you've got the looks,' to Brandes. She took it as a compliment but it was really an insult.

They drank until 5 a.m. The more he drank, the more relaxed he became. He loved being surrounded by women, the more the merrier. None of them wanted the night to end. It turned into a kind of mini-orgy. Krellner was probably even wilder than Bukowski. At one point she gave him a Dexedrine tablet. Brandes was getting a baptism by fire into the background world of the 'Freep.'

As they walked away from his bungalow they heard the sound of a typewriter clacking. 'Now that's a fucking writer,' Krellner said. This was a man who could work as hard as he played. She thought it might be the Dexedrine kicking in.

A photograph of the night has survived. In some ways it's as iconic as the one of Jane Cooney Baker from her High School. It has Krellner standing beside Bukowski at his fridge. She's dressed in a mini-skirt and a skimpy top. Her tights are rumpled, signifying the recent weight loss, and she's in killer heels. The pair of them look a sight.

What makes the photo even funnier is the fact that she has cigarettes in both hands. She also has a beer in one of them. She has her arm around Bukowski. He's holding a beer too. His stomach is sticking out from under his T-shirt as he stands in his bare feet grinning at the camera. (Some other photos from the night have them in slightly different poses, indicating they may have posed for them. Neither is Brandes credited as the photographer, so who took them?)

Two weeks later she called on him again. She'd had a bad day at work and needed someone to talk to. This time they were both sober so the conversation was less frivolous. She told him she worked at the candy counter of Pussycat Theaters. He was familiar with the place. 'They show porn films there,' she told him. He hadn't been aware of that. She was surprised when he told her he didn't like porn films. 'They remind me too much of open heart surgery,' he remarked.

Brandes had grown up fast. By the age of fifteen she'd had a daughter, Stacey. She was 32 years younger than Bukowski.

On the night she met him she thought she'd fly to the moon sooner than date him but this was a different kettle of fish. She warmed towards him as she got to know him better.

They began a relationship. At first it looked as unlikely as the one with King had been, another 'beauty and the beast' scenario. When they went out together there were wolf whistles, usually because of the revealing dresses Brandes wore. She looked like she was poured into her dresses and forgot to say 'When.'

She told Bukowski to call her Cupcakes. 'All my friends do,' she said. Sometimes he just called her 'Cups', or 'Red.'

He was fascinated by her red hair. He called it 'lightning from heaven.' He'd been fascinated by Linda King's hair too.

He wrote about the night he met Brandes and Krellner in his *Free Press* column. In it he said they were hookers. Brandes was disgusted but Krellner was delighted to be mentioned in any capacity by 'the great Bukowski.' He used their real names – though not their surnames.

Brandes thought Bukowski behaved like a child when they were out together. She said it was 'as though he'd been locked away somewhere for years.' He became infatuated with her very quickly. 'She'll be the death of me,' he told Carl Weissner, 'but it will be worth it.'

He liked her zany attitude to life but he wasn't too keen on her hippie friends. He was also fiercely jealous of her looking at other men. This was always the way it was when he went out with pretty women. He knew the men looking at them would be thinking: 'If he can get her I must have a chance.'

One night when Brad Darby called around to see him he accused Brandes of flirting with him. She couldn't believe what she was hearing. She said she didn't even like Darby, that there was something off-putting about him. But Bukowski wouldn't let go of his suspicions.

He roared at her, working himself up to a pitch. 'Women are all alike!' he screamed, 'You're all nothing but fucking goddam whores!' She was dumbfounded at his reaction.

'Because he considered Brad an attractive man,' she said, 'and me an attractive woman, he figured we'd have no qualms about jumping into bed together. He thought good-looking people lacked character, had never suffered, had never experienced rejection, had it easy in life and got by on their looks.'

When Brandes came into Bukowski's life, Linda King had started to go out of it. King became pregnant towards the end of her relationship with him. She'd been sleeping with other men at the time but she firmly believed the child was Bukowski's. The tensions she was experiencing with him at the time – coupled with a house move - caused her to miscarry the child.

The miscarriage caused severe problems to her health. She could even have died. She was in trauma from the experience but in a strange way relieved. Having a baby by such a volatile man, she thought, would have been traumatic. She once said to him, 'The one thing that saved me having your baby was that your sperm was pickled with alcohol.'

She told him about the miscarriage on a phone call. He was with Brandes at the time.

'I almost bled to death,' she said, feeling herself on the point of tears. Bukowski didn't seem too concerned and changed the subject.

213

'Pamela has agreed to sleep with me,' he said, 'but she won't do it until I get a cleaner mattress.' She wasn't with him at the moment, he said, because she was gone out to buy the mattress. 'She's getting some champagne as well,' he added, 'Do you think she'll come back to me or run off with the money?'

This was poor behavior even by Bukowski's standards. King hung up on him. She was in a rage as she put the receiver down. She'd almost died carrying his child and all he could talk about was mattresses and champagne.

The following night she got drunk. She decided to get revenge on him so she drove to his bungalow on Carlton Way. When she got there she broke in through his kitchen window.

She decided she was going to take the things she knew were most valuable to him. She fastened on his typewriter first and then a bunch of books she saw lying around. She grabbed them and went back out through the window.

As she was making her way through some bushes that were at the back of his house she heard his car coming into the driveway. She called out to him.

'Who's there?' he said. When he came round the back she started throwing his books at him.

'What are you doing?' he said. She flung the books at his windows, picking one window for every girlfriend she thought he'd had besides her. Bukowski stood there dumfounded as he listened to the glass shattering.

When the books were all gone, she went out to the street and started bouncing his typewriter off it. Bukowski gazed at her in dismay. He couldn't believe she'd destroy his precious 'machine gun.' She broke the carriage.

It was all very symbolic. A carriage for a miscarriage. He'd destroyed her insides and now she was exacting retribution by 'castrating' him, breaking up his 'piano', his penis substitute. ('If

214

that baby could talk,' he liked to tell people, 'It would turn the walls blue.')

Tina Darby was watching all the action from her house next door.

She'd met King once before. It was on a night when Brad was exhibiting some of the raunchy photos he'd taken of Bukowski with her. King had barged in on them and gone wild when she saw them. She attacked Tina and injured her finger in a scuffle. She had to go to hospital to have it treated.

Remembering the incident, Bukowski told Tina to go inside for her safety. She did that as King continued to rant and rave at him. When she didn't show any signs of cooling down, Bukowski called the police. This was a first for him. He was usually on the receiving end of police calls.

She was handcuffed and taken down to the precinct. Bukowski didn't press property damage charges on her but she was tested for drunk driving.

'If your children aren't asleep,' one policeman warned her, 'You could have them taken away from you.' When she was released she phoned Bukowski.

'If you ever call me about your women again,' she said to him 'I'll come over there and do the same thing all over again.'

Bukowski told Brandes about the incident and she was sympathetic. She'd never met King but she'd heard about her temper.

Bukowski said he didn't mind too much about the books but he was heartbroken about the typewriter. He'd typed over a thousand poems on it, even dedicating one of them to it. 'I feel like I've lost a piece of my soul,' he said. John Martin had paid for a new one for him but it wasn't the same.

Brandes had just been evicted from her apartment at this time after falling behind in her rent. Bukowski said he'd try to get her into an apartment adjoining his bungalow. He knew the landlord

215

and thought he might be able to get her in without having to pay a deposit. She hadn't enough money for one. Brandes was always running out of money, being a creature of the moment like Bukowski.

She asked him where his old typewriter was.

'In the trash can,' he wailed. 'It seems wrong leaving it there,' he said, 'I feel like I should bury it and have a funeral service or something.'

'Maybe we can have a wake for it,' Brandes suggested, 'with an open casket.' She was always able to cheer him up with a quip like that.

Bukowski spent most of the next two years with Brandes. It was an on-off relationship like the one with King but with slightly less tortuous exchanges.

King knew she'd lost him to Brandes. It was no big tragedy; they'd run their course.

After what came to be known as the 'mattress christening' incident, she'd got him out of her system. She knew he was bad for her, that he'd turned her back to the person she'd been all those years ago when she'd had her nervous breakdown.

That was why she went so crazy at his apartment. She couldn't afford to let it happen again. She knew she had to stop thinking about him and move on with her life.

She did that, selling her house in Utah and moving back to Phoenix, where she'd grown up. It was a move she knew she had to make, no matter how much a wrench it was to her system.

The first thing she did when she got there was go to a doctor. She felt as if her body was ready to fall apart. She was dizzy and looking as white as a ghost. He put her on penicillin for peritonitis. She spent two weeks in bed and lost twenty pounds. That was the price one paid for having a relationship with a crazy poet.

Meltdown.

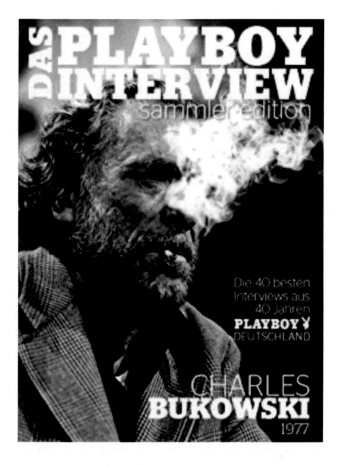

Bukowski came to see her once. It was when he was on the way home from a reading he'd done in Texas. He thought she looked well. 'You're better off without me,' he said. She agreed. 'The intense feelings were still there,' she said, 'but I was no longer emotional about him.' He stayed with her for three or four days but the spark was gone.

'Come back to L.A.,' he said to her the day before he left, 'It's not as much fun without you. Come on back and fight my women.' She replied, 'Is that the best you can offer?' They had breakfast in a café. She was too upset to eat as she remembered all the good times they'd had together. Now it was over, ending on a whimper rather than a bang. He seemed more laconic, eating her breakfast as well as her own, just as he'd done with Raymond Carver some time before. He was so nonchalant she became enraged.

Was this the same person who said, 'I'm fifty Christmas trees inside' when he was with her? She started to scream at him but it had no effect. He was gone from her in his mind. He wrote about the incident in his poem, 'I am a Reasonable Man.' Perhaps a better title for it would have been, 'I am a Cold-Blooded Man.' At times like this he seemed to have no feelings whatsoever. They never saw one another again.

Bukowski became as obsessed with Brandes as he'd once been with King but this relationship was much more one-sided. King was more flattered by Bukowski's attentions to her than Brandes was. She enjoyed his company but it didn't go any deeper than that for her. Neither was she as taken with his poetry as King had been. Anytime he showed her one of his books she appeared uninterested and this offended him.

'Why do you think people read my work?' he asked her one day.

'Shock value,' she said bluntly.

'That's the only reason?' he continued.

'Sure,' she said, 'Where else can they read about fucking, shitting, pissing, vomiting and death all in the same poem?' Bukowski was aghast that this was all it meant to her.

He told a friend about what had happened and the friend was aghast too. Bukowski reported back to Brandes what he'd said to him: 'He told me I should smack you around and then dump you. I'm beginning to wonder if he's right.' He loved shocking her with remarks like that, but Brandes wasn't affected by them.

He also loved pulling down self-important people when he was with her. One day a friend of Brandes called Janet Marino called to see her. Marino was something of a snob. They'd been at school together but drifted apart afterwards. When Marino heard Brandes had moved to Hollywood she looked forward to dropping in on her to see her in what she thought would be her new fancy apartment. Little did she know what was in store for her.

From the moment she entered the apartment - which was now beside Bukowski's one - she got a bad feeling about it. This wasn't the Hollywood she'd had in mind - 'bougainvillea, lemon trees and Spanish tiles.' Instead it was 'vagrants, sex shops, hookers and strip clubs.'

And Bukowski.

He was dressed in scruffy jeans and a T-shirt. And, because he was on his third or fourth beer of the day, looking like something the cat dragged in.

How had her old friend sunk so low? Marino wondered. Whenever Bukowski encountered people like this he overdid his slovenliness, turning on the 'bad boy Bukowski' bit.

Marino grew increasingly more uncomfortable as the visit went on. She couldn't wait to get out of the apartment but Bukowski was enjoying her discomfort and he decided to detain her. 'Like a vulture spotting his prey,' Brandes said, 'I knew she was about to get a royal dose of the Bukowski shock treatment.'

That she got. As he took a swig of his beer he let it spill down the corner of his mouth onto his T-shirt. Then he belched. 'Don't worry, kid,' he said to her, 'You'll get used to the dirt. It'll grow on you. Before you know it you'll be craving it. You'll embrace it like a long-lost lover.'

Marino's eyes darted around the room as if she was expecting rats to jump out of the walls. 'Is this a fucking joke?' she whispered to Brandes when Bukowski was out of earshot. She thought she was on an episode of *Candid Camera*, that they were putting on a show for her.

When she realized they weren't, she made a bolt for the door. Before she could get to it, Bukowski pulled down his jeans and flashed his 'big white hairy butt' at her. Marino screamed. She ran out of the apartment saying, 'You're both sick!'

Brandes went into hysterics after she was gone.

'Why did you do that?' she asked Bukowski. 'I don't like her type,' he told her flatly.

Despite having a lot of fun with Bukowski, Brandes knew fairly early on in their relationship that he wasn't going to be the Significant Other in her life. She was too young for him, and too flighty. Bukowski was as much a father figure to her as a boyfriend. She was also afraid his addictive personality would rub off on her. 'He reminds me too much of myself,' she said.

As well as laughing a lot they fought with one another, usually about stupid things. No relationship with Bukowski was conceivable without that. He always brought out the beast in his women. 'He didn't encourage me to misbehave,' she said, 'It just worked out that way.'

One night she put her heel through the windscreen of his car in a panic when she thought they were about to crash. He didn't bother having it fixed. There were so many bumps on it by now it was starting to resemble his own raddled face. Her own car was pretty beaten up too. The door was hanging off it and the side windows were missing. He said it reminded him of the inside of a sofa. Brandes didn't care how it looked.

It wasn't registered either - and she drove without a license. When she got parking tickets she tore them up. If she was stopped for drunk driving she was usually able to charm the police into letting her go. In some ways she was more casual than Bukowski about things like that. (He had a horror of getting pulled over, she said, or even getting a ticket).

One day he presented her with a book of poems he'd written for her. It was published by Black Sparrow Press in a limited edition of 180 copies. He called it *Scarlet*. He was excited giving it to her but when she read it she was shocked at the content of some of the poems.

One of them documented an incident where he accused her of not being a natural redhead, of dying her hair a henna color. Insulted at the slight, she pulled off her panties to prove to him that 'the carpet matched the curtains.' (This incident presumably occurred early on in their relationship). Other poems in the collection dealt with sex and bodily functions. Fairly typical Bukowski fare but not something a girlfriend would have expected as a love gift.

Neither were their dates the stuff of Victorian niceties. He brought her to boxing matches. They went to the track. They watched football matches on television. 'In some ways he treated me as if I was another man,' she said. He was used to doing that with Jane and Linda King. It was expected. If Hemingway brought his women hunting, Bukowski could bring them racing.

She was on pills a lot of the time. She showed the effects of them by dozing off in the most unlikely places. When they went to New York for a reading he was doing they stayed in the Chelsea Hotel. That was where Janis Joplin died. Brandes almost died there too. There was no air conditioning in the room so she opened a window and sat at it. She was feeling weak from the effects of the pills she was taking at the time and almost fell out. She was half way out the window before she managed to haul herself back in.

'I've lost a lot of women in my time,' Bukowski reflected, 'but never that way.' Maybe he was thinking about the man he saw falling through the sky all those years ago when he was with Jane. In a poem published in the posthumous collection *The People look like Flowers at Last* there's a poem called 'bewitched in New York' where he says he saw Brandes falling out of the window in his mind.

Slightly more disconcertingly, he adds that he wanted that to happen and that they had a bitter argument afterwards resulting in her refusing to sleep with him. This contradicts Brandes' version of events, leading to the old debate of just how much he used poetic license in his poems and how much of them were direct recall.

He said to John Martin, 'She's a speed freak, a pill-head and on the smack.' He spent a lot of his time in pharmacies with her as she handed in amphetamine prescriptions to be filled. She'd started taking them to lose weight but continued after it fell off.

The main problem with the relationship was that he felt too old for her. He also suspected she was seeing other men every time she was out of his sight. Whenever he called around to her house looking for her she seemed to be out. Sometimes he left poems on her doorknob for her to read, tying them onto it with one of his shoelaces.

'Why are you never home?' he asked her one night.

'Because I'm 26 years of age,' she replied.

Another night he accused her of being a prostitute. She vehemently denied this.

He wrote about her in his short story 'Work-Out' where he refers to her as Nina: 'She had gone the route: borne a child at sixteen, then had two abortions, a marriage, a slight run at prostitution. Barmaid jobs, shackjobs, benefactors, unemployment insurance and food stamps all held her together. But then she had a great deal left. That body, humor, madness and cruelty. Nina was a rifle shot into the brain of the psyche.'

They went on a break towards the end of 1976. She started a relationship with a dental student at this time without telling Bukowski.

They still saw one another but it was only platonic now. She didn't seem to be aware how much he was pining for her – or maybe she didn't want to be. Bukowski knew he was punching above his weight with her. He knew she could never have the same feelings for him as he had for her.

The following year was torture for him. He kept pursuing her without getting anything in return. She was like all women, he concluded. Their main talent lay in torturing men.

One day he decided to bring things to a head with her. It was August 16th, 1977, his 57th birthday. It was also the day Elvis Presley died.

He brought her back to his apartment and sat her down on his bed.

'Listen, kid,' he said, 'I can't do this anymore. We've got to end the madness. You're tearing my guts out. I can't think. I can't eat. I can't sleep.'

'Okay,' she mumbled. Afterwards he drove her back to her place. She'd been drinking champagne so she felt woozy. She went straight to bed. She woke up briefly at 8 p.m. and turned on the television.

There were two doctors on the screen. They seemed to be holding some kind of press conference about the 'death' of Elvis. She was too woozy to take the news in and fell asleep again. When she woke up the next morning she wondered if she'd dreamt it all but then the news came on and she realized she hadn't.

Elvis was gone. And so was Bukowski.

**Cupcakes' relationship with Bukowski ended
the day Elvis Presley died**

He used sex to recover from his infatuation with her. Women
entered and exited his life like revolving doors in the next few
months. Were they interested in him for himself or his notoriety?
He didn't know. Neither did he know why so many of them were

224

calling to him. His mailman passed one day and saw three women on his porch. The next day he said to Bukowski, 'How do you get 'em?' 'The problem isn't getting them,' Bukowski told him, 'The problem is getting rid of them.'

He didn't know where his attractiveness came from. A lot of it was due to his personality, what King called his 'aliveness.' She said there were always a hundred things going on in his head that life was never dull with him around. He was also someone who was open to anything that might happen on a given day.

Sex wasn't the ideal recipe for getting Brandes out of his system but it seemed to work. It was the old cliché: The only way to get over a woman was to get under another one. His emotions ran so deep he had to cauterize them out of himself by the distraction of the bedsprings. He'd been doing that for years now to protect himself from being hurt.

John Martin remembered calling to see him one day in the early seventies and finding two teenagers sitting on the porch outside his apartment. When he asked them what they were doing, one of them said, 'We came from Amsterdam to fuck Bukowski.' (The translations were obviously selling well).

Another lover he had at this time was a young woman called Amber O'Neil. She was from San Francisco. She wrote to him in care of City Lights to tell him how much she loved his books and said she'd like to meet him. The letter was forwarded to him by Lawrence Ferlinghetti.

He didn't always answer communications like this but the timing was right for O'Neil's one and he responded to it. A flood of letters followed both ways. Then one night he rang her and invited her to come and see him.

'I'm very short,' she said on the call. He told her that didn't matter.

He met her at the airport a few days later.

'Hello, Mr. Bukowski,' she said formally. She was indeed very short, not even five feet in height. They went back to his apartment. They were hardly in the door when she started unzipping his trousers and performing oral sex on him. It was a stormy session. She had to lie down to recover from her exertions afterwards. Other exerting sessions followed.

She spent three days with him in all. She was usually up first because he'd be sleeping off his hangovers. 'He seemed tired a lot of the time,' she said, 'He was looking his age.'

After she went back to San Francisco he took up with a restaurant manager called Jane Manhattan. He met her at a reading in Vancouver. Afterwards she visited him in his apartment in L.A., spending a week with him there.

They had a riotous time together. Anything she did he made into a drama. One day she bought a pair of high heels for herself. When he saw them he took out his penis and put it into one of them. He started bumping and grinding and pretending to have sex with it. Manhattan was in convulsions. Then he threw it down in disgust, saying, 'You don't love me, you bitch!'

He was always doing crazy things like that. It was why women loved him so much. He put them into good form. He would have made a great stand-up comedian if he wanted, someone along the lines of Lenny Bruce.

In fact he *was* a great stand-up comedian – or rather a great sit-down one. Many of the readings he did at this time turned into comic evenings. A lot of it went back to his deprived youth. 'My father taught me to be a writer,' he said once. He also taught him to be a prankster.

In his poem 'high school girls' from the posthumous collection *Slouching Toward Nirvana* he says women were always giving out to him about being negative when he was young but as he got older he became more positive and they turned negative. All their positivity has burned itself out. Because he started late at happiness, it lasted. Another poem from the collection, 'golden boy,' took up a similar theme. It concerned a classmate who promised much in school but after he graduated he was never heard from again.

By now Black Sparrow was starting to make a real mark on the publishing world. Bukowski's monthly stipend increased from $100 to $300 as the royalties flowed in. There were more and more offers for readings but these meant little to him.

He'd never viewed poetry as a spectator sport. Neither did he need hero worship to persuade him that what he was doing was worthwhile. Reading one's work aloud, he believed, was hucksterism, a performance for The Great Unwashed. More often than not the audiences applauded at all the wrong places, which really annoyed him. He did them for the rent rather than to 'expose my soul's genitals.'

The people who came to the readings weren't the clean-shaven breed that usually proliferated at such gatherings. Many of them were leather-jacketed troublemakers who tried to pull Bukowski down to their level by their repeated heckling.

He was usually able to out-heckle them but sometimes it got too much for him. He felt like an actor delivering the same dull script night after night: a tale full of sound and fury signifying nothing, as Shakespeare put it. 'This will be my destiny,' he wrote, 'scrabbling for pennies in dark tiny halls, reading poems I have long since become tired of.'

Even worse than the leather-jacketed brigade were the 'respectable' poets who came to gloat. They looked at him as if to say, 'Have you become reduced to this?' but deep down he knew they would have given their right arms to be where he was, having oceans of people hanging on his every word.

Many of these evenings had 'big fight' atmospheres. Sometimes actual fights broke out. He didn't mind too much if the poems were sidelined on such occasions? He'd served his time in the trenches.

He'd earned the right to be someone who charged megabucks to abuse people from a rostrum.

By the mid-1970s he was making up to $2000 for the readings. The more of them he did the more he grew to hate them but he needed the money. And there was always the hope of getting laid by a co-ed afterwards.

Many people left them claiming they'd been sold down the river by a man who seemed to be more interested in guzzling beer than reading. He never felt he had anything to apologize for in this regard. He wasn't twisting anybody's arm to attend them. He didn't set any standards of behavior for himself so he had none to live up to. They should have gone to hear Robert Creeley or T.S. Eliot if that was the way they felt. With this man a poetry reading was never going to be a parlor-room experience. It was a performance.

This was Bukowski Live and Unleashed. Five good minutes of him lasted longer in the memory than an hour of a poet who delivered genteel vignettes to the measured applause of the anal retentive.

It all depended on what somebody was looking for. With Bukowski one learned to expect the unexpected. One night at a reading in Michigan he put down his poems and started to arm-wrestle with a student in the audience. The 'big fight' atmosphere justified itself that night.

He played the court jester because he knew that was what they wanted. It was emotional striptease but it beat working for the sex magazines. Or starving.

The more the audiences poured in, the less he seemed to be bothered what he did – or didn't do. He knew a lot of them were bored by him and his work. Many of them would have passed him by if they saw him in a trashcan on the street. It was a kind of inverted snobbery, this elevation of him into some kind of dope god.

Bukowski's poetry readings were more riotous than literary. (Al Berlinski)

The readings usually ended when the wine ran out. 'I'm making some bastards rich,' he would say, 'and killing myself in the process.' Drunk or sober, though, he had the status of a living legend. He delivered his poems in the kind of drawl that suggested he didn't really give a damn. It was the same thing that explained his success with women. The less you seemed to care, the more interested they were.

He bantered with audiences as if he was going out of his way to make them hate him but the more he insulted them the more they cheered. If they abused him back, that was okay too. 'Fuck you!' roared a heckler at one reading. 'At last!' he replied, apparently relieved.

As his notoriety gathered steam he hiked his fee up to $1,000. This wasn't out of greed. It was probably more to scare promoters off. If that was the motive, it didn't work. They always acceded so he continued to do them. If they were dumb enough to offer him a grand a go - plus air fare and accommodation - he could hardly say no. It was blood money, (im) pure and simple.

The size of the crowds meant nothing to him. Though Walt Whitman was one of his heroes, he disagreed with his notion that poetry depended on large numbers of people to listen to it for its justification. 'To have great poetry,' Whitman once pronounced, 'we must have great audiences'. For Bukowski this was putting the cart before the horse. 'Bad poets create bad audiences,' he said, 'Death brings more death.'

After the readings were over he went back to what might we might advisedly call his normal life. The crowds dispersed and he was faced with nothing but a blank piece of paper. He enjoyed putting it into the typer and hitting the keys again, getting back to that original simplicity.

Sometimes he didn't get home immediately. If a groupie sidetracked him he might stay somewhere else for the night. He still couldn't believe his luck. No matter how many times this happened it was always a surprise to him. Were they jerking his chain? Why would they want to flirt with a man whose stomach spilled over his trousers, who slouched across rooms with the buttons of his shirt undone, whose face looked like the craters of the moon? Did they not notice his boils, his rotten teeth, a beer gut that was going on for a career of its own?

'Peacocks don't usually sleep with crows,' said the man who didn't lose his virginity until he was 23 – and then to a prostitute – but he didn't want to look all those gift horses in the mouth. He'd heard the word 'No' so often from women in his youth, their 'Yes' was now doubly sweet. The boy whose breath fogged the windowpane at the prom concert was now on the inside looking out at all the other poor souls wandering around in the dark. This time there was no night watchman to tell him to go home.

A notch on a bedpost, however, couldn't fulfil him in the long run. Nothing lifted his spirits like women but nothing dropped them as fast either. They were like poetry or horses or anything else in his life: unpredictable.

He was always on the look-out for 'gentle' women, he insisted, but the whores kept finding him. They told him they admired him because he was different to all other men but within a week they usually tried to mold him *into* those other men. You couldn't win.

Women worked him into a frenzy, he claimed, by making him think he needed them. Then he came to believe it. When they left him he was devastated, thinking it was them he missed, whereas what he really missed after they were gone was the routine of companionship. Once he got over that he was relieved. He had to keep telling himself this every time another one left him or her absence would have destroyed him.

A certain amount of attention from women was flattering but there were times he had to get away from it all. He needed to go into a room, lock the door and turn the light off in order to get his identity back. It was as if he had a preservation order on his heart, as if there was an invisible wire mesh around it that said 'Beware of Entry.'

'People in love become edgy,' he said, 'They lose their sense of perspective. They lose their sense of humor. They become nervous, psychotic bores. They even become killers.' Love was for 'guitar players, Catholics and chess freaks' - not Bukowski. He didn't want 'Will You Still Love Me Tomorrow,' just 'Help Me Make It Through the Night.'

'I'd love to live in gentle peace with a woman.' he told Al Winans, 'but I've never met the one yet. It's getting more now that I just need a housekeeper instead of a soulmate.' He thought relationships were doomed to disaster from the get-go. Neither party could keep up the charade they practiced when they first met. It wasn't long before they went from 'I really dig you,' to 'Jesus, you left a turd floating in the toilet bowl!'

He knew a lot of the attention he was getting came from his fame. This had crept up on him almost without him realizing it. He was like a tired old prospector who suddenly found gold and didn't believe it, imagining he was too long in the sun. He felt he deserved it but when life kicked you for long enough you expected that pattern to continue. When it didn't, you had to adjust your mindset.

From the Stygian darkness of an Atlanta cabin to this. Was there any single thing that had catapulted him into the A-league? No. There was no formula for success. If there was, somebody would have bottled it. Having his books sought as collector's items was a long way from the hand-printed Loujon Press days. After thirty years of being on the Pause button, his life had suddenly gone onto fast forward. He was an overnight success after three decades knocking on the door. He'd spent too long in the underground for success to give him 'the fat head.' It had come refreshingly late for him. If it happened in his twenties the bleeding ulcer might have killed him.

Fame meant that when the nails came up through his shoes now he didn't have to beat them out with a hammer. It meant his car started in the mornings. But it also meant more people recognized him at the track. And asked him for his opinions on things. Interviewers continued to come to visit him as well, their numbers multiplying according as his book sales went off the scale.

Their questions were even more banal than the ones he faced at the track. What did he think of literature? ('It sucks.') What about his own writing? ('That sucks too.') Did he read the critics? ('No. What they say tells you more about them than yourself. People usually see on a page what they want to see. It's like a self-fulfilling prophecy.')

Official America hadn't recognized him when he was struggling but when his books started to sell worldwide the goalposts shifted. The Old Guard still held firm but the sycophants sucked up to him for favors. The adulation was a novelty for a time. When it wore off he reverted to his old habits, creating scenes in public places even for the sake of it. The difference now was that his commotions sometimes made the papers. He liked it better when they just locked him up for the night. Now the police were as likely to ask him for his autograph as a statement.

He was flattered that he was read widely in jails and asylums. 'Hell,' he laughed, 'some of my best friends used to be crazies and ex-cons.' A prisoner from Australia wrote to him to say his were the only books passed from cell to cell. 'I allowed myself feel good about that for two days,' he admitted. His style was so compulsive you couldn't put him down. Other prisoners read him for a different reason: 'If that guy made it, and he's so fucked up, maybe there's a chance for me.'

John Martin had transformed him into a semi-corporate entity, which bothered some of his poetry friends from the past. There was a groundswell of discontent from his former fellow laborers at the underground vineyard.

Martin published him, they said, because he was a 'known' writer. Bukowski replied that people got known because they were good. That was how the game worked. You couldn't draw a line between quality and commercial success but neither could you equate obscurity with merit. He knew a lot of his critics were simply suffering from 'the green-eyed monster.' They couldn't do it like he could. 'People seem to like me,' he said, 'from Kansas City whores to Harvard professors.'

The professors wanted to know the secret of how he wrote but there wasn't any secret: 'It's just work, day by day.' Some offered to bring six-packs, which didn't work for him either. 'I'm a circus animal,' he complained, 'They wanted me to behave like a performing seal, to say they drank with Buk.' Some of them even brought their poems. 'That was the worst part.'

And the questions went on. How did he get out of the post office? Did he really nearly die once? Did he know someone who could get them into print?'

One man who pretended to be a journalist from Germany engaged him in a 4-hour conversation. At the end of it he said, 'I only pretended to be a journalist. I just wanted to meet you.' A wealthy man wrote to him offering to leave all his money to him when he died. A woman in Australia sent him the key to her house. Someone else sent him a knife in appreciation of his work. He didn't know if she was being sarcastic or not. Was he meant to stick it into himself?

He never understood fan worship of him, or indeed of any writer. He never sought out writers he admired, feeling what they had to offer him was inside the spines of their books. 'Don't meet your idols,' he said with Balzac, 'The gilt will rub off on your fingers.' His experiences with people like William Corrington and Doug Blazek strengthened him in this view.

His home became a shrine for pilgrims anxious to touch base with one who'd suffered like they had – or thought they had. At the onset of his career he was even too low on the totem pole for *The National Inquirer,* but now even *Time* magazine was seeking him out. In the old days people saw him drunk in alleyways and helped themselves to what was in his wallet. Now they were happy to browse through the books on his shelves.

Some of the unscrupulous ones stole them, waiting until he was gone to the can to help themselves. Rich man or poor man, he was still the victim.

'The Germans,' he said, 'think I'm a cross between Hemingway and Hitler.' Was there any other writer who could call up such dissonant echoes? For others he was the master of the *single entendre*, a writer whose work was more suitable to toilet walls than library shelves.

He was immune to his bad press. Some of the articles were little more than personal attacks on him. There were rumors that he failed to pay child support for his daughter that he never washed. Another one claimed that he beat his women. 'I'm not my image,' he said.

That was one of the things he had against The Beats. They worked too hard to be the characters they were purported to be. Bukowski didn't want to fall into that trap.

The Beats were too bourgeois for him. He hated their cheery solidarity, the way they always had to hunt in packs, leeching off each other. He was also unimpressed by the fact that so many of them seemed to be gay. (Was this a prerequisite for membership?) They played the fame game and became corrupted in the process, ending up as part of the very things they originally set out to exorcise. Like so many exhibitionists, they backed their way into the limelight.

Neither did he have much time for their championing of pot. If you took LSD, they reasoned, you were automatically deemed an intellectual. Thus ran the bullshit credo. He had no moral objection to drugs - how could Charles Bukowski have a moral objection to *anything*? - but they didn't give him the same buzz alcohol did.

Maybe they acted too quickly on the system for him. With booze you knew where you stood. You had at least some control over what it did to you. But drugs sneaked up on you. He preferred blackouts to bad trips.

Another reason he preferred drink to drugs was because it created energy. Pot just made people moribund. It made them go around the place saying things like, 'Hey, man, what's happenin'? Or, like Timothy Leary, another man who bored him hugely, 'Tune in, turn on, drop out.' For Bukowski the appropriation of these kinds of clichés deadened the brain if pot hadn't deadened it already. 'What a sick mob,' he told Steve Richmond, 'I'm building a machine gun in my closet now to take out as many of them as I can.'

His main gripe with the Beats was the fact that they became political animals, something he could never do. He felt closer to the punk movement but even this too was posey. Every group almost by definition was. Once you nailed your colors to any sort of mast you lost something.

All he wanted to be was himself, a tough task for any writer in the public eye. Most writers, he thought, compromised in some way in this department. Ginsberg was a classic example of the syndrome in his view, selling out his gift after he became the property of the establishment. Cummings also succumbed to this, falling prey to a self-serving style of writing that eventually superseded what he was trying to say. Celine lost his way after *Journey to the End of the Night* and Hamsun after *Hunger*. Henry Miller ended up making love to Japanese girls in showers. Artaud tried to cut his pecker off on a boat going to Africa. Even Pound went loopy with all that fascism business. Sooner or later everyone fell victim to the machinery. Which was why he preferred to write in a vacuum.

He thought Hemingway sold out most of all. Hemingway was a favorite target of Bukowski. He often said he became corrupted by the beast of fame and soon lost his loyalty to the 'pure hard line.' Bukowski had grown up on this. When Hemingway disowned it, Bukowski disowned Hemingway.

The tight-lipped style of many of Bukowski's early stories is almost indistinguishable from the early Hemingway. His debt to him is huge but he rarely acknowledged it, probably for this reason. Every time he focused on Hemingway's shortcomings it looked as if he was protesting too much. There could also have been a fear inside him that he would end his life as Hemingway had, by his own hand. And for similar reasons – depression and drink.

He was drinking so much at this point of his life that his landlord gave him two garbage bags every week to dispose of his empties instead of the single one he offered to all the other tenants. He loved the sound the breaking bottles made as they were loaded into the dump trucks almost as much as he loved the noise his typewriter made as he pounded on it with his fingers.

Most casual observers of Bukowski's life imagine alcohol destroyed him. He never saw it that way. As a young man it came to his rescue anytime he was feeling depressed. When other boys of his age were discovering women, he discovered drink. He abused it all through his life but never saw himself as an alcoholic. In *Women* he wrote, 'If something bad happens, you drink in an attempt to forget it. If something good happens, you drink in order to celebrate. And if nothing happens you drink to make something happen.'

When Henry Miller told him drink was killing his muse he guffawed. He believed it was summoning it. If he stopped drinking he thought he might also have stopped writing.

He read Tom Dardis' book *The Thirsty Muse* and admired it. It dealt with the drinking problems of people like Hemingway, Eugene O'Neill, William Faulkner and F. Scott Fitzgerald. Bukowski drank as much if not more than some of these but he refused to see himself in the same league as them. 'Miller advised me not to drink alone,' Bukowski said, 'but that's the best time for me. I use drink to help me write. How can you write when someone is with you?'

O'Neill came across worst in Dardis' book. Scott Fitzgerald wasn't far behind. The other two writers he dealt with were Faulkner and Hemingway were both raving alcoholics but they seemed to be able to contain themselves for creative splurges. That was the dividing line for Bukowski. It wasn't the damage you did to your body that counted but whether you could get up the next morning and hammer out another novel.

Hemingway could because he was such a giant of a man. Faulkner also seemed to have miraculous recuperative powers but Fitzgerald eventually reached a point where drinks were drinking him rather than vice versa. The difference between Bukowski and these four was that all his life he drank because he wanted to rather than because he needed to. Or so, at least, he believed.

No matter what condition he was in, Bukowski put something down on paper. He didn't suffer the DTs like O'Neill and Faulkner, or writer's block like Hemingway and Fitzgerald. Basically he saw himself as a 'two and a half bottles of wine' kind of writer. The poems written on the third one weren't usually up to scratch but that was still good going in comparison to the four writers Dardis featured.

The way he drank meant he got drunk quickly. He also liked to mix drinks. 'Let's all die quickly,' he'd say at parties. This was life – or death – in fast motion. Nights with Bukowski never took long to get going. The alcohol was like temporary insanity for him. It was as if there was an evil twin inside him that made him guzzle – and then do outrageous things.

Drink also made him clumsy. Linda King compared him to King Kong loping through a forest, knocking down trees almost without realizing it. Sean Penn said he was the most incredible drinker he ever saw. 'I mean that literally,' he said, 'I'm talking about the way he held the bottle. He usually held it above his head and then slugged it back to attack his system quickly. He lowered it almost vertically down his throat.' This wasn't a way of showing off, as one might do in adolescence. It was more like giving himself an intravenous injection of alcohol.

Sean Penn was fascinated by how Bukowski held a bottle

It was suggested to him once that Dylan Thomas drank himself to death because he felt his talent was waning. Bukowski's reaction to this was, 'Bullshit.' Drink for him wasn't so much escapism as a gateway to a higher truth. It was like the philosophy expressed in the film *The Fight Club*. Modern man had life sucked out of him by a grinding consumerism. The only way he could get it back was to revert to a kind of primal behavior: to become the hunter again, to seek real goals rather than the ones he'd been brainwashed into thinking he wanted by The System.

The destruction of the body was almost worth it to him for the preservation of his mind. Everything had its price. Sobriety perhaps exacted a bigger one. Drink, he said, saved him from madness. So did poetry. Poetry was the way he returned himself to his peculiar brand of sanity. It was his bowel movement, his nosebleed, his woman's period, his birth and death, his excavation of the tensions suppressed during all the years of his past.

Taming the Beast

Bukowski met Linda Lee Beighle, the woman who would become his second wife, at a poetry reading in 1976. He was attracted to her immediately. She told him she liked his work and he was flattered.

They exchanged phone numbers. Shortly afterwards they began dating. He was seeing other women for the first few months they were going together but then confined himself to her. She always felt she would be the one to tame him, having the patience the other Linda lacked in this department.

She ran away from home at the age of eleven when she was going through her hippie phase. Later on she worked for a TV station.

Eventually she became the owner of a health food restaurant. It was called the Dew Drop Inn. She swore by the 'If it feels good, do it' philosophy of the Indian spiritualist Meher Baba. This also appealed to Bukowski, though he emphasized the fact that he didn't need any figurehead to ratify his hedonism.

She refused to sleep with him at first because it was against the Meher Baba philosophy but she watched him romancing the other women. She seemed content to bide her time with him even when he abused her, or acted like he didn't care about her. Behind all the bed-hopping, she sensed he was looking for an anchor.

She also knew he needed someone to help him cut down on his drinking. He was having difficulty coping with his hangovers by now. He'd ignored the signals his body had been giving him since the 1955 experience in the L.A. County Hospital and she tried to get him to confront these. The other women in his life had a fatalistic attitude to his drinking. They didn't think he could stop, or even cut down. Beighle was more pro-active.

He'd never been with a pragmatic woman before. Most of them had either been self-destructive, like Jane, or young and flighty like King and Brandes.

Even Liza Williams, who held down a responsible job, was an eccentric. Neither had Beighle children, like King and Brandes – or Frances. He had her all to himself, which meant she gave him round-the-clock attention.

Despite her bohemian past, she had her head well screwed on. Bukowski could still spread his wings with her but not as much as he used to. Exactly how much he still wanted to was open to question.

Was the lion finally about to lie down with the lamb? With the first Linda, with whom Beighle would often be confused, life had been a rollercoaster of unpredictability. This one, in contrast, promised to make him 'fly low.'

She knew his body needed a break from the decades of abuse he'd given it. In the first few months they spent together she weaned him off spirits, encouraging him to drink wine instead.

'Why would I do that?' he asked her when she first mooted the idea..

'Because it has less alcohol in it,' she explained.

'And that's supposed to be an advantage?'

A few years ago he would have laughed in her face. Now he just nodded. Why not? He'd tried everything else. If nothing else it would be a different kind of buzz.

'Miraculously' he survived his first night on wine without breaking down any walls. He even managed to write a few poems on it. And he felt better the next morning. He didn't feel as if he'd swallowed 'wet cat turds.' Maybe she was onto something.

Beighle also got him off red meat. And she persuaded him to take vitamin tablets. Bukowski taking vitamin tablets was like Keith Moon drinking iced tea. But it happened. And continued to happen.

Bukowski the wino looking happy (Al Berlinski)

The Porn King had met the Health Food Queen and the liaison produced sweet music. 'I'm finally living with a woman who isn't a whore,' he announced. Of course that wasn't true. Bukowski referred to all women who weren't virgins as whores. It was the puritan in him coming out, the puritan Jane had often commented on.

The women he was seeing when he met Beighle dropped off over time. He didn't know if he was ready to settle down yet but she felt he was. She watched him becoming bored with all the craziness of the 'revolving door' routines. She even tidied his apartment sometimes. Often another woman would have just gone when she was doing so. She accepted that.

Eventually they bought a house together. It was in an area called San Pedro overlooking the Los Angeles harbor. It was a big move for him. Not many people thought he was ready for it. Anyone who read his work wouldn't have thought him a likely candidate for this. Beighle thought different.

San Pedro, the exclusive district where Bukowsk lived contrary to everyone's expectations

He lived a quiet life there without being pestered by people who knew him. There were no Hollywood wannabes, no would-be poets sipping their espressos. The only problem was the fact that the local liquor store closed at 9.30 p.m. (He had a solution for this: 'Let's buy it by the case.')

The house they moved into had a large garden with a hedge and lots of flowers. Being surrounded by flora and fauna was new for him. Only the grass was familiar. Beighle even got him to mow it now and again. 'You missed a blade!' she'd taunt playfully when he was finished, having heard the horror stories about his father innumerable times. And Bukowski would go, 'Oh no, it's starting again.'

The house also had a jacuzzi. Bukowski had once run errands for sandwiches. He'd begged for drinks. He even pulled a tooth out one time to save having to go to the dentist. Now he was about to spend his evenings lazing in a jacuzzi as he looked out at the ships on the harbor.

Such a view beat the corroded fire escapes he saw from the dingy rooming-houses. Did he deserve all the splendor? He thought so. He was now the most translated American author in print.

245

The most important item in the house was a writing desk. After all the years typing out his poems on the kitchen table in Mariposa and De Longpre he was suddenly becoming official. But there was a catch: 'I felt the fear, the fear of being like them.' ('Them' was other writers).

In another way the house was no different from the boardinghouses of yore because every night he retired to his study to pump out his poems. He may not have had to worry about people stamping on floorboards, or roaring at him from downstairs, but he was still 'barricaded in a small room' waiting for his muse to arrive. 'I used to be a poor bum,' he often joked, 'now I'm a rich bum.'

Some nights things went wrong. One of the cats he and Beighle started to collect might pee on his pages. The classical music that played in the background might not inspire him as much as it used to. The old days might not come across as good – or as bad – as he wanted them to be as he tried to excavate his memory banks for more material. But when it all came together for him it was the perfect storm. 'I have a party in my room most nights,' he said. The guests were the characters he created.

When they moved into the house the neighbors on both sides were polite. The old couple next door asked them if there was anything they could do to help them settle in. A younger couple on the other side were more subdued. The first few weeks were quiet but then Bukowski had a row with Beighle. He chased her through the garden one morning screaming 'You goddam whore!' at her. His words were heard by both sets of neighbors. The old couple became more distant afterwards whereas the young couple became friendlier. 'You never know with people,' Bukowski said. Some of them wanted the old Buk - even in San Pedro.

Love is a Dog from Hell, his new poetry collection, came out shortly after the relationship with Beighle became serious. It captures him at a time of his life where he allows his turbo-charged sexuality free rein. This is an entertaining book even if the sentiments appear slight at times. Whether he finds himself masturbating (a fairly common activity in the book), being a peeping tom (which sometimes leads to that) or indulging his various fetishes with those only too willing to respond, he adopts a jocose air, crystallizing a jumble of ostensibly trivial incidents into the tangled skein of his psyche.

He shows a moving side to his nature in 'an almost made up poem' — which isn't really a poem at all. He gives a mellow tribute to Frances in 'one for old snaggle-tooth', telling us she's hurt fewer people than anyone he knows. In 'another bed' he outlines his inability to live alone. It beats loneliness so he'll keep with it, keep on falling in love until he gets it right. He knows that somewhere on the planet the right woman for him exists for him. The problem is trying to track her down. In the meantime the whores and groupies will call. He'll continue to indulge and be indulged by them.

His predicament acquires an added twist in 'the price' where he asks a hooker how much she charges. She tells him $100 but later says she was only joking. When he asks the real price, she replies only with her eyes, presumably suggesting love. He tells her he isn't able to pay that price.

'Traffic signals' is one of many poems he wrote about his almost pathological fear of old age. 'The insane always loved me' deals with the manner in which he appealed to lame ducks in his life. 'The crunch' is unusually old-fashioned in tone. 'My old man' gives us an all too rare example of a bonding between himself and his father. The final poem in the collection is the best, ranging over a number of issues and also giving us the phrase 'locked in the arms of a crazy life' which Howard Sounes used as the title for his biography of Bukowski. All in all it's an uneven book lit up by occasional nuggets that keep you turning pages.

Confusion is part and parcel of its power. Bukowski never saw himself as having a mission to convert. In fact he usually didn't know what he wanted to say until he said it — and maybe not even then.

One book in which he knew exactly what he wanted to say, however, was *Women*, his next novel. Beighle regarded it as a kind of corollary to *Love is a Dog from Hell*. He worked at it intensively in the mid-seventies in his apartment in Carlton Way at a metal-rimmed table. He saw it as a tragicomic record of the 'crazy' years between 1970 and 1977, years he would never hope to repeat but which were invaluable for purposes of inspiration.

He wrote *Women* after his women phase ended just like he wrote *Post Office* after his post office one did. *Factotum* was written after he stopped being a factotum. Like most writers, he preferred to be out of the forest the better to see the trees.

It's more like a series of vignettes than a novel proper. It was originally going to be called *Love Tales of the Hyena* but he preferred the simpler title, realizing the other one would have suited a poetry collection better. (The elaborate titles of Bukowski's poetry books is equaled only by the succinctness of the novels' ones).

He envisaged it as a book of 'love, laughter and blood madness', a book that would stop people talking about *The Ginger Man* forever. Chinaski's bedroom shenanigans make Sebastian Dangerfield look like a choirboy. Love was ridiculous because it couldn't last and sex because it didn't last long enough. Somewhere between this Scylla and Charbdis he negotiated his tenuous trysts.

John Martin found parts of the book sluggish. He changed it (just like he changed segments of *Post Office*) to 'improve' it. Once again Bukowski was outraged. 'Would he have done that to Van Gogh?' he asked. Martin even advised Bukowski about what to say in interviews about it but he wasn't having any of that. 'Which of us is Bukowski?' he taunted. On the other hand, he never questioned Martin about how he presented his poetry collections over the years. Often he didn't even know what poems were going to be in them until he saw a printed copy.

Women was his most ambitious undertaking yet. He awaited its publication with more excitement than usual. He expected to get a lot of heat for it from the feminists but he also knew he'd put every interesting idea he had ever had about 'the female' into it.

It came out in 1978, confirming the anti-Bukowski brigade in their suspicions that here indeed was a chauvinist of the utmost proportions. Here was a man who treated women as sex objects and little else, whose idea of foreplay was taking off his shoes before sex. The fact that the female characters in the book didn't see themselves as sex objects was largely down to the fact that they were portrayed as being as highly sexed as he was. And about as vulgar as well - which was saying something.

That was the reactionary slant. Pro-Bukowski buffs said here was a book that put down things other writers fantasized about but didn't have the courage to express. It wasn't pornography as much as the demolition of myths about what Bukowski termed 'the man-woman thing.' It was also a riveting read. Chinaski – his alter ego once again - plays emotional musical chairs with a bevy of women who collect themselves around him like bees around honey. They seem to enjoy him all the more whenever he mistreats them, which is most of the time.

Bukowski had a virtual harem of women in the 1970s, as we saw, which followed thirty years of being a lounge lizard who only occasionally got lucky. On the first page he tells us that he's 50, that he hasn't been to bed with a woman for four years, has no women friends, masturbates regularly, has a six-year-old daughter born out of wedlock, was married once - to a woman who divorced him - and was in love once with a woman who drank herself to death.

This is a million miles away from what J.D. Salinger called the 'David Copperfield stuff.' Albert Camus once described modern man as someone who 'fornicated and read the newspapers.' Chinaski doesn't read the newspapers.

Voltaire is alleged to have said after a particularly passionate sexual encounter, 'There goes another novel!' It seemed to work the other way with Bukowski. Far from suffering writer's block, the more women he had sex with the more prolific he seemed to be.

'This is a work of fiction' he writes on the inside cover, 'and no character is intended to portray any person or combination of persons living or dead.' Which of course was baloney. Few of his conquests had trouble recognizing themselves in it. Linda King is Lydia, Liza Williams is Dee Dee, Beighle is Sara, Ruth Wantling is Cecelia and Pamela Brandes is Tammie.

Brandes was engaged to be married to a man called David Wood when the book was published. He was a stockbroker with three children from a previous relationship. When he read about the raunchy antics of 'Tammie' he almost called off the wedding. It took her ages to convince him Bukowski used poetic license in his depiction of her, that she hadn't said or done even a fraction of things attributed to her in the book. She burned a diary she'd kept of their time together in case it would surface in future years in the wrong hands. She also worried about compromising photographs of herself appearing anywhere. (Bukowski had a habit of snapping her when she was in the nude).

None of the other women he knew, who are featured in the same thinly-disguised fashion as Brandes, were any happier with the way they came across. Bukowski used his pen to get back at them in the same way as he'd written *Post Office* to get back at the people in his most long-lasting job - and *Factotum* in some of the more transient ones. This was fine because these people weren't recognizable or traceable.

The situation was different for *Women* because his former girlfriends were in other relationships now. Some of the material about them was so thinly disguised as to be transparent. It's as if he was busily taking notes all over the years. And, according to some of the women, trying to gain revenge on them for the fact that he spent the first 25 years of his life being virtually ignored by the fair sex. Was he secretly using them for raw material when he purported to be bleeding his heart all over them?

Amber O'Neil came in for a particularly rough ride – to coin a phrase. As he documented her strenuous attempts to please him sexually in the few days they spent together after she visited him from San Francisco, he wrote that she wasn't much good at oral sex. (This after saying she almost gave him a heart attack with excitement on another page).

She gave him a taste of his own medicine when she wrote her own book about their tryst. It was a self-published one called, appropriately enough, *Blowing My Hero*. 'That was all I seemed to represent for him in *Women*,' she said, 'so I thought it would make a good title.' It did, but it had the unfortunate side-effect of becoming the main thing people remembered about her afterwards.

She performed oral sex on a famous person. (Monica Lewinski would hold a similar distinction in a future era).

Bukowski's depiction of O'Neil in *Women* was shabby. She was a warm-hearted woman who thought she'd had a pleasant few days with him, only to see it transformed into a shoddy sex odyssey. He'd been 'kind and gentle' to her when they were together so she was surprised at the change in his attitude when he got behind his typewriter. 'I think he knew I was in over my head,' she said, which seemed to avoid the issue.

She felt Bukowski had a lot of bitterness in his heart towards women because of his past. Linda King also believed this: 'It started with his mother and went on from there.' But O'Neil wasn't bitter. She didn't hold a grudge against him. Her book reflects that. It's a collector's item today as only a limited number of copies were printed. She wrote it in longhand as she didn't own a typewriter. She brought it to her local library and typed it up on the library's typewriter. When she had it finished she rang a publishing friend she had and asked him for his view on it. He told her he thought it was wonderful. She asked him to print 500 copies. Half way through the printing he ran out of paper. Because of this, the last 25 pages were printed in a different color.

O'Neil had the misfortune to include some letters Bukowski wrote to her at the back of the book. John Martin said she had no right to do that as the letters were the property of Black Sparrow Press. He wrote to her to say she'd have to withdraw her book from sale. Curiously, in the same letter he also asked her if he could buy six copies of it from her. Did the collector in him twig that one day it might be valuable sometime in the future? Today, copies of it command large sums on eBay.

The cynical tone of *Women* fed into many people's belief that Bukowski wasn't much more than a sex machine. If we read between the lines, however, we can see that the sex scenes are counterpointed by a sense of yearning within him for something

252

deeper. It's too easy to read the book as *The Decameron Revisited*. We might be better advised to investigate the man behind the conquests. This is someone who's anxious to settle down but unable to tame the beast in himself. That said, Chinaski has all the subtlety of a barracuda in his seduction techniques, which makes it all the more incredible that the women in his life seem only too delighted to accede to his every wish.

Women was always going to be his most memorable book, the one that would confirm his status as the super-stud of the sewers. The other way he expresses his macho nature is at the track. Here he almost invariably seems to win. (If Bukowski was as successful a gambler as he claims in these pages he could almost have given up writing and lived off his earnings from the mutuels).

One gets the impression that if Chinaski didn't need women sexually he'd do just as well do without them. He rarely finds their presence appealing unless sex is hinted at. If women are predators, as he insists, maybe sexual violence is the only way to escape being victimized ('pussywhipped') by them. The fact that they seem to enjoy such violence suits Chinaski. Some of the sex scenes in the book resemble animals mating. There's no tenderness, no pillow talk, no sweet nothings. The motivation is always the maximization of pleasure.

'Was she liberated' he asks of Tanya at one point. He answers his own question: 'No, she was simply red hot.'

His women don't have plans outside the here and now. They speak about vague ambitions between their orgiastic frenzies but everything seems subservient to these in the boudoir. The zipless fuck (to use Erica Jong's phrase) is the Holy Grail. Everything else leads up to and away from this with varying degrees of jadedness. By the book's end, of course, the sex itself has become jaded, as if Chinaski has finally burned all of his testosterone out of himself and is ready to launch himself at life from a slightly different perspective. (Exactly what that is remains unclear as he feeds his cat a can of Star-Kist tuna).

Debra says to him at one stage, 'I think you fuck women in order to write about fucking them.' He doesn't deny the accusation. Sex occurs in almost as many variations as in the kama sutra. There's so much oral sex in the book — hardly a 'love' scene without it — one might imagine his girlfriend was called Linda Lovelace rather than Linda King. The relationship with Lydia is different. It's built on friction, a kind of sado-masochistic bantering.

At the end of the day we're left wondering what women represent to him. Are they beauties or beasts? Or both? He's hardly quite sure himself. 'I think it's a damn shame that a man who writes as well as you do,' Lydia says to him at one point, 'doesn't know anything about women.' Was she right or was he just pretending ignorance in order to get more out of them?

Bukowski put down everything he knew – and didn't know – about 'the female' in *Women*. (Al Berlinski)

At another point Dee says to him, 'You're good enough with the ladies and you're a helluva writer.' He replies, 'I'd rather be good with the ladies.' A few moments later he says to her, 'Don't love me,' as if this will spoil it all. He tells us Dee Dee's 'excited and happy reaction to life' irritates him. 'I was glad I wasn't in love,' he confesses, 'that I wasn't happy with the world. I like being at odds with everything. People in love often become edgy, dangerous. They lose their sense of perspective.' He oscillates between the two women, postponing the kind of commitment that could destroy what they have.

Sex, meanwhile, becomes the sinful joy of expiation: 'The thought of sex as something forbidden excited me beyond all reason. It was like one animal knifing another into submission.'

He courts prostitutes because they don't pose an emotional threat to him. Little is lost when they leave. And yet something in him pines for a lasting commitment. He's stuck between a rock and a hard place on his zany merry-go-round of skewed lechery and post-coital spats.

Love for him is an encumbrance, a monkey on his back that he has to get rid of as soon as possible. He's happier with evanescence: 'You were with one person a while,' he writes, 'eating and sleeping and living with them, loving them, talking to them, going places together, and then it stopped.' On the following page he tells us he'd prefer if someone stole his woman than his car. The nihilist needs his space. Tenderness has an unhappy habit of cutting in on that.

In *Women* Bukowski created a character who lives in a moral limbo. There's no message in the book. 'People just blindly grabbed at whatever there was,' he tells us, 'communism, health foods, zen, surfing, ballet, hypnotism... and then it all evaporated and fell apart.'

It's only in Chapter 92 he comes out of the closet about his real feelings. Here he outlines all the things he enjoys doing with his girlfriends, how he likes to explore them to find the human being inside, but always with the option of being unfaithful to them. The understanding seems to be that all relationships are open. Only thus can they succeed, for however brief a time. It's only when he meets Sara and she denies him immediate sex that he's forced to re-evaluate things, to realize he might be getting bored with sex. Or is it simply that he craves the challenge of her unavailability? Whatever, she transforms him into the man he becomes at the end of the book. This is pretty close to what happened between Bukowski and Linda in real life. The tired old war-horse needed somewhere to rest his head. After having Everywoman he wanted his Chosen One to ease him into old age.

Was he old-fashioned at the back of it all? He hints as much when he attacks the casual sex of the Bel Air set: 'a gymnasium of bodies namelessly masturbating each other.' Such swingers sicken him. He sees them as 'the dead fucking the dead'. There's no gamble in their relationships; they're just cozily liberal. 'It was like a garden filled with poisoned fruit and good fruit,' he writes, 'You had to know which to pick and eat, which to leave alone.' It's not exactly the Book of Genesis but we know what he means. He needs the passion of desire, the torture of the end if and when it comes. He refuses to be bland even with hookers. You have to put your heart on the line each time you make love, along with your libido.

Women don't *only* represent sex to him. He writes about the way they walk, the way they dress, the beauty of their faces. But just so as we don't get our hopes up that the petrified Chinaski heart is about to finally melt, he tells us that while men are engaging in typically male pursuits like drinking or watching the ball games, their female counterparts are already planning their demise: coolly, clinically and without mercy. One might imagine forewarned would be forearmed but he doesn't shy away from them on that account. Just as he knows booze is bad for him and still drinks it to excess, so also he dives headlong into relationships like a kamikaze pilot.

A later passage in the book takes his feelings into a wider context, embracing everything from the trivial to the profound as he makes us aware relationships aren't all sex and acrimony for him. They're simply togetherness, being there with your partner, each an extension of the other as ordinary things happen.

He outlines the things he's sentimental about: 'A woman's shoes under the bed; one hairpin left behind on the dresser; the way they said 'I'm going to pee... '; hair ribbons, walking down the boulevard with them at 1.30 in the afternoon, the long nights of drinking and smoking; talking, the arguments, thinking of suicide; eating together and feeling good; the jokes, the laughter out of nowhere; feeling miracles in the air; being in a parked car together; comparing past loves at 3 a.m., being told you snore, hearing her snore; mothers, daughters, sons, cats... jails, her dull friends, your dull friends, your drinking, her dancing, your flirting, her flirting; her pills, your fucking on the side and her doing the same, sleeping together... ' Who else but Bukowski could put miracles, suicide, divorce and urination in the one paragraph and still not appear incongruous?

Relationships carry a large price tag when they end, however, as end they must. He pushes himself through the pain barrier of emotion as a ballast to shore against the ruins of his meltdown when yet another lowlife calls it quits with him or when his 'ordinary madness' makes him long for some breathing space outside the confines of trailer trash high jinks.

The women kill his longing but they fail to drive out the subliminal beast. They make up for the years of want while he's with them but nobody, not even Cleopatra, could give him an experience that would last the pace. How could she? He was, after

257

all, the Last Man Standing, the Last Hard Bastard from the bad end of town, sucking up on thrills to kill the enemy inside himself until another binge loomed, another binge that would intuit a different kind of death.

In the meantime he'd check out every available woman within spitting distance of Sunset. Maybe the Perfect Moment lay beyond the next bedpost. Maybe the next piece of ass, the next whore, would be... therapeutic. Or, failing that, would pass an hour or two for him as he sat looking into space, dreaming of someone who'd take him up where he belonged; to hog heaven. And so the circle turned. But one of these days he might leave them all, leave them as he once left Jane.

Women sold 12,000 copies within the year, becoming a *succes de scandale* for its controversial author. It flew off the shelves even faster than *Post Office* had. Not everyone worked in a post office but everyone was interested its simple title let people know that's what it would be about. Bukowski was pleased with the way it was received even if he wasn't expecting any rave notices from the feminists. He didn't plan to defend himself against these. 'I do not,' he proclaimed, 'like arguing with women who wear moustaches.'

He felt many of those who accused him of sexism hadn't even read the book. They were basing their assumptions on preconceived notions people had of him, people who'd already made up their minds he was Public Enemy Number One when it came to female sensitivity. Their beliefs, he felt, were based on half-baked attitudes to sexuality gleaned from cursory readings of his other books or potted versions of his life peddled in thumbnail profiles.

It was one of his most assured works but it went on to become his most vilified one. He might have got away with if it was published before the women's movement took root but not in the late 1970s when feminists had become seriously empowered.

His chauvinism flew in the face of the time. 'I don't like New Men,' he said, 'what are they going to do for women except sleep in the wet spot?' He wasn't fond of feminists either. 'I'm an extinct species,' he declared, 'someone who still believes a woman can be rotten to the core.'

Too many feminists mistook Chinaski for Bukowski. 'He's only one-tenth of me,' Bukowski explained. He could be an animal with women when he was drunk but maybe the reason he drank in the first place was because he was too sensitive to face them sober. He wouldn't be the first writer to have raised a glass to his lips to try and give himself some iron in the soul.

Such was the power of the writing that not even the feminist broadsides against it carried much weight. Once again the old bastard had gotten away with it.

Steve Richmond defined him as a 'radical masculinist,' a description he liked. He subsequently told Richmond: 'The female is skilled at betrayal and torture and damnation. Never envy a man his lady.' He followed up by saying one shouldn't blame women for these qualities. It was simply the way they were made.

'Horses, booze and the typer' were his three priorities, he told Gerard Locklin - in that order. Women came a poor fourth. He needed them but he didn't want them. The reason he didn't want them was because he didn't trust them. You knew where you stood with booze, even when it wrecked your head. With the horses you played the percentages. They may not have been fair but at least you went in with your eyes open. Women were different because they made promises they never intended to keep and then they sucked your soul away. The honeymoon might last a month and then the long knives came out. Writing was the most reliable of the three because you were in control of it.

'I get it off with the word,' he told Clive Cardiff. No woman could be as glorious to him as the hours he spent at his 'piano.' When it was going well it was infinitely better than sex. It was a rush, a mindfuck, a time when all the world's petty excesses and casual cruelties made sense. What he hated was when it became a business, or when he had to talk about it. On occasions like this he did his best to demythologize the whole process.

That happened one night in Paris when he was on a rare trip to Europe in 1978. Against all the odds he found himself on a TV chat show called *Apostrophes*. Here he managed to disgrace himself in the kind of way Brendan Behan had done a decade or so before in London. Bukowski did it for the same reason as well, refusing to allow the cattle call regimentation of TV subdue his personality.

He once said that if anyone ever saw him on a talk show they had his permission to shoot him on sight. 'It's like swallowing you own vomit,' he claimed. How could anything real get said in a sanitized environment presided over by the likes of Johnny Carson or Merv Griffin? It was a canned culture, the mass hypnosis of mom's apple pie. You dished out sensationalistic scandals to lobotomize people. Nobodies talked to other nobodies about nothing and you watched it paralyzed until you got sense and hit the remote. 'Conversation destroys talent,' he said. The silence of a graveyard was even more profound.

On the show in question he was put sitting between a woman who wrote animal stories and a psychiatrist who'd once given electric shock treatment to Antonin Artaud. The psychiatrist kept staring at him and that unnerved him. Was he next for the treatment? They started speaking in French. Bukowski was given earphones to hear their comments translated into English but he couldn't hear properly through it. His microphone wasn't working properly either. He said to the make-up woman, 'I feel like a fucking astronaut with all these things hanging out of me.'

Bernard Pivot, who was hosting the show, got off on the wrong foot with him before it began because he refused a glass of wine Bukowski offered him. He'd been swilling it since being presented with it in make-up. After the cameras started to roll he became hot under the television lights. Then he got irritated by the people who were talking and started to interrupt them. He said he wasn't too enthused about being on the show. Pivot didn't like the way things were going. He tried to get him to stop talking. Bukowski ignored him.

Then Pivot told him to shut up. There was no problem translating this because he said it in English. Bukowski froze. Nobody spoke to him like that on television – or even off television. He decided to walk off the program. He stood up – or rather stumbled to his feet. He started to say goodbye to the other guests but in a confused way, as if he didn't know what he was doing. He looked as if he was about to fall. Everyone looked at him wondering what would happen next.

He yanked off the earphones and slugged back what remained of his wine. Before he left he put his hand on the head of the woman who wrote the animal stories. She jumped up in fright. He slouched away.

When he got to the door of the studio he pulled a knife on two security guards who were standing there. It was a natural instinct for him. He always carried one with him, usually producing it whenever he felt threatened. At this stage everyone started to get hysterical. Pivot tried to recover the situation by announcing that Bukowski was a disgrace to his nation but by now it was too late. People who were watching the show on their TVs chortled at his pathetic attempt to save the situation. They were glued to their sets. They saw Bukowski as the hero of the hour.

'The next thing I remember,' he said later, 'is I'm in the streets of Paris and there's this startling and continuous roar and lights everywhere. There are 10,000 motorcyclists in the street. I demand to see some can-can girls. I'm taken back to the hotel upon the promise of more wine.'

The story was all over the papers the next morning. Over fifty million viewers had seen Bukowski humiliate Pivot. People who'd never watched the show in their lives couldn't stop talking about it. They all wanted to know who this weirdo was who cut a swathe through French protocol on an upmarket literary show. For Bukowski it was just another night. How many years had he behaved – or misbehaved – like that with fellow barflies and nobody thought anything of it? So he was drunk on television. So what?

Bukowski became a sensation in France after appearing on the TV show *Apostrophes*.
(Al Berlinski)

He forgot most of what happened on the show – and after it. When a critic from *Le Monde* rang him to say, 'You were great, bastard', he hadn't a clue what he was talking about. Beighle tried to jog his memory but she might as well have been talking to the wall. His alcohol intake had combined with the hot studio lights to make the night into a blur for him.

Later in the day Beighle and himself visited Nice. Beighle's uncle lived there. When they got there he told them he wasn't going to see them, having been disgusted with Bukowski's exhibition of himself the night before. Beighle's mother was already in the house but it made no difference.

They went to a cafe instead. There they got a tumultuous reception. Six waiters lined up in front of Bukowski and bowed to him. He was enthralled. On the way out of the café a group of women shouted out at him from a bus. 'I could get used to this,' he told Linda.

His little adventure over, he went back to the 'day job.' His next book was one of his smallest but had one of his longest titles, *Play the Piano Drunk like a Percussion Instrument Until the Fingers Begin to Bleed a Little Bit.* Another anthology of poems, it betrays its amorphous origins more than once but there's a clarity and immediacy in the writing - and enough biting imagery to keep you turning the pages.

A mocking tone is evident in poems like 'a little atomic bomb' and 'interviews.' There's an interesting poem about Jane Cooney Baker called 'fire station' where Bukowski offers her sexually to a crew of firemen for money to play card, an arrangement she seems more than happy to comply with. Sex is also trivialized in the hilarious 'blue moon, oh bleweeww mooooon how I adore you!' where he sends up his stud image. He has a go at D.H. Lawrence in the ambiguous 'I liked him', a poem with a sting in the tail.

In '12-24-78' he reminds us how much he despises Christmas. The consumption of alcohol was always a very serious occupation for Bukowski. He had little patience for the 'They tell me I had a great Christmas' set who treated it as a kind of seasonal *divertissement*. Drink is also celebrated in 'some picnic,' a poem that features probably the only pleasant get-together ever experienced between Bukowski, Jane and his parents. Here he raises a toast to Jane's beer belly, which his parents have mistaken for pregnancy.

The most poignant poem in the collection is 'the proud thin dying,' which deals with the humiliations of old age. If he'd written nothing else but this in his career he would still have been remembered. It's hugely powerful.

Shakespeare Never Did This, also published that year, was a record of the trip he made to Paris and another one to Germany. The ostensible reason for the latter was to give a poetry reading in Hamburg but the highlight for him was meeting his 90-year old uncle Heinrich, his mother's brother. Bukowski hadn't seen him since he was three. He was everything his father wasn't: good-humored, broad-minded, in love with life and behind him every step of the way. If he'd grown up as Heinrich's son, his writing career - which was largely born out of pain - might never have happened.

It's a mellow book, the work of a man who's found the woman he's going to spend the rest of his life with and is patently aware of this fact, which gives the acerbic asides a softness they wouldn't otherwise have had. He wrote it without signing a contract and that seemed to free his writing hand. But Bukowski wasn't happy with the book. He thought it read too much like a travelogue.

The poems that he threads through his memories are more restrained than usual. Michael Monfort's photographs, which accompany the text, provide further proof the beast has finally been tamed. Which isn't to say he doesn't get up to some wild antics on the trip. The point is that the anger is gone — even against his father. He's at the point of his life where his reputation is established and he's surrounded by the people he loves most: Linda Lee, Uncle Heinrich, Barbet Schroeder, Carl Weissner and Monfort.

He leaves us in little doubt that it's the human parts of the trip that make it memorable for him. These take precedence over the architecture, the cathedrals, the castles, even the poetry.

Bukowski didn't have much time for the castles of Andernach

The Germans seemed to understand his poetry better than Americans. While he was there he made no secret of his admiration for a nation that had been laid low by two world wars and still managed to preserve their dignity. Whatever about the other changes wrought in him, the neo-Nazi in Bukowski was still alive and well.

The trip was full of activity. He signed his autograph on *papier maché* napkins in nightclubs. He flew on 'wings of dizzy laughter' as the paparazzi snapped him and fans shouted out his name. His interviewers he treated with disdain, either fobbing them off with incoherent rambling or smart-alecky one-liners. The reading attracted 1,200 people – in a venue that was supposed to seat only 800. When the chants of 'Bukowski! Bukowski!' started up he replied simply, 'It's good to be back'... after 54 years. According to Weissner the reading drew a bigger crowd than Hitler. People came from as far away as Denmark to be there.

Afterwards he was taken to the house where he was born. He was gratified to learn that it operated as a brothel for a time. 'I knew I got it from somewhere,' he joked. When Heinrich showed him photographs of his parents in their youth he broke down in tears.

Towards the end of the year he discovered that the contract he drew up for his 1972 publication *Erections, Ejaculations, Exhibitions and General Tales of Ordinary Madness* had a clause in it that was handwritten by him on the side of one of the pages. This entitled him to 75% of the foreign rights of the book rather than the more customary 50%. It meant he was owed $4500 from the last year alone. This revelation lifted his spirits mightily as the book had been flying off the shelves in Europe. The money would come in handy as the mortgage on his home in San Pedro was high. 'I mustn't have been drunk that day,' he reflected. It would have been an unusual one. He was still hitting the bottle as hard as ever, even under Beighle's strict regime. He'd recently fallen down drunk in front of his fireplace and smashed a coffee table.

He did another reading the following year in Redondo Beach, a suburb of L.A. He introduced it by saying he hoped it would be a 'dignified' evening, his tongue was firmly planted in his cheek. There was a police presence there, surely a first for a poetry reading. It wasn't long until things hotted up. After a rambling discourse from him, a member of the audience groaned. 'Read your poetry.' Bukowski replied, 'I'm running this show, not you,' to wild cheers.

He assured everyone that the beer he had in his hands was a necessity rather than a prop. 'I'm Humphrey Bogart!' he roared at one point, 'I'm carrying steel, man. One more beer and I'll take all of you. I've been lifting weights.' He then said, 'Don't ask for your money back because I've already got it.' When a member of the audience said, 'You're drunk,' he replied, 'I wish *you* were.'

Bukowski saw himself as a literary version of Humphrey Bogart

He told the gathering he was doing the reading for the money rather than to 'conquer' Redondo Beach. But of course he did conquer it. His attitude to his listeners was that of a man who knew what they really wanted. He may have been standing on a pedestal looking down on them but he was coming from the same place they were. There was a shared experience of life's insanity.

His self-deprecating lyrics exposed the sham that so much poetry was built on. Many people in the audience were from factories and the trailer parks but that didn't mean they were any less intelligent than a literary audience. For Bukowski it probably meant that they were *more* intelligent than one. What it also meant was that they'd been sold short by a self-congratulatory clique.

His irreverent antics brought the fun back into literature. He chortled both at life and himself, only too happy to play the clown prince. Ten years ago he was doing this sort of stuff for nothing, or the price of a rooming-house for the night. Now he could almost buy another car with what they gave him. It was a form of whoring, to be sure, but a hugely enjoyable one. 'Don't give me any shit, man,' he droned, taking on all comers, 'or I'll come out into the audience and cut your nodules off your earlobes.' The place erupted with glee. Everyone seemed to enjoy being insulted. As Humphrey Bogart might have said while slapping his latest moll about the place in a *film noir*, 'You'll take it and like it.' And they did.

Later in the year Joyce Fante read Bukowski the last chapter of her husband John's latest book, *Dreams from Bunker Hill,* over the phone. It was an emotional reading and he was moved by it, almost as moved as he'd been by Fante's earlier *Ask the Dust.* By this time his health was in a chronic state. Retinal damage to his eyes had made him so near-sighted he was hardly able to see book contracts. Ulcers and running sores had made his feet gangrenous. He had toes on both of them amputated. Then the left leg below the knee was amputated and finally, when this didn't stop the problem, the left leg above the knee. He bore with it all manfully, telling his friend Ben Pleasants that bitterness over one's fate was something every writer had to fight against. If they didn't it would shrivel him up. No matter how miserable his plight became he refused to cave in. Hollywood friends like Francis Ford Coppola and Martin Sheen buoyed him up, all the more so if they discussed the possibility of future screen work.

When Bukowski met him he told him he meant more to him than any writer he'd ever read, living or dead. Fante was touched by the praise. By now Bukowski had introduced John Martin to the rich reservoir of Fante's works. He brought him to his notice after mentioning him briefly in *Women*. Martin rang Bukowski to ask him if he was a real person or not. He thought it might have been a made-up name as he'd never heard of him. When Bukowski told him he did indeed exist, Martin took it upon himself to check out *Ask the Dust*. When he read it he was as impressed with it as Bukowski had been. He set about re-publishing it with Black Sparrow, thus opening up Fante to a whole new generation. The book had been out of print for twenty years by this time.

He asked Bukowski to write the preface and he obliged. He wrote about the first time he'd seen the book on a library shelf. That was in the days when he used to go to libraries either to hide from landladies looking for rent or to avail of the toilet facilities. He'd been browsing through a number of books when he spotted it on a shelf. He pulled it down and started reading it. It entranced him so much it changed his life.

He couldn't believe a book could have that kind of effect on him. The way Fante chiseled his syllables, his mix of humor and passion, his sense of structure — this was writing at its most captivating. He read all of his other works afterwards and saw in them the same textured luxuriance shot through with an aching melancholy. But *Ask the Dust* always held a special place in his heart. It was his first exposure to him. He'd read it first in 1940 and now, 39 years later, it still 'did it' for him.

There was a spin-off effect on Fante's other books as a result of Martin's action. These would also appear under the Black Sparrow imprint in time. Bukowski even dedicated his book *Love is a Dog from Hell* to him. Fante in turn helped Bukowski with a screenplay he was working on at the time for Barbet Schroeder. (This would become the movie *Barfly*). What a pity that he wasn't in a fit condition to enjoy his literary renaissance. He'd spent so many years in the doldrums, so many years working thanklessly on meretricious scripts for television and the movies.

Bukowski visited him a few more times in the hospital. It had another celebrity patient: Johnny Weissmuller of *Tarzan* fame. Weissmuller was suffering from dementia. He spent most of his time running up and down the corridor screaming 'Me Tarzan!' like his jungle hero. It was black comedy, like something out of a Bukowski short story. Eventually they took him off somewhere to be treated. When he came back the life was gone out of him. The other patients missed his jungle calls.

Fante's right leg had now become diseased and the pain was excruciating. Afterwards his nightmare got worse as the same problems he had in his left leg started to hit the right one as well. More amputations above and below the knee were necessitated. It was like death by a thousand cuts — literally. Joyce's support was constant but she didn't need a doctor to tell her it was the beginning of the end for her husband. As if all this wasn't enough, he also had to contend with bouts of paranoia. After being released from hospital on one occasion he got it into his head that Joyce had kidnapped him. He sat bolt upright in his wheelchair with a loaded gun in his hands, his eyes on fire with the internal demons that plagued him.

Everyone knew it would be a blessed release for him when he finally died but that didn't make the prospect any easier to bear.

When he eventually did die, Bukowski knew he'd lost not only a role model but a dear friend, despite the limited time they spent together.

His career was now advancing in leaps and bounds. As well as the money coming in from 'the sparrow' he'd become huge in Europe. He was able to buy Linda a sports car out of the royalties from Germany and France, the two countries where he was most popular.

Dangling in the Tournefortia, another collection of poetry, was published in 1981. The first poem, 'the stink', reminds us yet again what an incredibly rich memory Bukowski had as he writes about a childhood experience of a woman who seemed to be permanently drunk. She disgusted him at the time but forty years later, as he himself has succumbed to the power of whisky, he can. The poem that follows this, 'The lisp,' is also set in the past, documenting Bukowski's first literary efforts at the gentle behest of his English teacher. She gave him the encouragement every fledgling writer desperately needs and he responded in kind, flooding her with compositions. All these years later - partly thanks to her - he's still scribbling. It's called 'the lisp' because she had one. It's a panegyric that celebrates her early vote of confidence in an insecure boy.

'Parked' has him looking at a boring young man on the street who's almost physically perfect, imagining that this is how his parents wanted him to turn out. In 'notes upon a hot streak' he's at the races, playing the horses 'like other men play chess.' He's there also in 'do you use a notebook?' and 'suckerfish'. He leaves us in little doubt in these poems that parking attendants rank much higher on his list of desirable people to meet than writers.

'Order' makes the point that creativity can easily be stifled in a room that's too tidy. In 'contemporary literature, one' he starves in a paper shack in Atlanta, writing in pencil on the edges of newspapers as his father ignores his requests for money. He's more

271

prosperous in 'the secret of my endurance.' Now other starving scribes are writing to *him* for advice. He's their working class hero but he wonders if they realize he's now living in a big house with a long driveway behind a six foot hedge. His ability to laugh at his sudden wealth suggests corruptibility by its blandishments is probably unlikely.

There are a few poems about alcohol but not as many as usual. 'Night school' casts a jocular look at a drunk driver's class where he shines. (At last he gets a chance to marry his two favorite hobbies: writing and drinking). In 'produced and bottled by… ' he informs us that you can trust a drink much more than you can a woman. 'Slow night' has him confessing that wine is now destroying him in the way his father once did. Bukowski wrote a lot of poems about his father during his life and 99% of them were negative. This is no exception.

He once said his father was responsible for his writing career: 'If I hadn't suffered so much at his hands, there would have been no poems, no passion.' He told Neeli Cherkovski: 'Fear made me a writer.' It was as if every lash of the razor strop he gave him as a child was an extra poem, every temperamental outburst a new short story. Pain was the whetstone from which he minted his sentences. Without it he might have remained just another prissy introvert with boils. His father gave him the aggression he needed to circumvent the host of problems life dealt him. It formed a continuum with the later aggression of life, stopped him running from it to his mother's apron-strings for solace.

The point he was trying to make is that he had no hiding place from him. The only solution was in himself. No God or family member could protect him from what was coming to him. He had to learn to become immune to it, to assert himself over it.

'The father never leaves,' he told an interviewer once. 'Mine was always with me, not in my heart but under my toenails. Sometimes he even took on female form.' Every time he found himself with a mad woman he thought of her as his father reincarnated. It was almost as if he was the devil in human form. He once raised a glass to him with this dubious tribute: 'Thank you for my poetry and stories, for my house, for my car, for my bank account. Thank you for those beatings that taught me how to endure.'

Such endurance had an almost literal manifestation in his next book. It was as close to an autobiography as he would come. It was a book he resisted writing for many years for obvious reasons, feeling it was bad enough having to have all that pain inside him without dredging it up again in print. It was John Martin – who else – who eventually prevailed upon him to write the book, to slay the dragon for once and for all.

Most childhood memoirs, he felt, were boring. That was why he agonized for so many years over doing his one. It was also why he went out of his way to make it different.

Ham on Rye appeared in 1982. If one wishes to divine the essence of Bukowski, this is where to begin. He called it a horror story but it's also cathartic.

His devotees were already familiar with many of the anecdotes from his stories and poems. Seeing them together here - and with the glue of a lengthy narrative - they gell with near-mathematical precision. The book contains all of his disgruntlement, all of his alienation and all of his humor. It's as important a part of the literature of adolescence as anything that ever appeared before it on a similar theme. '93% of it is true,' he assured his readers.

In these turbo-charged pages Bukowski explodes most of the myths of the all-American childhood, basing us in Nightmareville where his demonic parents make life even more miserable for him than it would have been if he weren't afflicted with walnut-sized boils, a resentful disposition, an unscholarly nature, a diffidence with girls, a nascent hostility and a pronounced discomfiture of temperament.

The early sexual leanings are here, the locker-room banter, the derring-do, the peer groups, the irreverence, the generation gap, the fake jingoism, the macho imperatives, the jealousy, the crippling depression - lifted partly by booze - the long slow slide into post-graduation lassitude.

He waited forty years to write the book and it shows. If he tried to tackle themes like this before he'd honed his craft he mightn't have done them justice. In his other books he's often amorphous but here he had to get everything to fit. There was too much angst to play around with.

His life begins with screaming all around him. His grandmother threatens to 'bury' everybody in a way that lets you know she means business. An introductory reference to the young Bukowski informs us that he's unhuggable. When the aforementioned lady attempts such an act, he hits her on the nose. (Even this early he was a good judge of character).

His father believes children should be seen and not heard. He barks at him continually, so much so that 'Heinie', as he's called, feels he must be an adopted child. At school he has few friends but he doesn't seem put out by this, content to brood alone about the sad lot life has dealt him. Football games on the street provides a temporary respite from this as he grows up but at home there's the roaring, the nagging, his father beating his mother and his mother taking it.

There are also endless lectures. Lectures about his future, about what he should be doing with his life, about how he should be grateful for being fed and clothed. Would the day come when he'd be charged for staying under this roof? (It would).

He forms a friendship with a boy missing an arm. They click, one outcast appreciating another. His life has moments of tranquility but then the lawn-mowing episode raises its head. He's beaten for missing a blade of grass, beaten senseless by a man who's either as insane or as evil as Hitler. He takes what's dished out to him as if it's his destiny.

Later on he feels it's his destiny to be the school tough guy. His sullen manner can have no other outcome. Being bad has an allure for him. It gives him the cachet missing from the rest of his life. Being bad makes him a somebody.

Then comes his initiation into drink, the most magic experience of his life so far. Alcohol takes all his pain away, all his feelings of resentment and deprivation. It's both soothing and uplifting at the same time. 'We sat on a park bench,' he writes, 'and I thought, well now I have found something. I have found something that is going to help me for a long time to come. The park grass looked greener, the park benches looked better, the flowers were trying harder.'

His father loses his job but he pretends he still has one so people won't look down on him. Each morning like clockwork he drives somewhere. Heinie's mother works too. Heinie pretends to go to school but doubles back home when the house is empty. Upstairs he spies on a scantily-clad woman across the street, masturbating as he does so.

Acne is his next crisis. It hits him just as he's beginning to be accepted as a roughneck. Circumstance has played another cruel trick on him, denting his rebel status by transforming him into a creature people will be disgusted by. Now they'll avoid him not from fear but revulsion. Especially women. What woman would date a boy whose face looked like the Grand Canyon?

In Senior School he becomes even more conscious of his maladies. He watches the Beautiful People taking their dates to the beach in convertibles and wonders why he was born so ugly. There's no logic to it. When it comes to gym class he's too embarrassed to take off his clothes. He joins a military squad instead. There he doesn't have to. At home the pus spurts out of him. He bursts his boils in frustration. His parents cover him with ointments that stink and burn. There seems to be no let-up to his suffering. At the hospital they drill him with needles. Back home he misbehaves. His grandmother thinks a devil is inside him. She sticks a crucifix into his back to drive it out. Heinie screams at her, sending her out of the room. Then he curses God.

What little joy there is in his life at this time comes from reading. He begins to write a story about a German aviator called Baron Von Himmlen, an ugly man with scars on his face, 'but beautiful if you looked long enough.' He drinks heavily. He's a military hero, shooting plane after plane from the sky.

Heinie's father finally finds a job. It's at the county museum. His medical treatment has been free up to now but it has to stop because there's money coming into the house as a result of the employment. He has mixed feelings about this. He won't have any more drilling but he'll miss a kind nurse at the hospital.

He starts reading in the library, filling his mind with the stories of other people as badly off as he is. They become his soulmates, as close to him as anyone he knows. At school he continues to attract misfits. Girls are still out of reach for him. He pretends they don't exist for fear he'll go out of his mind pining for them. When he goes to the beach he feels uncomfortable with his body again. He decides he'll never be able to live with people. He thinks maybe he should become a monk. Or maybe he should go to sleep for five years. A third option would be to drink for a living.

He starts attending an elite high school. His father tells him that with the right opportunities they could become rich. Anyone can, he insists. Heinie doubts this will happen. He knows the poor always be poor and the rich will always be rich. All you can do is accept it. Nobody is going to change the system.

The ugly will always stay ugly too. He realizes that at the school prom when he stands outside watching the people inside. They're dancing together, looking pleased with themselves with their easy manners and fine clothes. After a while the night watchman comes along. He asks him what he's doing there. He tells him he's a pupil but he isn't believed. The man tells him he looks too old to be a pupil, that he looks at least 22. He tells him to go home, which he does.

On graduation day he's depressed. He decides all the future holds for him is a 'hairy crawling turd.' The land of opportunity won't be that for him. It will only be one dull job after another.

He starts working in a company called Mears-Starbuck. It cripples his spirit. The tough guy crumbles. His father couldn't break him and neither could the teachers in the school but the world of employment does. He has no future and no past, no anything. Neither does he wish to *be* anything.

His father twists the dagger at home, telling him he's a nothing. He looks for other jobs but they don't materialize. When World War 1 breaks out he doesn't want to sign up. Everyone is giving out about Hitler but Heinie has a sneaking regard for him. He becomes a proponent of Nazism even though he knows this will make him into a pariah with everyone he knows. But then he thinks: Why should he care? When you have nothing you have nothing to lose.

The last straw is when his father finds his writings and declares them to be repulsive. He throws them out the window along with his clothes and his typewriter. There can be no going back on this. No way can he live under the same room as this man again. He's accused of being a dirty writer by a man who doesn't even know what good or bad writing is. He decides he can do either one of two things: leave or kill him. He decides to leave. It's the lesser of two evils. Slightly.

The place he goes is no Shangri-La. It's Skid Row, where all the misfits hang out. For some reason he feels at home among them. He always knew he was unusual but here everyone is unusual so he doesn't stick out. Even if he was a murderer or a bank robber he wouldn't stick out. Nobody preaches to him here.

They allow him to sit in his own space. If he said he was going to kill himself he feels they'd even allow him to do that. It's as close to peace as he's ever been.

The Japanese bomb Pearl Harbor but he's unmoved by the event, as unmoved by it as he has been by most things in his life up to this. He still doesn't want to sign up. Let the others kill and be killed. It's not his war. He decides to have a drink instead. That's much more important than war.

The bombing of Pearl Harbor meant little to Bukowski

Ham on Rye was a huge undertaking for Bukowski and he rose to the occasion admirably. Most people agree this is his most ambitious undertaking, the novel where he outgrows his bad narrative habits and gives us solid meat instead.

There are lyrical interludes and a well-rounded narrator. It's the poor man's *Catcher in the Rye* if you like, which may explain why he chose the title. It's the only one of his novel titles that's open to

278

interpretation, all the others being straightforward. Ham on rye bread was the typical working man's lunch of the time.

Bukowski admired Salinger. He particularly liked the way he walked away from the literary world after writing his masterpiece.

'The good ones stop,' he said, 'The bad ones just keep on going.'

He reminded him of the Chinese poet Li Po, someone who was more interested in the process of composition than the end product of publication. Li Po was alleged to have burned his poems after writing them.

'I don't think he was that stupid,' Bukowski said, 'I think he only burned the bad ones.'

He had a different approach to the difference between writing and publication. For him book were like smoking a cigarette. The writing was the drag, the publication the ash. Readers were the ash tray.

Ham on Rye remains his most ambitious novel. Time has been kind to it. The question he must have been asking himself now was, could he top it? He'd spent many years building himself up for it and he was drained.

A new dimension was added to his career with a film based on his work came out the following year.

1983 saw the release of Marco Ferreri's *Tales of Ordinary Madness*, a film based on some of his stories. It featured Ben Gazzara as the thinly-disguised Bukowski. It was his first time seeing someone play him on screen and he was wondering how it was going to pan out.

Sadly, he was disappointed, Gazzara being totally miscast. The pair of them got on well but Gazzara failed to convince as an alcoholic.

He was 'always hitting on the wine bottle,' Bukowski said, 'but never getting drunk.'

Ben Gazzara

The film was doomed to failure because it played things the safe way, i.e. choosing a pretty actor to 'open' it. Bukowski despised it. He thought his vision was muzzled. He liked the intensity in Gazzara's eyes but unfortunately it was the wrong kind of intensity. His expression, he said, reminded him of a man 'straining to have a shit.'

Madonna attended the premiere with Sean Penn. They'd just got married. Bukowski liked Penn but the chemistry wasn't good between him and Madonna. It got worse when she refused a drink from him. (This was probably the moment he decided she was wrong for Penn).

Madonna seemed threatened by Bukowski. It was as if she felt he'd draw Penn away from her into his sleazy world. She didn't appreciate the raw beauty of his poetry like Penn did. And she wanted to be in control. Seeing her husband chortling with Bukowski wasn't a good prelude to the marriage for her.

Hot Water Music, another collection of his short stories, appeared the same year. Sexy and outrageous, they seemed like a cross between Damon Runyon and Elmore Leonard. Few holds are barred in these pages. The stories seem like one story told thirty or forty different ways. Maybe this quality could apply to all of his work.

Writers figure strongly in them, most of them resembling the author. In 'The Great Poet' we get his familiar diatribe against 'liberated' women. Elsewhere his rogue's gallery of likeable lowlifes throbs with familiar energy.

An autobiographical element is apparent in the two stories entitled 'The Death of the Father', numbers 1 and 2. He writes about that man as if he were a distant relative. After the funeral wards he has sex with his father's girlfriend, the final example of his hatred for him. In Part 2 he writes about the nonchalant manner in which he disposes of all his father's possessions. An auction sees the house emptied of all his effects, most of them being given away for nothing. (A bottle of whisky, significantly enough, is held onto). A strange sense of tranquility is apparent as the main threatening influence of his life is removed from it forever.

War All the Time, another collection of his verse, appeared in 1984. It's impressive in its authority. In 'talking to my mailbox' he berates a young writer for sending him material for vetting instead of submitting it to a publisher. Bukowski himself never solicited the aid of middlemen. You've got to do it on your own, he advises finally, the wise words of a man who's clawed his way to the top without any help from middle men.

In 'the last generation', the poem that follows this, he makes a contrast between the 1980s and the 1920s. He presumes - rightly or wrongly - that it was easier to be a genius in the twenties because there were fewer writers about. 'A Love Poem' sees him reflecting on the women in his life with an uncharacteristically cool voice. He's back to his irascible old self in 'a beginning.' Here he suggests mischievously that women should only be entitled to talk about liberation when they stop carrying mirrors with them.

'On and off the road' is an interesting insight into his views on poetry readings. He compares peddling his wares in this fashion to being a travelling salesman, with the added bonus of being allowed to insult his clients (his invariable response to hecklers) and, hopefully, get laid. 'Eulogy to a hell of a dame' is a tribute to Jane, a woman he believes was destroyed because she realized everything around her was meaningless and took that thesis to its inevitable end. She was given little in life and gave little back but she had style and character. She imprinted herself on Bukowski so much that since she died he's left with nothing but 'the rotten present.'

The other women in his life, the 'girls from nowhere' can't compare to what he had with her. Sitting with her in a cinema with a bag of popcorn in his hand was infinitely preferable to the rollercoaster ride his life has been since. Living in the tawdry rooming-houses, sex was the only thing he had to look forward to. It was the poor man's polo for him. But it sufficed. He had, after all, failed at almost everything else.

In 'oh yes' he says there are worse things in life than being alone but seclusion helped him hone his art, even if the pickings from his writings were slim in the early years. In 'an old buddy' he says that after he started to become successful he had to contend with begrudgery, he explains in 'an old buddy.' Now he's in 'Who's Who in America', as he reveals in 'our curious position.' Begrudgery isn't the only thing that bothers him since becoming famous, however. In 'a note to the boys in the back room' he says there's also the problem of those he half-knew jumping on the bandwagon as 'old friends' when they were far from that. But what a long way he's come since the days when, as a mailman, he delivered a letter to a 'famous writer' and was ignored when he mentioned that he too wrote.

'Practice' is a funny and yet profound rumination on death, a subject that also crops up in 'suggestion for an arrangement.' Here he tells us he wants to die with his boots on rather than with his ass stuck in a bedpan or, like John Fante, blind and ripped apart. He told Fante once that the gods were punishing him because he wrote so well, an unusual statement from a man who believed in no God at all.

Bukowski's collections were now coming out thick and fast. *You Get So Alone At Times That It Just Makes Sense* was published in 1986. Two of the poems deal with his father. In 'retired' he writes about his gluttony, his boring life and shock death. 'My non-ambitious ambition' outlines the manner in which his Reader's Digest bromides had the effect of pushing the young Bukowski in another direction entirely.

We flash forward to him as a 21-year-old in New Orleans in the poem 'my buddy.' Here he befriends a disabled old man in a seedy apartment. The man tells him, 'Nothing is worth it', a remark which makes him conclude that he was a sage. One might have imagined a comment like that to depress him but so great is his hatred of his father's Positive Thinking he regards the easy decadence of this affable old soul as a welcome antidote.

Many of the other poems in the collection take up this theme, most prominently 'bumming with Jane' where he writes about the wild years he spent with her. Their time together is a smorgasbord of car crashes, hospitals and drunk tanks but he looks back on such times now as the most wonderful of his life. He paints a different picture of their liaison in 'my first affair with that older woman,' describing her as somebody who lied to him, stole from him and was both abusive and unfaithful.

After she died, he writes, he drank alone for two years. There's no hint of sentiment or self-pity. As he puts it in another poem ('well, that's just the way it is') no matter how grim thugs get, he'd still prefer to be himself than anyone else.

'Beasts bounding through time' is a powerful poem dealing with the huge price fame exacts from artists. He trawls through the pages of history with a grocery list of tragic cases. 'The lost generation' is more specific. Here he castigates those Paris writers from the 1920s who irritated him with their 'rich dumb lives.' Bukowski had often criticized this breed. 'How were they lost?' he asked, 'All those poor idiots were moaning about were ants in the picnic basket.'

In 'final story' we get the Bukowski take on why Ernest Hemingway committed suicide. His contention is that Hemingway was destroyed by the juggernaut of fame rather than anything in himself. This is a simplistic thesis because Hemingway had a host of problems. He was an alcoholic depressive with writer's block, as Bukowski well knew, so it's surprising he takes this reductive stance on a man he knew to be so complex.

We're presented with an unusually nostalgic Bukowski in 'O tempora! O mores!' One can be excused for blinking twice at this poem which harks back to the days when the glimpse of a stocking was looked on as something shocking. It's hard to believe the man who wrote *Women* would admit a preference for a well-turned ankle to a selection of girlie magazines, particularly after reading 'love poem to a stripper' where he gives a more expectable green light to a red light district, writing with affection at tarts with hearts.

Nostalgia also turns up in 'Glenn Miller', a poem one finds hard to square with the rest of Bukowski's canon, and even in 'magic machine', where he writes about the wonder of listening to a

Victrola back in the 1930s. The former ends with a piquant image of the world around him opening its mouth in an attempt to swallow everyone.' The latter has a more recognizable sting in the tail, Bukowski emphasizing the fact that part of the magic was listening to it when his parents weren't around, which makes us wonder if the poem is a tribute to the music or how he heard it.

'The Master Plan' is a humorous piece about him deciding to give up poetry when he realizes he's getting nowhere fast, content to devote himself instead to the much less arduous practice of drinking for a living. In the latter capacity he doesn't have to worry about bothersome details like rejection slips, or even paper. All one needs to be a card-carrying drunk is a good elbow - and hopefully a liver to match. There's no money in it, unfortunately, but neither is there in writing. So what really, has been lost?

This is a much more preferable scenario than the one he depicts in the harrowing 'death sat on my knee and cracked with laughter,' a poem about poverty. One night things are so bad he decides to spend the last of his money on a loaf of bread, planning to eat all the slices slowly and pretend they're pieces of a delicious steak. When he gets home, however, he realizes the bread is too stale to eat. The mice help themselves to it instead, creeping over his 'immortal' stories as they chew around the mold.

In the title poem he writes about the hungry years and his famous 'ten year drunk,' at the end of which he's ready to give life 'another shot in the dark.' Editors are still as ignorant as they were a decade ago in his view but he refuses to allow them to faze him.

At this time Bukowski was a supersonic success overseas. By the late 1980s over two million copies of his books had been sold in Germany alone. A few years earlier, three of his books appeared on the best seller list in, of all places, Brazil. He was translated into countless languages but was still relatively obscure in America. It was the old story: a prophet was never recognized in his own land.

Barbara Frye died at this time. The circumstances were mysterious. Involvement in a drug cartel was rumored. Bukowski had only rung her twice in the last twenty years. The first time she said, 'You're drunk,' and hung up on him. The second time they spoke for about twenty seconds. He was amused by the fact that you could live with someone for two years and not have anything to say to them. But that was Barbara.

He shed few tears at her passing. She'd been too cruel for him to grieve for her. Neither did her family grieve. In fact they didn't even have her body flown home from India. The daughter who'd burned down her house in Japan eventually committed suicide. 'Barbara was the only woman I ever met,' Bukowski said, 'who was even more messed up than I was.'

Moving Towards the 21st Century

The toughest thing about success is that you've got to keep on being a success. (Irving Berlin)

Bukowski may have become tamer as he got older but he never lost the fire in his belly. He would have continued to write on park benches with the grimy stubs of pencils even if he was never discovered. Fame was just the way the cards fell and he accepted its comforts accordingly.

He never romanticized obscurity. If somebody didn't make it to the top he usually felt that was because they weren't good enough. As against that, there were many famous writers he despised. He never reconciled these two viewpoints. When a colleague suggested he got big publishing contracts because he was 'known' he became annoyed with him, arguing that one only became known because one had talent.

He enjoyed the luxury of San Pedro and didn't feel he had to apologize to anyone for it, least of all the people who wanted him back in 'The Row.' Here he was lord of his demesne. No longer had he to haul a black cardboard case from pillar to post, dodging irate landladies on rent day. It was his turn to laugh at the people voted 'Most Likely to Succeed' in the College Yearbook. Many of those wonder-boys were now selling salami to make ends meet while Bukowski was chewing on expensive cigars and living off the fat of the land. 'People still expect me to jump off balconies,' he said, 'but I can't do it anymore. I'm just an old guy sitting out the years.'

He was surprised to find he could write as prolifically in his new environment as he had in the 'dull whispers of nowhere.' 'Poverty isn't ennobling,' he said, 'It's destructive.' He could just as easily have been in Carlton Way or De Longpre Avenue. The sights and sounds of the world outside his window nudged the muse towards the short crisp sentences at which he excelled. The words still came out like bullets. He could still write about men like himself at war with their bitches, their jobs, themselves. And write about them just as intensely. 'You have to hit the typewriter hard,' he said, 'Hate won't come through on a dinky portable.'

The fact that money was rolling in now meant that he got a call from Internal Revenue. They wanted a chunk of it. 'Where were these people when the pages were blank?' he protested. Where were they when the rejections were pouring in, when he had to sell his blood to eat? Now they wanted to piggyback on his good fortune.

He asked an accountant for advice. 'You have to spend your money,' he told him, 'or they'll take it anyway.' He decided to buy an expensive car. He went down to a garage and picked out one costing $16,000. When he told the salesman he was interested in it he looked at him as if he was trying to make a fool of him.

'How do you plan to pay for it?' he asked him.

'With a check,' Bukowski replied.

The man froze. Was he joking? He rang the bank and discovered he had the credit to cover it. 'It was worth it just to see the look on his face,' Bukowski said. He was remembering all the times he'd been refused drink in bars because of the way he looked, all the times he'd been treated as a poor relation, a fifth wheel. His mind even went back to the night at the prom concert when the night watchman banished him from the premises. That was the first time he was 86ed but not the last.

The fact that he had a BMW made people think he'd sold out but he didn't see it like that. It was just a tax write-off. The government was going to take the money if he didn't. But some people who knew him from the old days were disappointed - as disappointed as diehard Bob Dylan fans were when he got rich singing about the poor. Bukowski hadn't much time for Dylan, seeing him in the same light as most rock musicians with their comfortable upbringings and stylized angst, but he liked some of the Dante-esque imagery in his songs.

A lot of people couldn't wrap their heads around the fact that Bukowski now owned a BMW

His accountant told him he should invest in property too but he didn't like that idea. 'I like to see what I have,' he said. He asked the accountant if he could claim alcohol as a tax write-off. The accountant thought he was joking and he probably was. (The snooker player Bill Werbeniuk suffered from a condition called hypoglycemia, which meant his body burned off alcohol too quickly. To preserve the balance he had to drink lots of it, sometimes up to twenty pints a day. The Inland Revenue treated such expenses as tax-deductible. How Bukowski would like to have had that disease). Jane would surely have turned in her grave at his new circumstances. 'I'm all straightened out now,' he said.

But he confessed in a more frank moment, 'I miss the dirty action.' Every plus had a minus attached to it.

Gone were the clip-joints, the whores, the mad ballet of a life lived on the edge. Gone were the ghost poets and the romantics who burned themselves out with the fire of excess. He'd been there and maybe he'd go there again but for now he had a good lady engaged in keeping him alive for a while more.

Life was quiet in San Pedro. He stood in line at supermarkets. He clipped the hair out of his nostrils. He even got early nights on occasion. And, dread of dreads, looked at TV.

He'd survived. How could he have done that when the graveyards were strewn with the corpses of so many others who hadn't taken a fraction of the liberties he had with his health, or a fraction of the drink he'd imbibed? He'd spent his days on a 'live now, pay later basis since as far back as he could remember but so far nobody had called for the bill.

He told the journalist Paul Ciotti, 'The wine does most of my writing for me. I just open a bottle and turn on the radio and it comes pouring out. I have no plan. The typewriter gives me things I don't even know I'm working on. It's a free lunch. I don't know how long it's going to continue but so far there's nothing easier than writing.'

One piece of writing he found particularly easy to do was a script he'd written for his friend Barbet Schroeder, a jazz impresario turned film-maker.

Schroeder had also made documentaries - on everything from the life of Idi Amin to a gorilla that was taught to communicate in sign language.

Bukowski liked him for his eccentricity. Why shouldn't he? He was one himself. Schroeder liked Bukowski too. He was never judgmental about his lifestyle or his drinking, more amused than shocked by all his excesses.

He appeared at Bukowski's door one day and told him he wanted him to write a screenplay about his life. He gave him an advance to do it, sight unseen, knowing he'd amassed enough experience in his life to compose something that could easily be adapted to the screen.

He called it *Barfly*. Schroeder loved it from the moment he read it. His only problem with it, he told Bukowski, was that the main character needed to 'evolve.' Bukowski didn't know how he could solve that problem.

'My characters never evolve,' he told Schroeder, 'They're too fucked up.'

They had a lot of fun bringing it to fruition. When Schroeder flirted playfully with Beighle, Bukowski said, 'Fuck off, you French frog.' (He was actually part Iranian). Schroeder replied, 'If I bonk Linda you can kill me. You won't be prosecuted because I'll write a suicide note first.'

This was the kind of talk Bukowski enjoyed. Schroeder's personality was like a breath of fresh air to him. He gave him faith in the film world in the same way as people like John Martin and the Webbs had in the literary one, ensuring him that there was still room for people who had talent.

But there were problems with *Barfly*. Schroeder found it difficult to raise the money for it. When he felt it wasn't going to get made he asked Bukowski if he could shoot some documentary footage of him instead. Bukowski agreed. The resulting footage became *The Bukowski Tapes*. He shot over four hours of Bukowski sounding off on all his favorite topics: women, booze, horses, Hollywood, work, etc. This has become a documentary much loved by Bukowski fans. It contains some of the best interviews he ever gave. His merry eyes twinkle as the fiery convolutions of his scabrous past are paraded before us.

Schroeder isn't seen. He fires questions at Bukowski from behind the camera. We get his genial essence in 52 vignettes. He talks about everything that ever intrigued him in his dizzy path through life. It's like an autobiography on celluloid. Though his tone is often crabby, he seems happy behind it all.

In one hilarious episode he talks about Elizabeth Taylor, an actress upon whom he spews especial venom. He tells us he thinks she's ugly - and she can sue him for saying that if she wants. It's unlikely that anyone in history has ever called Taylor ugly but Bukowski seems convinced of it. He says her alleged beauty is simply a result of where different parts her body have been arranged, that it's nothing more than how the chips have fallen. In essence he's really just reiterating the old saw about beauty being only skin-deep but, being Bukowski, it sounds much more convoluted than that. (He only liked one of Taylor's films, *Who's Afraid of Virginia Woolf?* It's not too hard to see why).

It's difficult to see how Bukowski thought Liz Taylor was ugly based on the evidence of this photograph

In another segment he talks about his reclusiveness. He tells Schroeder he likes him but he'd like him more if he wasn't there. People bother him, he says: the way they look, the way they dress, the way they walk, the way they talk. He's really only happy when he's as far away from them as possible.

The part of the documentary that most people talk about is where he has a row with Beighle. They're sitting on a sofa together. The segment starts quietly with Bukowski saying he doesn't like being pushed around by people in life. She says he's an idiot if he allows this to happen.

At this point she doesn't seem to realize it's her he's talking about. When she does - after he tells her she's been spending too much time out of the house and he's fed up of it - she thinks he's joking.

But she's not quite sure. She starts to laugh nervously and Bukowski gets angrier as he listens to her. His tone becomes more threatening.

He narrows his eyes as he puffs on a cigar. His voice is low but there's no mistaking the anger in his voice. He tells her he's going to get an attorney and have her 'ass' moved out of the house for good.

It's only at this point she realizes he means business. He's on a roll now. He's been drinking all day and his ugly side comes out, the side he always said he inherited from his father, the side that was accentuated by alcohol. It's as if he's on a path without any logic attached to it. The same paranoia he showed with King and Brandes when they were away from him comes out now.

He turns to Schroeder and says, 'She thinks I can't do without her.' Then he roars at Beighle herself, 'You fucking cunt! You whore! You bitch!' He now starts kicking at her with his feet. Then he lunges at her. She leaps from the sofa. He appears to be about to punch her as they go off-camera. Everything is in stark contrast to the quietness of a few moments before. It seems almost like schizoid behavior on his part.

Beighle said she was 'mortified' by his behavior, especially since it was being filmed.

'It made for great footage,' she said wryly, 'but it wasn't so good for me.'

The sudden show of temper lets us know how much of a brooder he was, how he could work himself up into a frenzy within seconds. Beighle was obviously unaware how much her socializing bothered him until that moment. Otherwise she wouldn't have been so nonchalant with him before he erupted.

Bukowski had no memory of the incident the next day. That often happened when he drank too much, like when he was on the TV show in Paris. Schroeder asked him if he wanted the segment removed from the film when he edited it.

'That's up to Linda,' he said. He never minded how he came across in any aspect of his life, visual or otherwise.

Beighle allowed it to stay in, probably to let the world see that the so-called 'cuddly old bear', as the world now saw him, was still a handful.

She said he was never violent with her after that day but admitted he lost his temper on occasions. When that happened she always left the room, leaving him to 'fight with himself.' It was the only way to deal with him.

'He was so good with words, she said, 'He could crush you into a tiny piece of dust.'

The argument wasn't reflective of his personality at that time, or indeed of his life with Beighle. Schroeder said his main motivation in doing the documentary was to show that behind Bukowski's reputation as a degenerate - which he helped establish – was 'a poet of exquisite sensitivity.

He broke up with Beighle in 1983 but they got back together two years later. The split did both of them good, making them aware of how much they had going as a couple, how much they had to lose if they broke up.

The parting was therapeutic in that regard. It strengthened their relationship when they got back together again.

When they did, Bukowski asked her to marry him. It didn't seem in character but he knew he was ready now.

Bukowski got married in 1984, once again going against everyone's expectations of what he might do next

They tied the knot just two days after his 65th birthday. For this marriage, unlike the one with Barbara Frye, he wasn't going into unknown territory. He felt sure Beighle was the woman for him. He told her mother, 'I love your little girl. I keep her heart in my back pocket and sometimes I sit on it.'

The ceremony was as informal as one might have expected. He ordered everyone to drink their fill because he was paying the goddam bill. He dispensed mirth and goodwill like one to the manor born, an avuncular old goat at ease finally with himself after six decades battering down the walls of recalcitrance.

At the reception he took Steve Richmond and Gerard Locklin aside and warned them about the dangers of women: an action only Bukowski could have got away with at his own wedding.

Meanwhile the writing went on. Schroeder told him the *Barfly* project still had a good chance of reaching the screen and not to give up on it. The documentary had been a kind of insurance policy for him that he got 'something' on Bukowski but now it was looking like they'd get the movie as well.

The producers started looking for an actor who might be suitable to play him.

Kris Kristofferson – or 'Chris Christofferson' as Bukowski spelled it – was the first choice but he would have been playing a singer in the film and Bukowski couldn't have that. The prospect of a guitar-strumming Chinaski made him sick to the core.

James Woods was then considered. Bukowski had been impressed with Woods' work in *The Onion Field*. He liked his energy but thought he needed to tone his style down a bit to fit the world-weary Chinaski. (Woods' later *Eraserhead* would become one of Bukowski's all-time favorite films.)

Another possibility was Sean Penn. That option meant Dennis Hopper would have been directing the film. Hopper and Penn were friends. Both Schroeder and Bukowski liked Penn but neither of them were too keen on Hopper.

Bukowski thought he was shallow. Another thing that turned Bukowski off Hopper was the fact that he was a reformed drinker when they met. This was hardly the blueprint of Henry Chinaski by any stretch of the imagination. Neither did Bukowski have much respect for Hopper's 1969 cult movie *Easy Rider*. He thought it romanticized the flower power set out of all proportion, portraying them as the Beautiful People of Unofficial America. (Bukowski had more experience of the spaced-out members of the set).

Hopper believed the reason he was cut out of the deal was because he'd cast aspersions on Schroeder's directorial flair years before, telling him his main talent was for documentaries rather than dramas. Schroeder had a long memory, he said, and used Bukowski as an excuse to punish him for the slight.

In the end Mickey Rourke came on board. He seemed to tick all the right boxes for both Schroeder and Bukowski, even though he too was a reformed drinker.

'Trust me,' he told Bukowski, 'I can get back to my bad self-quick enough.'

Faye Dunaway was chosen for the part of Wanda, the character based on Jane Cooney Baker in the film. Bukowski disapproved of this decision. 'They could never find anyone like Jane,' he said piquantly, 'and neither can I.'

**Bukowski didn't think much of Faye
Dunaway's performance in *Barfly***

The studio wanted Dunaway because she was bankable. She saw the part as being a door back into the big time for her after some bad film choices in the recent past. 'I haven't felt such passion for a character since *Network,*' she said, seeing the promise of a comeback in Wanda, a woman of 'sweet vulnerability.'

Dunaway had only made one movie in the previous six years, Michael Winner's camp period farce *The Wicked Lady*. One had to go back to 1981 for her last acclaimed performance: the biopic *Mommie Dearest* where she went totally OTT to play the child-bashing Joan Crawford. With Wanda, she thought, history could repeat itself.

Before the cameras started to roll there were some obstacles to be overcome. Executive producers Menahem Golan and Yoram Globas of Cannon Pictures started to go cold on the idea again just as they were about to. Schroeder was devastated. And even more devastated when they told him they were putting a prohibitive turnaround figure on the movie. That was the amount that would have to be paid to them by another person who might like to buy the property from them if they decided not to proceed with it.

Schroeder conveyed his disgust at this cynical move to Dunaway. Both of them felt it smacked of a crucial lack of confidence. Dunaway offered to work for no money upfront to help the situation, foregoing her salary in exchange for a deferment or a percentage of the profits.

Schroeder went one better, going into Golan's office one day with a Black & Decker chainsaw. 'Do you see this finger?' he said to him, holding up his hand, 'I don't really need it.' He then turned on the saw. 'If you don't reach for your wallet and make this picture,' he said, 'I'm going to come in here and cut off a piece of it.' Golan was won around by the threat. He said, 'If Barbet thinks that much of the movie, it must have something.'

The film went into production in February 1987. It takes place over four days but Bukowski said it represented as many years of his life. He compressed them into that time frame for the purposes of the screenplay. He asked Schroeder to get him final word on every script change and this was arranged — no mean achievement, he realized, in an industry where the lead actor got '750 times' (sic) what the writer did. His contract stated that he didn't have to be on the set any day he wanted to go racing. 'They got their priorities right,' he said. As well as writing the script he had a small part in the film – as, what else, a barfly. 'Blink and you miss me,' he said, 'or maybe you don't even have to blink.' It was both the beginning and the end of his acting career.

The Los Angeles Times ran a feature of him in March of that year, describing him as 'a 66-year-old man with a sandblasted face, warts on his eyelids and a dominating nose that looks as if it was assembled in a junkyard from Studebaker hoods and Buick fenders.' Despite having lived in L.A. for most of his life, it pointed out, he was still relatively unknown outside literary circles. What made this even more astounding was the fact that he'd written over 1,000 poems, five books of short stories and four novels. Devotees of his work were willing to pay exorbitant prices for early editions of his poetry and he was widely translated. So how come more people didn't know about him? Would *Barfly* change all that?

It did. The film made him a more recognizable figure to those who didn't read poetry and had a spin-off effect on all of the titles he already had in print. What an irony that a film about a down-and-out would catapult him into the big time.

He liked the work he did on the screenplay but thought the film had too much 'designer destruction' about it. Faye Dunaway, he thought, chewed the scenery.

Of Rourke he said, 'If I looked that bad in my drinking days I would have been kicked out of even more bars than I was.' His clothes may have been wrinkled but they weren't dirty, as Rourke's were. Bukowski claimed he washed them every night even in his worst times. Neither did he ever have his pants hanging down the way Rourke's did, not even when he was in his worst stages of drinking.

He also had problems with Rourke from a physical point of view. Bukowski was a big man with rough skin. Rourke, for all his scruffiness, was more of a tenderfoot. Neither did his stubble compensate for acne vulgaris.

'If I met him in an alley,' Bukowski claimed, 'I would have blown him away.'

Bukowski thought the fight scenes in the film were too brutal, almost to the point of slapstick. Toughness would have been better conveyed by a tilt of the head than a pummeling of fists. 'They looked like they were trying to make *Rocky*,' he said. 'We weren't professional boxers. Some nights we could hardly stand. But that's Hollywood, always trying to goose things up.' Rourke also overdid the Sensitive Poet angle as far as Bukowski was concerned.

Bukowski's cameo in the film occurs in the scene where Chinaski meets Jane. 'I was surprised I wasn't nominated for an Oscar,' he joked. Further cameos were played by other real-life barflies. He knew the world these colorful personalities represented was fast disappearing. The presence of televisions in bars sucked the life out of them.

'We used to be the performers. Now everyone just sits and stares at the tube.' The world he grew up in had changed forever, especially the rundown districts. He remembered the pimps and whores who ate hot dogs at street corners with mustard dripping down their chins.

'When you clean up a city you kill it,' he maintained, 'The puritans and Christians have killed Los Angeles.' There were only a few characters left. This made them all the more treasurable to him.

The film was shot in just 34 days. Despite the above problems, Bukowski felt it had a core of truth about it, unlike most of the Hollywood drivel that was going around at the time. Bukowski used to drink in the actual bar used for his scene. Watching it made me feel thirsty,' he said, 'That must be some kind of recommendation.'

Rourke had just finished making the IRA movie *A Prayer for the Dying*. The final cut betrayed its intentions, he felt, so he disowned it. The experience gave him the kind of cynicism that was perfect for Chinaski.

Mickey Rourke shared Bukowski's disenchantment with Hollywood

Bukowski had a lot in common with Rourke, whose father deserted the family home when he was a young boy. He was subsequently beaten by his stepfather, a man he despised. As he grew up he drifted into jobs that almost equaled Bukowski's in the lowlife stakes: pretzel seller, nightclub bouncer, towel boy in a massage parlor. Bukowski liked his iconoclastic attitude to Hollywood. He liked the fact that he didn't run with the 'in' crowd that he wouldn't walk across cut glass to make a deal like some of the other Bratpackers. In a way Rourke was the Bukowski of Tinseltown, a man who refused to bend the knee. They were like two mavericks kicking against the pricks, two 'difficult' talents who kept on keeping on — despite being bad box office.

The only problem Bukowski had with Rourke was his aforementioned 'reformed drinker' status. His father had been an alcoholic and that gave him bad feelings about it. He realized drink worked for Bukowski but he saw this as the exception rather than the rule.

Bukowski would have preferred Rourke if he accepted the healing properties of booze. This was a hard pill for him to swallow but it was one of the things the film was about. Bukowski didn't deny the fact that drink was an escapist illusion but the world was such a cruddy place, maybe illusions needed to be valued. 'I come from a long line of drunks,' Rourke said when Bukowski when he tried to push drink on him. Bukowski told him to stop boasting.

To get into the character of Chinaski, Rourke decided to copy Bukowski's slow speaking voice. 'I made the choice to talk like him in about ten minutes,' he confessed, 'so you can say I'm winging it. I decided that unless I went all the way with this character I'd wind up being mediocre. I decided to make the guy real, not like he was in a Hollywood fucking commercial movie.' He got the drawl right but he pitched it too softly. His voice in the film is so soft, one could hardly hear it behind a matchbox. It reminded one of what someone said about Marlon Brando's rasp in *The Godfather*: 'It was like asthma set to music.'

In Bukowski Rourke saw his mirror-image, a guy who'd taken life's sucker punches every time they were thrown at him and still came up for more. 'This character is very close to how I feel about the acting world right now,' he said, '*Barfly* came along at the right time to help me get my shit together and rejuvenate my feeling for the profession.' He'd been unhappy not only with *A Prayer for the Dying* but also the quasi-erotic *9½ Weeks* which had been similarly bowdlerized by the studios. 'We set out to make a real film about real people,' he complained, 'but the studios reckoned the public would be more interested in seeing me hump Kim Basinger over a coffee table.'

He sympathized wholeheartedly with the character of Chinaski, a man who was at the end of his rope but still refused to sell himself out to the literary establishment. Here that establishment is represented by Alice Krige, who plays a literary agent in the film. She wants to get Chinaski into the big time with his work but he waves her check book away, opting to stick with the sewer bums where he feels more at home.

There were some problems with the editing of the film. In the opening scene a fight sees Rourke left for dead in an alley but the next night he's bright-eyed and bushy-tailed, making one wonder at his recuperative powers. In general he looks far too fit. Where's his beer belly?

Whatever faults Rourke had in his performance, they were nothing in comparison to Dunaway's. Looking like somebody who forgot to put her makeup on for a job interview at the William Morris Agency, she came across as far too 'together', a wiseacre with a flirty eye rather than a loveable loser. If Rourke needed a beer belly, so did she. (A character calls her fat at one point and she takes umbrage. She's right: she has an hour glass figure).

She talks about the 'penal system' in a scene where Jane would probably have preferred talking about the *penis* system. The scene where she collects the ears of corn is laughably amateurish. So is her claim of having seen an angel. The 'diamond in the rough' idea is so over-drawn as to be farcical.

Things become harder to take when Krige pays Rourke a surprise visit. She's interrupted by a stabbing incident from the s&m couple next door. Apart from this unlikely coincidence, the fact that Rourke shows little or no interest in having a piece of writing accepted by her flies in the face of his career to date.

Even the tattoo on Rourke's arm looks wrong. It's showy in the kind of way Bukowski hated - an appeal for a very obvious form of street cred. Neither is there any scene of him writing anything except epithets. The film is like a fast food guide to literature, the thing Bukowski's whole career screamed out against.

The film marked a watershed for Rourke. His star failed to shine in subsequent roles. Disenchanted with the glitzy lifestyle, he attempted a career in professional boxing but it didn't take off. A subsequent stint as a tattoo artist didn't go anywhere either. His film career rumbled on in fits and starts, his poor attitude to directors meaning he stayed low on the totem pole of desirability. Some years later he was arrested for beating up his wife Carrie Otis. He subsequently spent time in a psychiatric clinic and suffered a number of panic attacks. For a while he started writing poetry. This carried certain echoes of Bukowski. ('Most recently I have observed/That movie stars stink/And that nepotism keeps giving birth/To a new generation of scum). He had a mini-renaissance with an Oscar nomination for the film *The Wrestler* in 2008.Dunaway pursued a more mainstream path but her career never again reached the highs of *Bonnie & Clyde* or *Network.*

Bukowski didn't do any promotional work for the film. As a sop to Sean Penn he talked to him for Andy Warhol's *Interview* magazine. They covered the usual range of topics: women, the track, fighting, writing, drink. 'Alcohol is one of the greatest things to arrive upon the earth,' he told Penn, 'apart from me.' But he was with Linda now so he preferred to drink at home. 'Nowadays I just go into bars to piss.'

He ran into Norman Mailer during the filming. (Mailer was directing one of his own films at an adjoining lot). 'The Barfly meets the Champ' were his opening words. Both of them were almost as famous for their riotous lives off the page as anything they wrote on it. Mailer had recently knifed his wife Adele Morales, had recently head-butted his rival Gore Vidal. Bukowski liked his outrageousness but he thought he over-wrote. Mailer thought the same about Bukowski. Hostilities were suspended for the night's drinking. They hovered around one another like prizefighters at a title bout.

'It was nice of Hank not to say anything about my work,' Mailer said to Linda when he was alone with her, 'I don't think he likes it.' Bukowski laughed when she relayed his comments to him. 'Somebody needs to tell Mailer *no* writer likes any other writer's work,' he said to Linda, 'until they're dead. Only then do we not feel threatened by them.'

Another Bukowski-related film came out shortly after *Barfly*. This was *Crazy Love*, a Belgian movie directed by Dominique Deruddere. Bukowski liked it. It made me look better than I am,' he said. Deruddere based it on a selection of his stories, most of them dealing with the tarnishing of dreams. It's comprised of three separate segments featuring a character called Harry Voss at various stages of his life. The first one has him as a young boy from the country. His fantasies are nurtured by his mother, who tells him playfully that her husband loved her so much he kidnapped her. One night he sees a film in his local cinema featuring a chivalrous marriage. He's so impressed by the bride in the film that he steals her photograph from a glass case as he's leaving.

Thereafter he witnesses the vulgar spectacle of his parents having sex. An attempt to woo a young beauty at a carnival comes to nothing as a result of his bashfulness. His older friend tells him he can get relief from his sexual yearnings by masturbation, which he graphically demonstrates. The pair of them play peeping tom to a sleeping woman in a later scene but she wakes up as Harry tries to fondle her breasts. She screams at him, resulting in him running from the house. The film ends with him masturbating to the photograph he's stolen from the cinema.

In the second sequence Harry is nineteen. He suffers from such an acute case of acne that he draws reactions of mockery from those who look at him. In a scene reminiscent of the prom concert episode from *Ham on Rye* he finds his attempts to ask a girl to dance frustrated by his gross appearance. Things become farcical when he covers his face totally in toilet roll, leaving gaps only for the eyes and mouth. He comes back to the dance hall and again asks the girl to dance. Amazingly she says yes. Afterwards he gets drunk. He laughs uproariously as he lies down on the street cradling a bottle of liquor. When two policemen approach him with a poem he's written he tells them to destroy it and carry him into his house.

The final segment, based loosely on Bukowski's story 'The Copulating Mermaid of Venice, Calif.,' is the most evocative, and probably the reason he admired the film so much. Harry is now 33. After stealing a bottle of whiskey from a bar following a staged fracas, he and his friend see a corpse being put into a hearse. They steal it and Harry then has sex with the dead body, an experience he describes as 'the best fuck I ever had.' Overcome by grief afterwards, he refuses to bury the woman, instead taking her to the sea with him where he drowns both her and himself. By now we realize where the title of the film comes from.

It's a haunting vignette. The subject of necrophilia was never handled as sensitively as it is here nor is likely to ever be again.

Not too many people know about this film but it's a more faithful depiction of Bukowski's disenchantment with various forms of devotion than some of his more well-known work. Deruddere refused to tailor it towards a commercial audience. He sought to capture the pining lodged at the heart of desire without any compromises.

The screenplay for *Barfly* appeared the following year. Looking at the words on the page without images to go with them shows how contrived so many of the set-pieces were. Bukowski tried to make Chinaski and Wanda into two ethereal spirits misunderstood by the world but all the screenplay really succeeds in doing is portraying a pair of self-obsessed malcontents.

For much of the time he seems to strain at the leash to make a case for his protagonists. We see the beauty of the sewer in all his work to some extent but not because we've been bludgeoned into it, as is the way here. Two bruised souls bonding in the twin sanctuaries of boudoir and bar makes for a great storyline but the theme was handled with much more authenticity in films like *Ironweed* in years to come.

The screenplay is at its best when it demonstrates Bukowski's truculence rather than his self-righteousness. Simple lines which hit the subject on the head are what one remembers rather than the knowing tone of its weaker parts. Maybe Bukowski was too close to the material to do justice to it. A half-century of pain went into it and much of that it was still too raw.

1988 saw the publication of *The Roominghouse Madrigals,* a collection of his work from 1946 to 1966. There's a lot of metaphorical content here but little of the immediacy we see in the later work. It was comprised of material he published in magazines and chapbooks when he was starting out. In the Foreword he tells us he believes it's neither better nor worse than his other work - both opinions were proffered to him by friends - but merely different. This is the best way to approach it. If he'd always written like this it's unlikely he would have achieved iconic status but there's no gainsaying the book's inspirational content. It testifies to a more sensitive psyche than he usually vouchsafes us. 'I never revised or re-typed,' he also says in the foreword, 'To eliminate an error I would simply go over it thus: ########, and go on with the line. One magazine editor printed a group of my poems with all the ########s intact.'

At times the voice is bardic, at times muted to the point of unrecognizability. He writes about everything from death to the thoughts a man has while he's shaving. In later years he would adopt more of a 'commando raid' approach to his themes, landing on them briefly and then vamoosing, but the two-decade wingspan of this book gives us more pause. He writes about the ordinary in an extraordinary way.

The book is figuratively rich. Images lie clustered in on top of one another relentlessly. It's the kind of imagery that's more traditional in nature, more 'poetic,' if you liked, which is so unlike Bukowski.

Honesty is the keynote. This emanates from his past with 'whores and hospitals.' He refuses to play the 'culture vulture' game. The funniest poem in the collection is 'O, We Are the Outcasts.' He uses humor to demolish fatcat dilettantes who write poor work from comfortable studios and fiercely guard their womenfolk from the rapacious Bukowski, who may well corrupt them if he gets his grubby hands on them. There's a lot of anger as well. He channels it into a biting satire about those who believe there's only one way to write: the safe way. Nowhere more than here have we such an articulate exposition of his revulsion for those who've never had to go out on a limb for their art, who've never had to work shoddy jobs or miss a meal or sleep rough, which means they've had all that much more time to hone their skills – which are non-existent.

These poems *are* madrigals, as the book's title suggests. They're music - the sad, sad music of human pain. Bukowski's heart is a lonely hunter. He carves sentiments out of the dead wood of his past, the counterpoint of emotion drawing him into webs of language from which he doesn't always succeed in extricating himself. It's like a man silently screaming, soaking up the influences of different times and places in search of the jigsaw that is his life. But the jigsaw is missing a piece. If he was indeed a 'bastard angel', as some have suggested, it's his angelic self-that's on display here.

Even in such an ostensibly simple poem like 'Breakout' we see his desperation. Anger mixes with guilt when he's unable to come up with the rent for his landlord. It pushes him towards a premature exit. Forever on the move with his black cardboard case, he asks little from life and receives less. Something intangible keeps him going, some innate belief in himself, smothered between the depression and the fear. He may yet find a Jane Cooney Baker or a kindly editor. He may yet stave off hunger and thirst, may yet witness his work seeing the light of day before a heavy labor job has him back in the hospital or the madhouse. Or maybe the cemetery. He's always juggling absolutes like that. They give his work an edge of mania.

Bukowski published *Hollywood*, his third novel, in 1989. The *Barfly* experiences fueled it. Transcribed in the elliptical tones one had by now become familiar with, it had him being amusingly sardonic about the skullduggery that surrounds the movie industry. He hated most films he ever saw, he said once, so it comes as little surprise to anyone that *Barfly* is used to air some of his more treasured bad feelings about the movie cosmos.

He saw Hollywood as candy floss. The only reason people were entitled to praise certain films, he argued, was because the majority of them were so bad. (The cult of celebrity attaching itself to film stars also fazed him, so much so that when he met Arnold

310

Schwarzenegger in the early 1980s he told him he was 'a megalomaniac piece of shit.' Schwarzenegger appears to have been too dumbfounded to hit him).

If we expected *Hollywood Babylon* in *Hollywood* – and we were entitled to – we didn't get it. It isn't a corrosive tome. It would better be described as a laconic perspective on the deal-making ethos that permeates Tinseltown and the parasites that buzz around its perimeters. Although the names of the protagonists have been changed, such changes are slight enough to leave us in little doubt about who he's referring to. Jack Kerouac is Mark Derouac. Norman Mailer is Victor Norman. Jean-Luc Godard is Jon-Luc Modard. Taylor Hackford is Hector Blackford. Francis Ford Coppola is Frances Ford Lopalla. Weiner Herzog is Wenner Zergog.

Such changes, or rather non-changes, make the book more comical than anything else. It's significant that he doesn't even bother finishing the disclaimer in the frontispiece, which would prevent him from possible libel charges, writing 'This is a work of fiction and any resemblance between the characters and persons living or dead is purely coincidental, etc.' (One imagines him yawning as he wrote that 'etc.')

Mickey Rourke was Rickey Yorke in the first draft. He changed it to Jack Bledsoe afterwards because there was 'no use asking for a lawsuit. Let them work for one.' So why did he make the other names so recognizable then? His actions seem confused here.

What made the book valuable, he felt, was that he was in the middle of all the hoopla when he wrote it and he still managed to get a perspective on it. He was on nodding terms with the sharks but didn't become infected by them. He smelt their blood and they smelt his and then he went home.

The anecdotes featuring such sharks are amusing but the book leaves one with a flat aftertaste. That was no doubt part of his intention seeing as he's dealing with a soulless milieu but you don't have to bore people to convey boredom. He runs the risk of doing that here.

The fun he had making *Barfly* is evident in *Hollywood* but the book is a victim of its downbeat tone. He spills far too much ink on the nuts and bolts of contractual stipulations. This is perhaps understandable considering all the problems he had with Barbet Schroeder trying to get *Barfly* onto the screen but it doesn't exactly make for engrossing reading.

As well as castigating the people behind the scenes, Bukowski also casts a bemused eye on the people who live out their careers in front of the cameras, those darlings who spend so much of their time adopting poses they eventually forget which life is the real one. He doesn't become aggressive with such beings, content to satirize them from distance as he soaks up the celluloid experience like a sponge. At the end of the day, he concludes, acting is just another job, not entirely unlike working in a biscuit factory or a ladies lingerie department.

Two-thirds of the way through the book he utters a long overdue paean to screenwriters, the unsung heroes of the movie medium, the people without whom nothing could get off the ground in the first place and yet who are often relegated to the status of fifth wheel once the cameras start rolling. Bukowski himself broke that tradition, being treated almost like royalty on the set, but he was the exception to prove the rule.

The filming of *Barfly*, he tells us, gave him mixed feelings. He revisited old haunts to try and jog his memory for how it used to be but shooting in the bars where he once drank filled him with a certain emptiness, as if you killed something in the act of trying to recapture it. Even his relationship with his wife suffered as a result of this, he tells us. The pair of them are in a world that isn't their own, a world where even melancholy has to be formalized.

Hollywood, of course, isn't only about Hollywood. Bukowski could never resist the temptation to bring all aspects of his life into everything he wrote about a certain topic and this book is no exception. In addition to the deal-makers and the hangers-on we get the racetrack, the days when he slept in alleyways, and the short tragic life of Jane. He also includes his terrifying experience in the charity ward.

The most amusing parts of the book occur when he's meeting reporters, answering their facile questions with one-liners. He doesn't understand why they seem to be interested in soliciting his views on anything other than literature, which may strike us as surprising considering he spent most of his life sounding off on any subject one cares to mention.

He portrays Hollywood more as a banal world rather than a decadent one. The pages documenting the discussion of percentages are as relevant today as when they were written. As a reference book, however, it's too personal to be the definitive guide to a milieu it purports to unpick. He Bukowski-zes Hollywood rather than letting Hollywood Hollywoodize him.

He was now, technically speaking, a member of the elite. When Madonna came to visit him with Sean Penn the neighbors gawped.

He didn't know why. She meant nothing to him. So Madonna called. So what?

He saw her as being infatuated with the bitch goddess of fame. He quoted Pascal: 'Only things done in quietude are worth more than the applesauce shit of a turkey.' When she asked him if he might be interested in appearing in her book *Sex* - the title was about as imaginative as the contents - he gave her a flat no. He said he was bored with women who talked about the subject as if they invented it.

There was bad chemistry between Madonna and Bukowski on all fronts

He went out for a meal with Penn and herself one night and they let him pay. That pissed him off seeing as they were both millionaires and he wasn't too long out of the trashcan. He felt he was being used so he wrote a poem about it, which he then sent to John Martin for publication. But then Penn brought him out a few times and he realized he was generous after all. He asked Martin to pull the poem in case he was offended by it so he did. In time he came to see Penn like he did Barbet Schroeder: a person who lived in the shit of Hollywood but was somehow above it.

Bukowski also grew in Penn's estimation. Their friendship grew deeper and they started to see more of one another. Bukowski even became friends with Penn's mother. 'You're just an old phony,' she said to him, refusing to be taken in by his crabby credentials.

Notwithstanding the friendship with Penn, the only way Bukowski thought he could survive Hollywood was by keeping his distance from the glitterati. He thought this was what destroyed John Fante, so after *Barfly* and *Hollywood* he left it behind him. 'I took the money and ran,' he said, 'and ran and ran and ran.'

The day after he finished writing *Hollywood* he woke up with a fever. He shivered so much he thought he was dying. His temperature was 103 degrees. For the next week he couldn't eat or sleep. He could hardly make it to the toilet. When he started to lose weight he went to his doctor but he could find nothing wrong. All he said was that he had an iron deficiency. When he went for a second opinion he got the same diagnosis. It continued with a third. The last doctor put him on herbs and acupuncture but there was no change.

The mystery was solved shortly afterwards when he had to take one of his cats to a vet. He told him about his problems. The vet said, 'Maybe you have tuberculosis.' He was right. 'It took a cat doctor to tell me what was wrong with me,' Bukowski said, 'after visiting all the high-priced professionals. This confirmed me in a view I had about doctors already. They're all full of shit.'

He didn't know how he'd contracted it. It could have been in his system since youth – an uncle had died of consumption – or he might have picked it up from one of the rat-infested dives he lived in as a young man.

He was placed on a course of antibiotics. The first thing most alcoholics ask when they're put on antibiotics is, 'Can I drink with these?' In Bukowski's case the answer was no. In the old days he probably wouldn't have obeyed such an injunction but now he did. Neither did the abstention seem to bother him too much. He told Linda he didn't miss drink for the first time in his life, that he was too sick to care about it. This was surprising. (In a poem called 'a gigantic thirst' published in the posthumous collection *The People Look Like Flowers at Last* he contradicts it). He went back on the bottle when Marina got married in 1989 but it was only for a day. What doctor could have denied him the pleasure of walking his beloved daughter up the aisle with a beer in him?

By now Marina had become a charming young woman. She was definitely her father's daughter in her appearance - same shape of the face, same mouth, same kind eyes - but her personality was markedly different. The daughter of Los Angeles' most combustible man had grown up into one of its most tranquil citizens. Did she find her youth difficult? 'No, just different. I was glad it was different. Asked if she found it difficult being ferried between her mother and father during her formative years she said, 'I knew I was loved by both of them. That was all that mattered.' Speaking of Bukowski more generally she said, 'He's the most honest man I ever met.' Even his enemies would have agreed with that.

Septuagenarian Stew, another poetry collection, was published in 1990. Bukowski was coming up to 70 now but he was still refusing to act his age. 'I feel the same as did at 20,' he claimed, 'or maybe younger. At 20 I didn't know how to have fun. Your face changes as you get older but you don't change, especially if you're a writer. Writers are essentially children. For most of my life I've behaved as a child. Why should I change now?'

He dedicated the book to his friend and former co-editor Neeli Cherkovski. It was published to coincide with his seventieth birthday. It combined both prose and poetry, a format that would become a feature of future collections.

It's vintage Bukowski. There's a hilarious story called 'Bad Night' which features a man undergoing a midlife crisis. He negotiates the path from phone sex to the real thing with equally disastrous results. This is the ultimate sterility trip as Buk paints the sleaze industry with just the right amount of wry lunacy. Elsewhere we get revisions of the theme of the famous writer evaluating his new status. We move from the begrudgery of 'The writers' to the movie premiere horror of 'Mad Enough' to a man in a dentist's office (in 'Blocked') who ranges from pedophiliac fantasies to an old-fashioned grope to kick his brain into action so he can fill a porn mag writing slot.

Giving a voice to the so-called 'underclass' with his hard-bitten dialogue and his nickel-and-dime thrills, the stories find him in inspirational form. They engage us whether he's writing about his father (a man who was 'mean without even trying') or simply sending up his own myth.

In these pages we have a jaded Bukowski - or, as he refers to himself in 'The Writers', 'Fucktowski'. Jaded but not without joy. He dusts himself down from the flophouses and the crazy women for another hit of booze. He may be 'half-dead' from fame but that still leaves him half to play with before he reaches the drop zone. And for the time being, maybe that's enough.

He doesn't want to go under, like Manny Hyman in *There's No Business*, who's outstripped by gimmickry. Better to play the hacks at their own game, to bullshit the bullshitters. Poverty creates neither nobility nor great writers, he assures us, so he'll keep his BMW and his electric typewriter, thank you very much. This isn't compromise, baby, it's *survival*.

One of the more meditative poems in the collection is 'the burning of the dream,' which deals with the L.A. Public Library, a building which 'most probably' kept him from becoming 'a bank robber/a/wife-/beater/a butcher or a/motorcycle policeman.' He spent many years inside these walls sampling books like food as he immersed himself in the lives of writers for whom he felt an almost instant kinship. The bad ones spurred him on to create his own compositions. Most of these came back to him from editors' slushpiles in the early years but the very writing of them saved him from a depression that could have driven him under.

Writers who didn't appeal to him he lists as Shakespeare, Shaw, Tolstoy, Frost and F. Scott Fitzgerald. They shared a penchant for tameness and the well-honed phrase, two qualities that were anathema to him. Neither did they live rough, which seems to have beer a prerequisite for being appreciated by him. He admits his judgments in this regard have come from his 'forced manner of living' rather than his reason. One imagines he would have preferred to read a bad writer who'd been 'on the bum' rather than a good one who hadn't. You always had to win your spurs with Bukowski. He despised smugness.

'The summing up' takes us into the Jane Cooney Baker phase. He remembers the years when they lived in hotel rooms and shirked work, the alcoholic over-indulgences of each of them acting as the balm by which the other sought their alibi, or rationalization. Paid on Friday and broke on Monday, they rolled

318

out of bed to slake their thirst with the same passion as a starving person coming upon an oasis in the desert. It's a sweet paean to a lifestyle that killed one of them and ought to have killed the other, delivered in a totally unsentimental manner that's par for the course for him. He doesn't put a gloss of nostalgia over the time and neither does he coarsen it. The last phrase says it all: 'we did what we did.'

'My best friend' works a similar beat. One of his many 'life in miniature' poems, it deals with the years when he dragged his suitcase from boarding house to boarding house, taking up jobs when he needed them and dropping them just as suddenly. Jane isn't by his side this time but he drinks just as much as he did when he was with her, 'sucking on gin on the mattresses of nowhere.' He inhales the 'dirty game' of work and then exhales it again, drifting on to the next possibility as he leaves behind him all those who aren't aware of their own stultification.

'Sometimes it's easier to kill somebody else' performs the unique function of being funny about a suicide attempt of his that went wrong. When it doesn't succeed he decides that life, miserable and all as it was, was marginally better than gassing himself into oblivion. John Martin gets a tribute in 'moving up the ladder' as Bukowski relates the circumstances of his discovery by that man in 1965. It's taken him 25 years to write about the by now legendary rendezvous with Martin.

Another seminal moment in his life occurs in 'poem for lost dogs' when he finally stands up to a barman who's been using him as a punching bag for so long that he expects him to roll over. But one day he decides so fight back, to stop being the light relief for the other patrons, just as he decided he wasn't going to take his father's beatings one day.

'The drunk on the next bar stool' is a poem that illustrates how uncomfortable he feels in company. He said in an interview with Barbet Schroeder that it disturbed him if a person even brushed against him in a crowd. Here he outlines the discomfort he feels in an elevator: 'I am trapped in an airless cavern of madness — a dull, indecent madness.' He also exhibits his Garboesque persona in 'I like your books' where he fobs off an overly-curious fan at the track. He sometimes spoke to strangers there but only on certain subjects. His writing was off limits. The man in this poem crosses that line and gets put in his place as a result. Bukowski ends by musing resignedly that he's probably lost another one of his fans, adding dryly, 'Let 'em go back to Kafka.'

'My father' again brings us back to a theme with which he seems to have had an almost Freudian obsession. Each time he writes about this man, however, he puts a different spin on it, constantly re-evaluating his relationship to him for a new perspective on it. His father caused him to drop out of society because of his warped attitude to acquisitiveness, he alleges, but when he went to skid row he saw greed there as well.

As a result of this disappointment he surrenders himself to the world of BMWs and the American Express Gold Card in the poem 'gold in your eye.' It's set years after his hobo experiences. By now he's a celebrity, having attained the material comfort he never lusted after like his father but which he likes to wallow in betimes to annoy those people who've romanticized his barfly years out of all proportion and who are now resentful of his newfound prosperity. Are they worried about the condition of his soul or are they simply a group of sad fuckers eaten up with jealousy?

A more reflective tone is evident towards the end of the book. In 'the orderly' he writes about sitting on a tin chair outside the x-ray lab as death on 'stinking wings,' wafts through the halls outside. At this point of his life, as he writes in 'luck,' time is moving towards him instead of him towards it. In 'celebrating this' he assures us he'll outstay his welcome on the planet as long as he can - and hopefully expire at his typewriter. Three wheels on his wagon, he's still rolling along.

Exactly how long he could continue to cheat death was open to question. 'I don't feel I have too long left,' he said one day after coming home from the track. 'Even though I won $212 I feel the light is dimming. I looked down at my feet when I was coming out today and saw I was wearing a brown shoe and a black one.' He would have been amused by this a few years before but now it was a possible suggestion of impending dementia. Old age was creeping on. He said he found it tiring even getting out of bed in the morning, putting 'one foot on the floor and then the other.' Maybe he was finally getting 'the bill' for his profligate past.

As if old age wasn't bad enough – not to mention the tuberculosis – he now contracted leukemia. It was a shock but he seemed almost immune to shocks now. He accepted the news philosophically, or at least he seemed to. After the life he lived, every day was a gift from the gods. He had no right to expect to live as long as he did but having survived so long he thought he might have a few years left in him. Now that was in doubt.

He submitted himself to treatment for it. The trips to hospital for tests reminded him of those he'd taken as a child. The difference now was that he wasn't just facing embarrassment or humiliation. This was 'the big casino.' Was he on the way out? His negative thinking was made worse when his next door neighbor died. Then her husband broke his hip. He was 96. They'd been married 47 years.

The first full-scale biography of him appeared in 1991. It was called simply *Hank*. (A later edition amended that to *Bukowski: A Life*). It was written by Neeli Cherkovski, his friend of many years. He was the obvious choice to write it. He knew Bukowski better than anyone and had kept a record of many of their nights drinking together. He seemed to have a photographic memory for the details of such nights if his book is anything to go by. Bukowski also allowed himself to be 'interviewed' by Cherkovski for the book, and to have the contents of the interviews taped.

The first time Cherkovski met Bukowski he showed him some poems he'd written about him. Bukowski took a look at them and threw them into the fire. In the following years, however, Cherkovski's poems started appearing opposite Bukowski's in magazines. He then started talking seriously to him about literature. He mentioned Celine, Steinbeck, the early Saroyan. Many writers, he said, became famous too early and lost the feeling for why they wanted to do what they did. Others became corrupted by wealth or glory. What you had to do was ignore the paths of others, to stamp out your own ground.

Cherkovski saw Bukowski as a cross between Humphrey Bogart and a character out of Raymond Chandler. He wrote a brilliant profile of him in his book *Whitman's Wild Children*. It was because of this that Bukowski thought Cherkovski should write his biography. Cherkovski was honored to be given the job of being his 'Boswell.' The pair of them spent months preparing it. Bukowski told him everything he could think of about his life. He knew a lot of it already, obviously, by having shared so much of it with him.

When the book was published, however, Bukowski didn't like it. He felt Cherkovski cobbled together a hodge-podge of reminiscences in an overly-fussy way and didn't do enough with them. He had a point here. It was heavy-handed in parts and also devoted too much space to his early years. For Bukowski it lacked bite. The language didn't live. 'He didn't capture my madness,' he said. Cherkovski argued that much of the stories he'd told him were in such bad taste they were unusable. Bukowski didn't agree. For him, these would have been the best parts. (He put some of this into a later edition of the book).

Reception of the book was mixed. Some people praised it for its conscientious tone but others thought Cherkovski had missed a trick, that he failed to capture Bukowski's essence. Cherkovski felt he was never fully appreciated by the reading public for his closeness to Bukowski when they were both unknown writers. 'I was his friend then,' he lamented, 'but when he became famous I was seen as little more than a hanger-on.'

Bukowski had a major problem with the way Cherkovski portrayed the relationship he had with Linda King in the book. He thought King came across as the 'good guy' and himself as the villain. He was particularly annoyed by Cherkovski's narration of an incident involving King where she clawed his face to ribbons during a row. In Cherkovski's version of events Bukowski threatens King with a frying pan. Asked why he did this when he knew the real facts of the matter, Cherkovski told Bukowski he didn't want to offend King. 'But you don't care about offending me!' Bukowski said. Cherkovski laughed in embarrassment.

Later that year the Cannes Film Festival screened *Cold Moon,* a French film based on two of Bukowski's short stories, 'Trouble with the Battery' and 'The Copulating Mermaid of Venice.' Its most unseemly episode concerned two men having sex with a corpse. It had the dubious honor of winning the Worst Film Award that year.

The Last Night of the Earth Poems was the final Black Sparrow book to be published while he was still alive. It had an authoritative edge absent from much of his previous work. It was as if he was finally content to wear the mantle of Writer in Residence. Aged 72, one might say it was about time.

In the first poem of the collection, 'jam', he manages to invest a mundane topic (traffic gridlock) with significance. He conveys the monotony of his immobility so graphically that the final image of him as a dinosaur crawling home to die doesn't appear in any way incongruous.

'Days like razors, nights full of rats' is another rollercoaster ride through his back pages but with the added dimension that he now etches in his schizoid nature of 'library days bar nights.' Libraries and bars comprised the lion's share of his young life but they could hardly be more opposite. He was quiet in the former but in the latter his other self-came out. (Maybe the Bukowski idea of heaven would be a library that served whisky).

'Trollius and trellises' is a tribute to John Martin. Bukowski writes frivolously of their 'unholy alliance' and expresses a fear that Martin, being a decade younger than him, will soon retire from poetry publishing, thus making him into someone who'll have to totally re-invent himself for his successor. 'Thank you,' he ends up by saying, for locating him at 5124 De Longpre Avenue, 'somewhere between alcoholism and madness.' They were both relatively unknown in those days but together they laid down the gauntlet for a generation.

'Death is smoking my cigars' is one of the many poems in the book dealing with mortality. The Reaper first announced its presence 47 years ago when Bukowski was starving for his art and bleeding from both ends. Now that he's a 'minor success' it appears again: more threatening this time because he has more to lose.

Other poems explore more familiar themes. In 'hock shops' he reveals that no matter how much pawnbrokers exploited him in the past he never grudged them their percentage. Their scraps of money kept him alive when nobody else wanted to buy his typewriters or suits or gloves or watches even for a pittance. No more than the library or the bar, this was another 'marvelous sanctuary' where hard luck cases could keep body and soul together when a salary wasn't coming in.

In 'upon this time' he goes into the subject of writer's block, which isn't a condition one imagines this incredibly prolific man would ever have suffered from. The same theme is a concern in 'only one Cervantes' but this time he manages to exorcise it by writing about it. The next three poems are concerned with death in various degrees, most-specifically 'D' where his doctor tells him he has cancer, albeit of a non-life-threatening form. 'If I had cancer,' the doctor says, 'I'd rather have your kind'. (The poem doesn't give us Bukowski's real-life response: 'I'd rather you had it too.')

After these we get perhaps the most beautiful poem in the collection, 'in the bottom.' It deals with one of his many dark nights of the soul as he chronicles the 'suicide oceans of night'. Each verse begins with the same line ('in the bottom of the hour') and takes us through a catalogue of tragedies from the back pages of history, rounding itself off with Bukowski himself, who's become increasingly mystified by life. He reaches no conclusions but this is far from being a depressing poem. In fact it's curiously uplifting in its lyricism.

In Section 3 of the book he bathes himself in the trivia of his days. Life is a movie, he tells us, in which we're the willing or unwilling cast members. We negotiate its boredom with varying degrees of success, fending off pressmen ('the interviewers', 'between races') smoothies ('the aliens'), nonentities ('splashing') and insomnia ('darkling'). In the latter poem, again, failure to sleep brings on thoughts of The Big Sleep.

'Luck was a lady' is a confessional poem about the bad days when his vain attempts at chatting up women were summarily rejected. When he watched them being picked up by men better turned out than himself it was like the prom concert experience all over again. He seethed with resentment about this, imagining he would be 'the idiot in the schoolyard' all his life.

'Crime and punishment' also trades on his childhood, on all those days he was sent to the principal's office for misbehavior and forced to stand in a glassed-in phone booth for hours as a punishment. It ends on an upbeat note with him getting some degree of satisfaction from the fact that the principal is subsequently imprisoned for embezzlement of school funds. The irony is choice. The ostensible pillar of the community cooks the books as the supposed ne'er-do-well (who will one day become mega-famous) stands suspended in a claustrophobic space.

'Inactive volcano' is a typical example of a slender narrative that makes an interesting point simply. Now famous, he goes into a bar he used to frequent when he was a down-and-out. The bartender remembers him from the old days and is bewildered to see him with a member of the jet set. Bukowski gives no explanations to the barman about his new situation. There isn't any need to because he hasn't gone soft. He's the same man he always has been. He's wearing a more expensive suit but he still has the same heart. What's more, he may yet go crazy again, even with his glitterati friend. The poem ends with the playfully ominous: 'wait and see.'

Section 4 begins with 'dinosauria, we.' This has some interesting vignettes but for most of the time it's just assembly line apocalyptic fare. It isn't a bad poem but Bukowski is always more engrossing when he's being personal rather than issuing a polemic, however heartfelt.

A different side of his character is captured in 'my first computer poem.' Here we have a harbinger of the new Bukowski. He's been dragged kicking and screaming into the modern world by his wife, who bought him a present of the computer for his seventieth birthday. He wonders if Whitman would be laughing at him from the grave at such a compromise to technology. He decides to press on regardless, viewing his new machine as a beginning rather than an end.

Bukowski using a computer was the ultimate sell-out for some people. The 'purists' saw it as a betrayal but Bukowski had a different slant on the situation.

'Anything that corrects my spelling,' he joked, 'can't be all bad.' Even so, it's hard to think of him managing to 'bet on the muse' using such a contraption.

In 'young in New Orleans' he leaves us in little doubt about how reclusive he is, preferring the rats in his apartment to the humans. Even being crazy, he says, isn't so bad if you're undisturbed. Something else he prefers to people is music, as he makes clear in 'classical music and me.' He tells us he became hooked on that type of music as a young man, which resulted in him buying out the entire stocks of certain record shops for his 'fix.' After he went on the road he had to leave his records behind him. Thereafter he was dependent on the whims of radio stations to entertain him. When everything else in his life was going wrong, classical music got him through. Books also helped, as he makes plain in 'the word.' This punch-drunk hobo was an unlikely literary scholar but in the dark times his bibliophilia kept him from murdering somebody - or himself.

There are many other quality-studded poems in these pages. They usher in a more mature style even if he's still harping on many of his old obsessions. Sooner or later everything that ever happened to him seems to have found its way into one of his books, either as a straight incident or an excuse to make a point about an incident. The former scenario is always more effective.

His health was in tatters when the book hit the shelves. His body was finally putting up the white flag. He'd just come through a painful operation for cataracts and was battling the leukemia was well. He now started a course of chemotherapy for it, which caused him to lose his hair. The doctors told him things didn't look good but he didn't believe them. Why should he have? They'd been wrong too many times before.

He tried to treat himself with alternative medicine when they said the chemotherapy wasn't working. He embraced Buddhism, the healing methods of Deepak Chopra. He even started drinking herbal tea. He played with his cats in the garden like a benign septuagenarian, the Don Corleone of San Pedro.

He'd negotiated so many crises in the past he could have been forgiven for imagining he was immortal. His ambition was to celebrate his eightieth birthday in the eighth month of the new millennium. 'I intended to live to be 80,' he'd written in *Women*, 'so I could fuck an 18 year old woman.'

Bukowski had an ambition to live until he was 80 so he could see in the new millennium. (Al Berlinski)

He'd always believed good writers should be given longer lives than anyone else. In his poem 'the feel of it' he wrote that 69 was too young for Aldous Huxley to have died. Huxley had helped him through some dark nights. Did that not count for something? Did it not count for something that Bukowski himself had done the like by others?

He admitted he'd drunk more booze than most people had water but he was still around. The doctors who told him he was killing himself for the past two decades were now dead themselves. He'd supped with the devil using a short spoon and come away smiling. Was there going to be another twist in the tale?

In 1993 his doctor told him he had about a year to live. The way he said it stopped Bukowski in his tracks. There were no jokes now, no claims to see in the new millennium. He listened to his words without replying. For once, one imagines, he believed what a doctor was telling him.

Within that year he still continued to write and to send out his poems to magazines. No matter how famous he became – or how ill – he still carried an aura of the struggling scribe about him. Every time he saw his name in print, no matter how obscure the magazine was he got the same thrill as when he saw his first published work in *Story* in 1944.

He also had a poem published in *Poetry* magazine now. He'd been sending his work there for four decades without success and suddenly they said yes to one of his compositions. That seemed ironic to him. He'd got there by the scenic route. His first story was published in *Story* and now maybe his last poem was going into *Poetry*. There was a kind of arc to it, a completion.

He bore his ill health with fortitude, informing nobody outside his immediate circle that he wasn't well. The only inkling people had about his predicament was his failure to reply to their letters. He was usually prompt in this regard, replying generally by return of post unless there was some reason not to.

He claimed he had a yellow streak down his back but people who call themselves cowards rarely are and Bukowski was no exception. He proved that by the way he negotiated his final illness. His life up to now had been a crusade against self-pity. He wasn't going to change that now.

He always said he feared life more than death. He had reason to. Few people took as many chances in the course of it as he did. Now it looked like it was about to end.

He'd arrived at Terror Street but he showed no terror. 'Dying might be bad,' he said, 'but it can't be worse than hangovers.'

Life was a joke and death a bigger one. The coming in and the going out were equally absurd. The only thing human beings had to work with was that little dash between the date of their birth and the date of their death. Everything else was out of their hands.

A man could live eighty years and not have lived. A man could fly past your window in a dinner jacket, having jumped to his death for reasons best known to himself. A man in apparent good health could die reaching for a glass of water one morning, the tap still running as he fell. A woman could die in India and not have her body reclaimed by her family. A woman could be given a Christmas gift of one too many bottles of whisky for comfort and bleed her guts out onto the floor.

On the other hand a man could have a gun put to his head and not die. Or he could try to kill himself and fail. He could be sentenced to death in the charity ward of a county hospital and live for four more decades. He might even see off TB and leukemia as he once saw off a bleeding ulcer.

He still had some work to do. Did this not entitle him to a stay of execution? Or had he been given this already?

If he'd died in the fifties his life would have been as meaningless as that of his father. He was richer now than that man could ever have dreamed about but he'd gladly give back every cent for more time on this cursed earth. There were no pockets on a shroud.

He'd given death many clean shots at him in years gone by but it hadn't taken advantage of them. Now it was making up for lost time. 'Death, at last, is a bore,' he said, 'No more than pulling a shade. We do not die all at once but piece by piece, little by little.' No doubt he was thinking of John Fante and his amputations.

Hemingway was right. The world killed everyone finally, not only in the body but in the mind as well. It didn't matter if you were opening a can of beans or tying your shoelaces, it would get you and kill you. The secret was to know that and expect it. The cemetery had always been 'the best bet on the board.'

He could have died in any decade of his life after he reached adulthood and nobody would have been surprised. Each year he lived was like a present from whatever deity presided over hoboes. It was like a reprieve given out for whatever reason.

He'd lived five lives in one. He'd drunk the good wine and the bad, sampled the mad women and the sane ones, communed with angels and devils, and was still breathing. His burn-out, in a way, had been in his pre-fame days. He destroyed himself before 'Bukowski' arrived.

His life had been a revolt against death but now it was time to fold his tent. The boat would finally be stilled as it lay tethered to the harbor. Death was battering at him 'like a wild bat enclosed in my skull.'

Dying didn't depress him. What depressed him was what he was leaving behind: the drunken nights and the drunken days…and what he was leaving behind. A wife. A daughter. His work. He was more concerned about posterity's view of him than anything else. He feared the vultures more than the worms.

Was there another roll of the dice somewhere else? He didn't know. 'Maybe there's a hell,' he said, 'If there is, all the poets will

331

be there reading their works and I'll have to listen. I'll be drowned in their preening vanity, their overflowing self-esteem.'

He decided to do without what he called 'the God fix,' decided to take his chances with whatever apocalypse materialized or failed to. Faith was too convenient a way to make sense of the madness of existence. It was a comfort blanket people pulled around themselves in times of trial, a *deus ex machina* that served as hypnosis for those who couldn't face the world naked. 'Faith is all right for those who have it,' he said, 'Just don't load it on me. I have more faith in my plumber than I do in the eternal being. Plumbers do a good job. They keep the shit flowing.'

There would be no crucifix in this deathhand. Life was where it happened for him, life with its stinking furnace, where flowers occasionally dug their way through the cement, where occasionally a hard heart melted and gave you a blast of hope. But it was never meant to be forever. Only books lasted forever.

He died in Linda's arms on March 9th 1994. The official cause of death was pneumonia, the chemotherapy having played havoc with his immune system. Most people expected him to get cirrhosis of the liver. He dodged that particular bullet but another one had lain in the long grass.

He once said he wanted to die at the typer with a bottle of wine to his left and Mozart to his right. He didn't quite get that but he came close. Linda said his face looked so peaceful as he died that she was reminded of a new-born baby.

Pamela Brandes heard the news on the radio as she was driving to work. She was shocked to hear him described as a 'pornographic poet.' Could such a trivialization have been allowed for any other writer of his genius? She yelled at the radio, 'Is that the best you can do after over thirty years of prose, poetry and even a screenplay?'

Linda King didn't hear the news for a few days. She'd dropped out of his life completely after he got together with the 'other'

Linda. (She rang him once but he handed the phone to Linda Lee after speaking to her for a few moments, a signal to her that he was now gone from her). 'Without me,' she said, 'he wouldn't have written some of the best love poems ever.' That was probably true. And neither would she. 'He told me I'd never be able to write without him,' she said, 'so when I do a poem now I keep his sculpted head nearby. It's like my muse.'

The high priest of black art was gone. Every few years there were rumors that he'd died, usually put out by his enemies. Now those enemies could dance on his grave if they wished. Would they? Maybe not. He wasn't a threat to them anymore now.

He left a staggering 45 books behind him, a tally of near-Dickensian proportions. The demand for them would be constant in the coming years, as would the demand for even the tiniest bit of information about him from all the forums and websites devoted to him. (If someone told him this in the 1960s he would have referred them to the nearest shrink).

The newspaper obituaries were riddled with the kind of clichés Brandes heard on the radio, trotted out by those who quite possibly had never picked up a book of his in their lives. They referred to the bard of the bar, the laureate of low life, the dirty old man who spent his life worshipping at the altar of excess. Lazy copytakers spent their time digging up accounts of him that had been on file for up to twenty years.

He was buried in the clothes he wore to the track. A pen he used for filling in his racing sheets was placed in one of his pockets. In all the years at the track he'd probably broken about even, which was a lot better than most. He'd beaten the con. But the con of death was non-negotiable. It was a marked dice.

The funeral was a subdued affair presided over by three Buddhist monks. Bukowski had been studying Buddhism himself in his last months, seeking from it the tranquility that had come his way since meeting Linda.

Those who cared most about him were present at the graveside: Linda Lee, Marina, John Martin, Carl Weissner, Sean Penn, Gerard Locklin. Michael Montfort would have been there but he had to be in court. Red Stodolski, the owner of a bookshop that stocked many rare Bukowski titles, was there as well. The other mourners were non-literary friends from local shops and coffee houses. Neeli Cherkovski was barred from attending. He wasn't sure why. 'Hank and Linda drove up to my father's funeral a few years ago,' he said, 'and they were very sympathetic.' He thought the problem might have gone back to when he wrote his biography of Bukowski. He suspected Linda was still annoyed about the way he'd whitewashed Linda King at her husband's expense.

Penn and Martin delivered eulogies. Carl Weissner was too emotional to give one. Most people only knew Weissner as Bukowski's translator. They didn't realize how close he was to him, how much he poured his heart out to him in letters and phone calls over the years.

In a poem called 'eulogies,' published in the posthumous collection *The People Look Like Flowers at Last,* Bukowski said that he wanted to reverse the normal funeral procedure where people only speak well of the dead and let them speak badly of them. He was probably thinking of himself in his relentless quest for the truth but there was no danger of that here. The silence of the lambs followed the death of the lion.

At a short reception after the funeral, nobody drank alcohol. It was an irony that didn't go unnoticed. It was like the calm after the storm. The world had suddenly become sober. At Musso & Franks, his favorite restaurant, the barman cancelled all orders for Liebfraumilch for the day as a gesture of respect.

A few days later there was a reading for him. Penn was at this too. So was the Irish singer Sinead O'Connor. She sang a *capella* ballad about grief to commemorate him. O'Connor was one of the few feminists who liked his work. She ignored the façade of grossness for the complex man behind it. Penn went on to dedicate a film to him. It was his directorial debut, *The Crossing Guard.* It starred Jack Nicholson, the actor he always said he wanted to play him in a film about his life.

His tombstone carried the inscription 'Don't Try', a phrase that encapsulated his philosophy both of living and writing. Over-elaboration had been the bane of too many and they fell on their faces as a result of it. You had to live life like the grass that grew by the weir, he thought, taking it where it called you without asking too many questions. What would happen would happen and you had to deal with that. You had to look into the chasm and let your disappointments waft back at you without a murmur. Blessings usually only came when you pretended you stopped wanting them. This was life's sick joke on humanity. It was why none of us could ever be fully happy.

Was Bukowski ever happy? Maybe the answer to that question depends on what we mean by the word. Did he deserve to be? As Albert Camus said of his character Meursault, maybe he was the only Christ we deserved.

He was a cynic only in the sense that cynics are deflated idealists. Bukowski the dreamer was always trying to crawl out from under the mire. He was like a diseased romantic who stared into the abyss until the abyss stared back.

'Better always to have the reader believe you're a son of a bitch,' he said, 'That way he'll remember you longer.' Sean Penn took up the point. 'He was one of those guys,' he said, 'who was given every opportunity in life to become a prick but he didn't take it. He became more like a pussycat.' 'I know I'm good,' Bukowski had told Penn earlier, 'but I prefer people to think I'm bad because it gives me a dimension.'

The Dirty Old Man Lives On

All we gotta do is die. And after livin', that's a break. (Bukowski)

The year after Bukowski died, the BBC made a documentary of him called 'The Ordinary Madness of Charles Bukowski.' For many people in the UK it was their first chance to see how he looked, how he spoke, how he lived his life. It had commentaries from many people who knew him.

His friend John Thomas read one of his poems. The two Lindas spoke. King talked about the night she broke into his apartment and took all his books, firing them at his windows to punish him for his various infidelities.

She made it out to be a comic act but when she said, 'That was one of the last times I saw him,' you felt there was sadness burrowing under the surface.

The documentary set the tone for a wealth of material associated with him that appeared by and about him in the following years.

There were DVDs of poetry readings he gave, some of them rare, and CDs of a similar nature.

Memoirs and chapbooks appeared, and occasional literary magazines featuring work generally thought lost.

People like Bob Dylan read his poetry on the radio. Items associated with him began to appear on eBay, some o them fetching prices that would have made him turn in his grave.

His face adorned key rings, fridge magnets.

His quotes were featured on coffee mugs, on T-shirts.

Bob Dylan became a fan of Bukowski after he died

More important than all of these developments was the appearance of much of his previously unpublished poetry. The posthumous collections of verse put out by Black Sparrow Press are as fascinating as anything Bukowski published while he was alive. Many of these are huge. It's been said that some of his individual poetry collections are larger than the total collected works of T.S. Eliot. When you think of the number of collections he published, the overall tally is staggering. Some of the poems in them are mediocre, of course, but it's still worth reading them for the gems. Even bad Bukowski poems usually have some great lines in them. His mind was such a kaleidoscope he never ceases to surprise us.

Three volumes of letters have also been published. These rank with the most explosively frank discourses of any writer in any generation. He tears his heart out of himself and lays it across the page time and again, making us wonder if this is the same man who could be so cruel in many of his relationships with people. They read like antitheses to the poems and stories, filled as they are labyrinthine clutter instead of the simple diction he became famous for, the preferred Bukowski parlance.

He throws the furnace of his heart on the page like verbal napalm. The tumble of thoughts seems hallucinogenic at times. It's as if he's on a bad trip. Images flood from him like lava as he fulminates on everything from money due to him for books to the meaning of life. He avoids capital letters, avoids paragraphs, avoids any of the niceties of convention as he rants on about his predicament at the bottom of the totem pole — and, later, the top. If anybody is in any doubt that Bukowski wasn't a passionate man they should check out these volumes. In them he ranges from tortured pleading to cackling like a hyena from hell. They're written in blood, sweat and tears.

They're also awash with detail. He cashes a check in a bank and that gets a mention. He goes to pee in mid-letter in another instance. He drops ash on his one good pair of trousers and burns a hole in the leg. He gets hemmed in by his neighbor in the parking spot and blows a fuse. He waves to a child playing basketball. He overtakes a motorist on the freeway for a challenge. He sings songs from *Oklahoma* with his landlady. In themselves these incidents are hardly worthy of mention but he brings us so far into every aspect of his life they form an integral part of the patchwork quilt of his days. At this level we're not so much reading letters as diary entries.

Sometimes when a poet writes prose he does so in a prosaic manner but many of these letters could be turned into poems themselves. Did he ever consider this? Once or twice, he said, he saw a good line and thought, 'That might do.' But he never saved anything: 'It would have been wrong. And unfair to whoever I was writing to. So I let it go. Something might have turned up later in a poem but if it did it was by accident, something in my subconscious.'

The range of themes was wide. Bukowski was someone who could speak about classical music and hemorrhoids all within the one paragraph. It wasn't the large tragedies of life that destroyed us, he claimed, it was the daily anguishes that did us in. A bill. A broken tap. A car that wouldn't start. A bad poem. A bitch with a sore head. Such drip-feeds of misery ate away at our souls.

Screams from the Balcony, a selection of his letters written from 1960 to 1970, is easily the best of them. He teases out his tensions in these letters, using them almost like a psychiatrist's couch. He writes like a perverse monk seeking nirvana through profanity. Los Angeles becomes Sodom or maybe even Armageddon. The imagery of apocalypse is never too far away. Here's a man who's been burned at the stake, who's still being burned every which way. Drink nearly kills him but also saves him. Literature does too. In his friendships he goes from gushing over people to describing them as scum.

The same names crop up repeatedly: Doug Blazek, Carl Weissner, William Corrington, Jon Webb and of course John Martin. You can nearly see the high octane fuel rising from the pages as he unleashes his imagination on us. If he harnessed the energy from the letters and channeled it into his creative work, one feels he could have made another dozen books out of the insights he throws away so nonchalantly here. Like a primitive man hacking through the undergrowth in a jungle he fulminates against the posers and the preeners, the smoothies and the cliché-merchants, the easyriders and the bandwagon-hoppers. Each day is a struggle but he battles on, his shoulder to the grindstone, waiting for the snow to melt with a new book, a daughter, a woman, a drink, or simply playing the ponies.

In the 1960s rejection appears to be the norm for him. The letters he sent out from the seventies to his death (published in *Reach for the Sun*) show an upswing in his fortunes but he still can't seem to relax.

A gentler strain is evident in his middle age but whether he's struggling to get a poem accepted by an obscure magazine or writing a novel that will be translated into twenty languages he's still the same man. Even in his final years when he's afflicted by leukemia he still manages a cheery attitude, whistling in the graveyard as death hints. Chemotherapy is just another trip down the highway.

When Doug Blazek asked for his permission to print some of his letters he told him to go ahead, there was nothing he was ashamed of anybody seeing. Frankness, after all, was what his whole life had been about.

Occasionally, however, his missives did him no favors, especially if they were written when he was drunk, and many of them were. He gives an example of one such in *Reach for the Sun*, written to an editor who'd accepted some of his poems. After the letter was received the poems were then rejected. The unethical nature of this procedure is appalling. Bukowski may have had the right to take legal action on account of it. Either way it demonstrated to him once again how untrustworthy editors were.

Pulp, his final novel, was also published posthumously. Dedicating it to 'bad writing' it was nonetheless an ambitious undertaking. After decades of writing almost totally about himself he finally stepped out of that groove to create a different persona, that of a gumshoe.

It was a pity he didn't carry through on the possibilities the new guise afforded. Instead he seems content to give us some hand-me-down Hammett, some overly convoluted plot twists and the all-too-familiar by-numbers existentialism.

The three-times-married, three-times-divorced private dick Nick Belane takes cases others won't touch. Belane is Henry Chinaski with a gun. He may talk more eschatologically (and less scatologically) but essentially it's the same whimsical buffoon we're dealing with.

It's more a pastiche than a novel proper. Bukowski pulls the curtain down on his novelistic career in the same move as pulling the carpet from under the genre. Maybe it would have been better served in a limited deluxe edition presented to friends.

It's hard to care about the plot. It seems to have been made up as he went along. He gets Belane into scrapes and then he has to get him out of them. He's on the trail of a red sparrow, a not very subtle metaphor for Black Sparrow Press). Its discovery might mean death for him but it could also mean catharsis – just as John Martin's Black Sparrow meant regeneration for Bukowski.

This could never have been his first book. If it was it's unlikely it would have been printed. As his last it has a certain curiosity factor but it's difficult to see why he cared so much for it when he was writing much superior poetry at the same time. It would have worked better as a long short story about a misanthrope searching for some grubby significance in a crummy world but asking the reader to follow him through 200 pages of minimalistic intrigue was too much. Having said that, the Bukowski humor is alive and well through the book, especially in scenes which have nothing at all to do with the plot, like where a sex-phone lady hangs up on him for insulting her. (Surely a precedent in this industry).

Literary experiments are fine, especially when they mean dispensing with a character a writer has lived with for most of his working life, but dispensing with Chinaski isn't really justified. Bukowski must have realized when he started running into brick walls with the characters. He probably began it with great expectations. It's a pity he didn't abandon it when he saw it was going nowhere.

Pulp is the ultimate whodunit because the 'it' is life and the 'who' is God – or maybe the devil. Belane inhabits an absurd cosmos where lost souls beat their brains out looking for shards of significance in the muck of their existence. Bukowski's message is that there *is* no message but, as ever, humor is his weapon against the darkness. When you laugh at the fates you somehow stunt their power. As his world collapses around him it's one of the few weapons Belane has left. He can shuffle off the mortal coil with a grin on his face.

Two years later *Betting on the Muse* appeared. Bukowski is back to familiar territory here. Right away we're into battle mode in 'splash,' which he informs us isn't a poem (because poems are dull) but rather a 'beggar's knife,' an apt description of his approach to his trade. In 'to hell and back in a buggy carriage' he chronicles the 'dried, dead, useless' days when his classmates got the beautiful women as they drove to the beach on sunny days, leaving him to bemoan his miserable lot alone. This was in 1935. Bukowski wasn't to know then that the gods would smile on him in his magic twilight.

'An evaluation' has him speculating on the number of hours of his life he's spent at the racetrack, a place as surreal as the bar or the boudoir but one which he returns to relentlessly. The murderous repetition is as bad as any nightmarish job he's ever been in. He continues to return to it for the same reason he kept going back to the bars: because he has nothing better to do. '12 minutes to post' has a more balanced appraisal of the same scenario because here he captures the conflicting emotions of the track: the boredom of waiting which turns to excitement as the names of the horses are read out and 'the lightning flash of hope' descends, promising to make something out of the nothing of their lives.

In 'Lousy Mail' he writes about the number of literary hopefuls who expect him to carry him up the ladder once they submit their treasured writings to him, which usually turn out to be abysmally bad. Having struggled himself, he was never in the mood to treat such a breed with kid gloves. 'They don't want to write,' he says, 'they want fame'. So he consigns their work to the nearest waste paper basket. Bad writers are one thing' arrogant bad writers are even worse.

'Let it inflate you' is a beautiful poem which evinces a Bukowski who has the patience to ride out the rawhide years, developing a mellowness that came with a love of the ordinary.

The last dozen or so poems in the book touch on notions of evanescence and eternity. He's aware he's nearing the end of the road but it's been a good ride. He has his woman, his fame and his cats. Why should he complain?

A darker note is struck in 'decline' and 'so now?' the last poem in the collection. Here he looks forward to the future with some trepidation. He waits for Godot, wishing he could 'ring in some bravery' but knowing he has to face what's in store for him on his own. Life is a 'lousy fix', but, as he says in an evocative phrase, 'the tree outside doesn't know.'

Al Winans wrote a memoir of his relationship with Bukowski in 1996, *The Second Coming Years.*

It was published by Kevin Ring's Beat Scene Press. A fond tribute to him, it put things down exactly as they happened. There was no attempt by Winans to settle any scores or have a go at his unpredictable old friend.

The only problem with the book was that at one point he has Bukowski telling him he'd like to see him and giving him directions to his house in San Pedro so he can do so. Such directions, for Winans, were 'poetic' so he included them in full in the book: 'From airport go west down Century,' etc. Unfortunately, they were so precise they resulted in many readers of the book calling to the address where Linda now lived on her own since Bukowski died.

'I got all sorts of crazy bikers arriving at my doorstep for years afterwards,' she pined.

Betting on the Muse was followed by *Bone Palace Ballet* in 1997. Beginning, as is customary, with poems about childhood, Bukowski gives us cameos of his early feelings about religion ('God's man'), sexuality ('snapshot' and 'burlesque'), literature ('first love') and his initiation rite into manhood ('depression kid'). 'Field exercises' deals with his ROTC experiences against the backdrop of Nazism.

'What will the neighbors think?' presents us with a valley of the squinting windows where his parents show more interest in their image than anything else.

Section 2 has him starving for his art as he listens to classical music in a Philadelphia rooming-house and watches mice gnawing at his latest compositions. 'Society should realize… ' is a love song to a prostitute, a poem the prudish may see as so many pornographic ramblings but it's really just a slice of humor.

There are a selection of poems dealing with his much-publicized attitudes to writing in Section 3. In 'the weak' he inveighs against those who mouth up the books they're going to write but rarely do. 'A tough time' has him suffering rejection from a highbrow university magazine specializing in nonsense.

Section 4 is a mixed bag, containing the usual hodge-podge of reflections on women, the races, his past and the changes time has wrought on his life.

Section 5 is also a mixed bag. 'Finished?' allays the fears of Bukowski's faithful crew of fans from the old days about his perceived sell-out to a champagne and caviar lifestyle. This seems unlikely from 'the barometer', where he writes about the kind of people he alienated with his 'ugly' writings. His parents were his first critics, then came the contumely of editors and finally that of his mother-in-law. He says he doesn't worry about the abuse half as much as he would about the prospect of seeing his face on the cover of *Time* magazine.

'The good people' is a broadside against 'cause celebs', i.e. those supposed bleeding hearts whose main cause is actually themselves. It's similar in tone to 'safe', a poem that describes a world like that of his parents where nobody does anything out of line.

In 'life like a big tender glove', he ponders the issue of what his father would have said had he known that his crazy mixed-up son would one day be rich and famous. 'Night cap' has him reminiscing on the 'wild and lovely ride' his life has been up to this. He discusses the darkness of impending death in a number of other poems like 'welcome darkness', 'old', 'Bach, come back' and 'quiet in a quiet night.'

The last of these is the most poignant as Bukowski writes about 'the last minute arrowing in'. He can't postpone the inevitable ('death has one move left. I have none') but that still doesn't stop him enjoying the time that remains to him.

A diary Bukowski kept from 1991 to 1993 came out in book form in 1998. It was called *The Captain is Out to Lunch and the Sailors Have Taken over the Ship.*

In it he sounds off in genial vein about all the things that have kept him alive over the years - horses, writing and Linda Lee - and also the things that have driven him crazy - horses, writing and Linda Lee. His writing has been a celebration rather than a moan, he tells us, but he needed the backlog of pain for his raw material. He thinks he should have been dead 'thirty five years ago.' He believes he only writes a little better now than he did when he was poor and starving. This makes him wonder why he had to reach the age of 51 before he could pay the rent.

He rants against bogus interviewers who tricked their way into his house to meet him. Movies are another target. Even the racetrack comes in for a hammering. It isn't the same as it used to be, he complains. The atmosphere of irresponsibility is gone and so is the sense of adventure. There are no fistfights at the track anymore, no crap games in the parking lots, no chance of meeting a woman sitting at the bar. There are just masses of people looking like death warmed up, so many ciphers that seem to typify the brave new world we're living in.

Social crusaders also come in for a battering. He writes about people who are in love with causes for their own sake rather than the good that can accrue from them.

He tells us about a group who were apparently disappointed when the Gulf War ended because it meant they had no relevance anymore as anti-war protestors. Being anti-war, he said once, took about as much courage as 'hitting grandma with a two-by-four.'

He used to be anti-war himself, he added, but when it became fashionable he changed to a pro-war stance. (When Bukowski met Ron Kovic, the war veteran who'd lost both of his legs in Vietnam, he was unimpressed by him. Kovic was played by Tom Cruise in the film *Born on the Fourth of July*. He became a national hero but Bukowski sniffed, 'Only a fool goes to war thinking he won't get hurt.')

Some of the best writing in the book is about the track. He says he goes there mainly because he has nothing better to do. It's a way of trying to impose significance on the mess of his days. He knows he can't get rich from 'the ponies.'

His main motive in going there is to observe the other gamblers, so many people who are lost like himself. He moves with them towards the illusion of bucking the system, concluding that such an illusion is no better or worse than any other one. Elsewhere he says he goes there to 'earn' his nights. The 'imperfect' hours he spends at the track make way for the 'perfect' ones writing and drinking. They're a necessary nothing, a mechanical device. You have to kill ten hours to make four hours live.

Turning to writing, he says he's never been more productive than in the past two years. He's made his style softer and more accessible. He was never a believer in editing so the transformation seems to have come about by itself.

After years of using wine to summon his muse it's suddenly arriving without it. Why? He doesn't know. Maybe it's the wisdom that comes with age. But he doesn't want to become smug.

To keep his 'weaponry' alive he knows he has to stay away from the 'comfortable' poets, the ones who like to be entertained by him, who happen by and exchange pleasantries. They haven't slept on garbage bins or woken up with rats on their stomachs. They haven't had cancer or TB or had to steal food to eat. But they like words. They think they know about life because they don't have too much difficulty putting words together.

Hell, for Bukowski, would be having to listen to such a breed reading their work.

His days are simple now. No longer does he drink incessantly. He sits in front of a computer screen writing poems about being stuck in traffic, about buying groceries at the store.

He waits for an alarm system to be installed. He plays with his cats, who sleep twenty hours a day. He should learn from them. They know the secret of life is not to care.

He still listens to classical music. He prefers it to any other kind, especially rock music.

He relates an amusing anecdote about being at a U2 concert where he's the guest of honor. The lead singer, Bono, dedicates the concert to Bukowski and Linda. This means more to Linda than it does to him. He doesn't think any more of U2 than he does of any other rock band.

He meets Bono afterwards in the VIP lounge. He can't remember what they talk about there. They've played well in the concert, he allows, but for Bukowski these trendy millionaires who protest against establishment values are as establishment as the nearest realtor in his BMW. He doesn't want to spend the night chatting with them. Instead he chats with the barman. That's more fun. You don't have to adopt a pose. Spontaneous things have a better chance of happening when you do that.

He gets roaring drunk, of course, and has an accident when he gets home, falling on the steps of his house. What Bukowski night would be complete without a drunken accident? Why should these stop just because he's become rich and famous and has had rock concerts dedicated to him?

Bukowski saw U2s Bono as a proper-up of the establishment rather than a rebel fighting against it

In John Dullaghan's documentary *Born Into This*, Bono says, 'I think we got to the old fucker.' The remark seems to have a tinge of resentment in it. Bono was a great fan of Bukowski but the feeling wasn't mutual. Sean Penn was a friend of Bono's. When he was at his Dublin home one night the subject of Bukowski came up. Bono said he loved his writing. Penn said, 'I know him.' Bono was amazed at this. Penn rang Bukowski on the spot and they had a chat. He was amazed to discover he didn't know who Bono was. So was Linda. She'd been going to U2 concerts since the days they were a garage band. Bono joked, 'She's been at more U2 concerts than I have.'

1998 also saw the publication of Howard Sounes' *Locked in the Arms of a Crazy Life*, the most detailed Bukowski biography that's yet been published. Drawing on previously unpublished papers it gave us an unvarnished portrait of him in all his moods. Sounes conducted interviews with many of his lovers and fellow writers as background. His exhaustive research filled the gaps left by previous books on him. It was written in a lively manner and became a best-seller, opening up L.A.'s most vaunted hell-raiser to a whole new generation of readers. The muscular style is one Bukowski himself would have enjoyed. Sounes threads the poems nicely through the life and vice versa. There were also a large number of previously unpublished photographs in it.

As the century drew to a close, people stood back and tried to look at exactly what Bukowski had achieved with his massive output. His reputation seemed to grow exponentially with each year that passed, on both sides of the Atlantic. The books also continued to come out. *What Matters Most is How Well You Walk Through the Fire*, another large poetry collection, was published in 1999. Reflecting the maturity of his recent work in a more disciplined format, Bukowski once again re-visits old pastures and tries to make sense of new ones with a mixture of humor and rage. The syntax is as simple as ever, many of the poems resembling haikus in the brevity of the lines. A lot of them filter out on a dying fall.

He starts, as he often does, with a poem about his early life. 'My father and the bum' isn't exactly rhapsodic but it has an easy flow. He contrasts the quiet simplicity of his next door neighbor with his father's pretense of having a job, leaving us to wonder who the real 'bum' is. Is it the man who sits throwing darts at a wall or the one who courts the respect of others on fraudulent premises?

'The mice' is a poem which finds his father again in aggressive mood, killing some mice the ten year old Bukowski was fond of. This is another incident that must have paved the way for the night he turned on his father with drink some years later, having imploded so many times before.

By the time we get to 'Pershing Square, Los Angeles. 1939' he's started to develop his barfly persona, welcoming it as a way of dealing with the fractured coordinates of his existence.

In 'the 8-count concerto' he presents music to us as the still center of his life. In 'Christmas poem to a man in jail' he mentions Mahler in such a context. This is really a polemic about the necessity of poets spurning tradition in search of a freer way of expressing themselves. 'One more good one' is a livelier way of making this point, depicting the old crow still cracking out those crisp lines against all the odds, cigar in mouth, bottle on floor, and brain on fast forward as the computer keys click into first gear for another full frontal assault on convention.

Section 2 of the collection continues in similar vein, 'the last poetry reading' being a satire on the idea of the poet as performer. We get a non-personalized treatise on poverty in 'Carlton Way off Western Ave.' which is unique for Bukowski. He generally prefers to take us into his own life rather than that of a neighborhood, or at least to use the latter as a gateway into the former. 'Revolt in the ranks' has a humorous approach to writer's block, depicting his poems as ungrateful children who wish to punish him. It's not as funny as 'comments upon my last book of poesy' where he gives a grocery list of the wildly varying responses of the public towards his work, ending up with one reader exclaiming, 'You jack-off motherfuck, you're not fooling anybody'. The point is, he never tried to.

Open All Night was published in 2000. It features an amalgamation of the same themes that obsessed him since he first put pen to paper. It's a poignant mix of thwarted emotions, dismal loves, absurd tragedies. We get the in-your-face women, the loveable oddballs, the risible vitriol. There's also the fame, the fans, the hate mail, the celebrity status, the notoriety, the track, the insanity of success and the insanity of failure, the movies, the theatre, the bars, the music, the idiocy of the masses, the tug of the ordinary, the magic of the mad.

Writing has always meant more to him than anything else, he informs us in 'the best men are strongest alone'. In 'Manx' he rails against the 'sadly sane.' Genius is lonely, he says, but it's important to follow your lights into the dirty bars for moments of epiphany with others. Bars are still sanctuaries to him, the last refuges of the free-minded, at least until television kills conversation and drives him away from them. Afterwards he drinks at home, suffering the leers of the beer deliverers who stare at him, for now he's quote unquote Famous, this strange unkempt man who keeps harems of ladies, each more demanding than the last.

Some women, however, have a redemptive influence on him. They give him a 'warm grace' and help him lose the fear of loving that's been instilled into him since his youth.

His average relationship, he tells us, only lasts about 2½ years because of his 'degenerate personality.' But he doesn't, as is commonly believed, bury the women he dumps in the Hollywood Hills. He doesn't expect virginity from his women but he prefers it if they haven't been 'rubbed raw by experience'.

In 'for some friends' he has a foretaste of the delight he fears will attend his passing. In 'Thoughts on being 71', this has largely dissipated. Death is now a 'pet cat,' something neither to be feared nor sought after. It's just an event that's in the nature of things. He's got this far and he has no regrets about what happens next. He's young in his mind regardless of the craggy visage that greets him from the other side of a mirror each day.

'Fame' is one of the most interesting poems in the book. Here he tells us his life was never about wealth or celebrity. The years of oblivion were the same as the years of plenty for him. If he'd wanted to become famous the words wouldn't have come out as they did. In fact maybe there would have been no words at all.

353

Fame happened and he was grateful for it but it didn't change him, it merely gave him the latitude to be outrageous.

Writing gives him a sense of immortality; it oils the machine of his day. There's a beauty in language that's rarely replicated in the world and to that extent it's to be treasured. So are women — at least for 2½ years. And horses. These afford him a 'precise simplicity' the rest of his life lacks. All of these things keep him sane - but not *too* sane. If something goes wrong for him he can still be witnessed wandering round the garden naked and spewing expletives, usually to annoy the neighbors.

No collection would be complete without a Jane poem and there's one here too. In 'to Jane Cooney Baker' he tells us she went away from him many times in the past but always returned, at least until one day in January 1962 when she succumbed to the 'beautiful whore' of death. He used to wait for her many times in the past but now, suggesting a further meeting in the next world (does Bukowski finally believe in the next world?) he says, 'You must wait for me.'

Jane continues to be a bugbear for biographers as so little is known of her. She was never interviewed. Only one photograph has ever been found of her, the one that's in this book. Nothing is known of her children except for the fact that her son Jo died in 2007. Her daughter Mary wasn't mentioned in the obituary so one presumes she pre-deceased him. There may be grandchildren but nobody knows if there are or if they wish to be located. Howard Sounes tried his best to track down anyone associated with her when he was writing his biography of Bukowski but he only ran into blank walls. Her grave is unmarked to this day.

Another book that appeared from Black Sparrow Press at this time was *Beerspit Night and Cursing,* a collection of Bukowski's letters to the artist-cum-author Sheri Martinelli from 1960 to 1967. Martinelli edited *The Anagogic & Paideumic Review,* one of the magazines he submitted his work to. She was a former girlfriend of

Ezra Pound. Though she rejected his first effort, her detailed response to it impressed him and the pair of them struck up a relationship. They were polar opposites in personality, her rarefied nature totally at odds with his cynicism, but they had a respect for one another born of a mutual passion for good writing.

Martinelli tapped into Bukowski's feminine side. There's a lot of tenderness in these letters. His tone is generally upbeat in them, which is surprising since his personal life was in tatters during the sixties. In one of them he tells her he's sent poems to 17 different literary magazines simultaneously, an uncanny example of his output. Martinelli replies to his diatribes like Emily Dickinson on acid. Her verbal convolutions, like her thoughts, are quirkily refreshing and Bukowski responds in kind.

A flood of Bukowski books started to hit the shelves after he died

She's like his Number One girl, the woman who seems to understand him like no other. He confides his most intimate thoughts to her as well as teasing out the obsessions we see in most of his other writings: the need to go for broke in one's art, the

355

necessity of paying homage to Mammon in order to buy time for what's really important, the strengths and weaknesses of fellow writers. The pair of them range freely over the gamut of literature as they try to come to terms with their aspirations and disappointments.

They never met. He asked if he could visit her in 1961 but she demurred. Was she nervous of meeting her pen-pal for fear he mightn't live up to his reputation? We'll never know because she died in 1996. As things stand, the relationship between them is frozen in time, hermetically sealed from the greater world outdoors. Reading their crossflow of letters isn't so much yin and yang as two sides of the same coin. It was highly combustible fuel going in both directions.

They postponed meeting one another so many times it almost became like a joke between them. This was a pity. Bukowski expressed himself to her in a way he couldn't to anyone else. He could talk books with her in one breath and the darkness of his soul the next. He poured out the kaleidoscopic cluster of images that was in his head to and she shared her own kaleidoscope with him. At times she seemed like a demented schoolmarm. Elsewhere she seems more like a sister, or even a mother. Both of them were wired to the moon but also cerebrally plugged in to their own psyches. Out of such anomalies they created a kind of fodder unparalleled in any collection of letters you're ever likely to read. *Beerspit Night and Cursing* is a rare treat.

Their relationship hit a bump in the road in 1967 when Bukowski accused her of lying when she said she'd been in touch with Ezra Pound. How could she have been, his friend John Thomas said to him, when Pound was incarcerated in a psychiatric institution? The fact that Bukowski let himself be sucked in by Thomas' thoughts was surprising. His relationship with Martinelli went back a long time. Why would she lie to him?

She was insulted by the accusation. She didn't try to defend herself against it but she was deeply offended by it. How could he communicate with her on such an elemental level for seven years and then suddenly turn against her on such a flimsy pretext?

It would be convenient to surmise that Bukowski lost interest in her after his career took off but it didn't quite happen like that. It's more likely that her repeated criticism of his poetry (well-intentioned as it was) began to grate on him more progressively as the years went on. In the early 1960s he was willing to take her barbs on board but as his work became more widely published he started to see her views as off-the-wall. It was a sad end to a very unusual friendship.

The next book to come out from a seemingly interminable tsunami of reserved material was *The Night Torn Mad with Footsteps*. It was published in 2001 and made one wonder yet again how Bukowski found time to live such a frenetic life amidst all the writing. Here the Czar of Cool looks back on the past with a mixture of nostalgia and cynicism.

The opening poem, 'one writer's funeral' captures the end of an era in its documenting of the funeral of John Fante. 'A drink to that' lays the ghost of his parents again. Elsewhere he writes about the track, drink, poetry, strippers, landladies, pulverizing jobs, the down-and-outs who kept him going when everything else failed. Mad whores and nudie dancers come and go. He loves and hates them and they love and hate him back.

There are cat poems, Jane poems, post office poems and even ones about mainstream figures like Humphrey Bogart, Marlon Brando and Brigitte Bardot. The collection finds our anti-religious, love-bashing Chinaski alive and well, laughing at life and death as he tries to keep both of these beasts at bay.

In the midst of all these collections a man called Jean-Francois Duval joined the growing list of Bukowski devotees with his book *Bukowski and the Beats*, published in 2002 by Sun Dog Press. The title made some people raise their eyebrows but Duval made a persuasive case for it.

Bukowski couldn't be construed as being a Beat by any stretch of the imagination because he didn't adhere by any of their credos. He didn't trip out on drugs or write mystical poetry. Neither did he intellectualise poverty or regard bohemianism as anything to be aspired to.

He felt the Beat dream was hijacked by those who lived in the comfort zone of economic solvency. This wasn't so much countercultural angst, he thought, as emotional bankruptcy. Life was about getting through the day, not seeing magic in a flower.

He never lost himself in beat-ific illusion. 'I felt more like a punk,' he said. Maybe that's why he outlived the Jack Kerouacs and the Neal Cassadys of the world. He existed in the dull centre of experience, more comfortable here than on the radiant rim. Kerouac always had his head over the parapet looking for a metaphorical pot of gold at the end of the rainbow. For Bukowski a rainbow just meant rain.

The Beats had a fractious relationship with him just as he had with them. In a lot of ways they were misinformed about him. Allen Ginsberg thought he lacked a sense of the spiritual. This wasn't true. You just had to look harder for it than with most people. 'If there's darkness in my writing,' he said, 'it's darkness trying to walk into the light.'

When he met Ginsberg after a reading he did with him in Santa Cruz in the seventies, Ginsberg made fun of him. Bukowski miss-pronounced certain words due to his lack of a formal education and not mixing in literary circles.

He miss-spelled other ones – including Ginsberg's name, which he usually spelt as 'Ginsburg.' This isn't anything to do with intelligence or talent but Ginsberg seemed to think it was. His frivolous attitude to Bukowski annoyed him. Bukowski retaliated by criticizing Ginsberg's tone of high seriousness, telling him he hadn't written anything of worth since his 'Howl,' a poem he felt had been over-praised.

There was a bomb threat at the reading and Bukowski took this as another opportunity to get a dig at him. 'I'm not afraid,' he said as everyone started to scuttle to safety, 'I'll just hide behind Allen. His karma will protect me.'

Bukowski liked William Burroughs' work but the feeling wasn't mutual. Burroughs seems to have blanked him at Santa Cruz when they were both there to do readings on subsequent nights. In the ironically titled poem 'My Friend William Burroughs' from the posthumous book *Slouching Toward Nirvana* Bukowski suggests they both ignored one another, despite staying in adjoining rooms in the Holiday Inn. From a close reading of the poem, however, it seems Bukowski was more interested in meeting Burroughs than he admitted.

He gave a different version of events to Harold Norse. Burroughs' ignoring of him, he told Norse, annoyed him so much he felt like knocking him on his ass. Norse said that wouldn't have been a good idea. If he tried it, he told Bukowski, Burroughs would probably have shot him. (This was a reference to the fact that Burroughs had accidentally shot his wife during a game of 'William Tell' that went horribly wrong in 1951. He'd placed an apple on her head but he missed it, hitting her in the forehead instead. He was drunk at the time. She died from her wound).

Duval interviewed Bukowski when he was writing his book. The resulting conversation contained the nucleus of the Bukowski myth. He re-cycled the anecdotes that were indissoluble from him, helped by some coaxing from Duval and Linda.

'Trying to be kind to others,' Duval quotes him as saying, 'I often get my soul shredded into a kind of spiritual pasta.' (That was before he traded bad beer for fine wines - and nihilism for a spiritual peace).

Duval sees him as a Quasimodo figure, the 'Hunchback of East Hollywood' as I put it in the original title of this book, a rough diamond who saw beauty in ugliness. He was Charlie Chaplin, Buster Keaton, the hobo clown laughing through his tears.

Sun Dog Press followed up Duval's book with another Bukowski title the following year, *Sunlight Here I Am*. This contained some of the most revelatory interviews Bukowski ever gave, from his first in 1963 to one he did shortly before he died in 1993. It was edited by David Stephen Calonne.

That year also gave us John Dullaghan's aforementioned documentary *Born Into This*, a traipse through all the old haunts and obsessions of Bukowski.

With some rare footage of him from the old days and a brilliant selection of interviews, this was a visual recall of most of the seminal events in his life. It captured him in all his moods, the contentious and vulnerable.

The movie critic Roger Ebert spotted an interesting moment in it. It's when Bukowski is speaking about how he lost his virginity at the age of 23 to a '300 lib whore', an encounter that ended up breaking the bed they were sleeping on,.

'He blushes,' Ebert remarked, 'This man who's reputed to be the hardboiled soul and the great Lothario actually blushes.' Bukowski featured Ebert as a character in *Hollywood*. He'd met him on the set of *Barfly*. Ebert thought it was a faithful depiction of him.

Ebert's remark is just one in a host of insights into Bukowski by most of the people who were important in his life. Dullaghan put his life's savings into making the documentary and we have him to thank for it. It captures him in all his moods, the good, the bad and the ugly. He spent seven years working on it in all and it shows.

John Dullaghan made the definitive Bukowski
documentary in 'Born Into This.' (Alamy)

This is a compulsive depiction of Bukowski's life. There are telling contributions in it from almost everyone who knew him: Linda Lee, Marina, Frances, Neeli Cherkovski, Brandes, Liza Williams, John Martin, Tom Waits, Steve Richmond, Taylor Hackford, Jack Micheline, John Bryan, Lawrence Ferlinghetti, Sean Penn, Joyce Fante and even Bono.

Linda King is the most notable absentee from that list. She would probably have liked to have been in it. As his most important girlfriend since Jane, she should have been. The incident where she trashed Bukowski's apartment, seen earlier in the BBC documentary on him, could also have done with a re-run here. But the 'other' Linda, Linda Bukowski, didn't want her in the final cut and Dullaghan acceded to her wishes.

He went against her on something else and suffered for it. In an original cut of the film he showed an incident after the U2 concert that was dedicated to Bukowski where he gashed his head on the front steps of his house after falling down there later in the night, as mentioned. Linda felt it wasn't appropriate to show this because it made Bukowski out to be a drunk. This may sound amusing to anyone who knows exactly how much he drank during his life, especially when Bukowski himself wrote about the fall in *The Captain Is Out to Lunch and the Sailors Have Taken Over the Ship,* but Linda was now intent on softening her late husband's image. She felt its inclusion would detract from that ambition. Dullaghan showed the segment at the Sundance Film Festival without consulting her and she was upset about this, refusing to talk to him as a result. It was later excised.

Books, Movies, Debates

In 2004 Sun Dog Press released another interesting title: *Visceral Bukowski: Inside the Sniper Landscape of L.A. Writers.* It was written by his friend Ben Pleasants. They'd known one another for over twenty years. Bukowski always referred to him as 'the Beverly Hills Anarchist.' He wanted him to write his biography. This book was originally intended to be that biography but instead it just became a memoir.

Bukowski put Pleasants in touch with a lot of people he knew to help him write the book but Pleasants discovered many of these people were enemies of his. Others were owed money by him or fell out with him in other ways. One of them even had his furniture smashed up by him. No doubt this was intentional mischief on Bukowski's part.

Pleasants wrote a fond account of his old friend and the times they had together in *Visceral Bukowski.* He chronicles the many nights they spent drinking together as they discussed everything from the Meat School of literature to Bukowski's troubles with the draft. There are revelatory asides on his troublesome relationship with his parents and his salacious feelings about 'the female.' Pleasants throws a lot of light on his early years as well, having tracked down a childhood friend, William 'Baldy' Mullinax, who recounts spirited drinking sprees with him. Mullinax recalls nights with Bukowski and Jane where Jane showed him more than a good time sexually It was her custom, he says, to humiliate Bukowski in this way.

The most contentious pages in the book document Bukowski's pro-Nazi leanings and his apparent disappointment that he had Jewish roots. Linda wasn't happy with this depiction of him. At a signing, it was reported that she wrote a note to Pleasants with just two words on it: 'Fuck you.'

I was in contact with Pleasants at this time and I offered to review his book. He was glad of the publicity. After I sent the review to him he wrote back saying he was now working on a new book about Bukowski. It was going to deal with his relationship with John Fante. It was going to be called *Bukowski, Fante and the Maserati Moon,* The book, he claimed, was going to discount the idea that Bukowski was as enthusiastic about the re-printing of Fante's books as he's always been reputed to be. The truth is that it was Pleasants himself who was most instrumental in bringing that about.

Black Sparrow Press closed down in 2002, selling the rights of Bukowski's books to HarperCollins

He enclosed a letter from Fante's son Dan which corroborates this. Dan wrote from Pacific Palisades in 1983: 'You are truly the one responsible for the renewed interest in my father's work. I just wanted you to know how very much I appreciate what you've done for my dad's career and for his spirit. I want you to know that the life and work of an often difficult, ungracious, proud, egotistical genius would probably have gone all-but-unnoticed were it not for you. Thank you for being who you are. God bless you, Sincerely,

Dan Fante.' Unfortunately, *Bukowski, Fante and the Maserati Moon* was never published. Instead Pleasants wrote *A Conversation with John Fante.*

Black Sparrow Press had closed its doors by now, having sold the rights of all Bukowski titles to HarperCollins for a reputed seven-figure sum in 2002. John Martin had refused previous overtures from them but now he felt the time was right. The industry was changing. Who knew where the next curve ball was coming from?

He assured Linda that her husband's back catalogue of material would keep the royalties rolling in for some years. The first Bukowski title to appear from HarperCollins (under its Ecco imprint) was *Sifting Through the Madness for the Word, the Line, the Way.* It was another huge anthology with a wide range of themes – everything from cats to colonoscopies, drink to death. It was an auspicious beginning. As usual the back cover gave no description of the contents of the book. The name Charles Bukowski was enough to sell it. People knew what they were going to get: rare writing about a rare life. He stepped into the wrong end of a jacuzzi and twisted his right leg, he tells us at the beginning of one of the poems, just to let everyone know we're getting the 'new' Bukowski here, even if his heart is still with the old haunts.

This is life in small doses delivered by a man who's been to hell and back. The evacuee of Desolation Row serves up a mélange of joy and pain from the belly of the beast. As is the case in all good writing, the allure is in the detail. This is evident in a poem like 'upon reading an interview with a best-selling novelist' where he becomes bored by the blandness of the interview but finds his spirits lifting when he sees a fly buzzing around his room. 'Life at last,' he writes.

There's an embarrassment of riches in these pages. One could be forgiven for asking why Martin withheld it from public consumption for so long. Bukowski would love to have seen every word he wrote published in his lifetime but he accepted the fact that this wasn't the way Martin worked. He knew he was afraid of 'overkill.'

Martin used the same word to me when I approached him with the idea of writing this book in 2000. He wrote back to me to say there were other books coming out on Bukowski at the time and that he would prefer if I didn't do it. I couldn't see his point at the time as he'd put out such a vast amount of books by Bukowski himself. Surely a biography, I thought, would keep his name alive in the public's mind.

The Flash of Lightning Behind the Mountain appeared the following year. All the old themes were here again - the gambling, the women, the fighting, the track. He's served his time with the bitch goddess of life but he isn't quite ready yet to become Yeats' 'smiling public man.' He still has the fire in his heart but mortality hints. He approaches the final curtain. It's not dark yet, as Bob Dylan might say, but it's getting there.

In 'first poem back' he tells us he always expected to die in his sleep but 'the gods' have decided instead on leukemia, chemotherapy and blood leaking into catheters. This is dark humor but not as dark as, say, someone like Samuel Beckett. In Bukowski's dark humor the humor usually over-rides the darkness, unlike with Beckett.

'Nothing here' is another poem dealing with impending death. In the old days he used to worry about being turned out of premises because of failure to pay the rent but now his 'final eviction' looms as the ultimate landlord waits for him.

In 'good try all' he writes about his relationships with women. Many of them were abused - and abusive Others he got on the rebound from previous relationships. He ended up losing them to other men because he arrived in their lives too late with too little to

366

offer. But he doesn't regret a moment he spent with these 'fragile tulips.'

'Proper credentials are needed to join' is a poem in which, again, he champions drink and gives out about amateur drunks. He was always snobbish about this subject. He didn't like pioneers much and reformed alcoholics angered him even more. In fact he never really accepted the fact that such a breed existed. In his eyes those who stopped drinking weren't alcoholics. They were only dabblers, people untouched by the real glories of alcohol. Bukowski would never have been a candidate for Alcoholics Anonymous. If a person told him they had a problem with drink he'd probably have suggested they drink more, not less, to 'cure' it.

This is another significant collection of verse from the old master. He doesn't look back in anger so much as resignation. 'I liked your poems better when you were puking and living with whores,' another poet tells him in 'a visitor complains.' He doesn't argue with the man but he says he thinks he's writing just as well in his new environment.

That isn't to say all the poems are up to par. Some of them are trivial. In the poem 'born again' he makes a far too large claim for changing a tire on his car, speaking of it like a reincarnation. In instances like this he seems to be reduced to making big points from small experiences, unlike in the past when he used big experiences to make small points – or none at all.

2005 saw the publication of *Slouching Toward Nirvana*. He was still getting the line down, still hitting the keys hard. 'In case of accident,' he writes in one poem, 'please get in touch with Henry Chinaski.' Is this real toughness or an old man trying to pretend he's tough?

He experiments with different writing styles in the book. He takes on a woman's voice in 'she lost weight.' 'Something's knocking at the door' ends like Yeats' 'Second Coming.' (Had

Bukowski read this poem? It seems like he has but he once said he never bothered with Yeats).

He liked writing about well-known people without mentioning them by name and he continues that practice here. 'A clean well-lighted place' is about Hemingway. 'Some people ask for it' is about Tchaikovsky. 'I'm no good' seems to be about Liza Williams. The tone in these poems is more placid than usual. Ironic humor appears in 'A note upon starvation' where he tells us he once almost starved to death from poverty and he now finds himself being advised to go on a diet by his doctor. The wheel has come full circle. What would Knut Hamsun think?

There's a pleasant tone to the book. One imagines him looking out over the boats on the bay, the electric light glinting on the page, cigarette ash burning his trousers. The gods still smile on him as he watches the lights of cars glinting on the freeway, as he digs into the motherlode of his past so he can strip-mine gold from it, carving the words onto the page while classical music hums away in the background.

In 'vulgar poem' he tells us he writes better than the young brigade coming up. Does he really believe this or is he trying to convince himself – and us? He often gives himself pep talks in poems to bolster his confidence. It's as if some kind of insecurity is being dampened down, as if he's protesting too much. When people look better than him on the street with their toned bodies and handsome features he criticizes them, telling us what they might look like in years to come.

In 'beach boys' the strain is most evident. These people may have the world at their feet today but what's in store for them in the future? Linda King once said she was with him at a beach one day and commented on the fine body of a young man passing by. She said he went quiet as she said it, perhaps feeling he was too old for her and not in good shape. Is this the part of him he's trying to cover up in poems like 'beach boys'? Was he still resentful of his adolescence when he couldn't get women because of his boils? In 'New York New York' he even manages to convince himself that a young man talking to his girlfriend on the phone is actually making it all up, that he's speaking to nobody at all.

Slouching Toward Nirvana is a book of two halves. The good half features brilliant poems about his past like 'I don't know about you but,' while the bad half contains ones like 'IBM Selectric,' a kind of ode to technology. In the latter poem, as he praises his electronic typewriter, you feel he's become a little too fond of his new-won comforts. That's not to say he isn't entitled to them, but a poem to his Underwood would have worked better. When he boasts about how much tax he pays, or how much he's won at the track that day, he seems strangely adolescent, strangely right-wing. In 'good news' he tells us we'll never find him at literary gatherings or on television. Fair enough, but is writing poems to electronic typewriters any better?

In 'dusty shoes' he writes about the way he brought color and sparkle to women's lives even thought he had nothing material to offer them. Linda King often talked about his aliveness, his humor, how nobody could ever be the same after meeting him. A later poem has Jane expressing remorse about the fact that she's lost touch with her son. This is interesting because we know so little about her relationship to her children. Did she really try to get back with him? She sounds almost desperate to do so here. She's put him through college, she says, but he refuses to communicate with her. Maybe too much damage was done by her desertion of him during his formative years. (He's called Billy-Boy in the poem instead of his actual name, Jo).

'There are four parts in the collection but the order seems arbitrary. 'Private screenings,' for instance dates from when Bukowski was filming *Barfly*. It features him having to suffer the screening of a film he hates. He tries to be polite about it to the director. He wants to walk out of the film but he can't, for fear of hurting his feelings. He looks forward to being in a public cinema where this will be possible. Such a scenario unfolds when he goes to a film with Marina and – presumably – Linda King in 'Academy Award?' He walks out and feels good about the fact that he's taking control of his destiny. (This poem should have been placed immediately after 'private screenings' instead of in a different section).

The feeling that Bukowski was indeed becoming too fond of his creature comforts, as suggested in 'IBM Selectric', is buttressed by the poem 'swimming pool' in which he refuses to allow his photographer Michael Monfort snap him beside the pool because he's afraid it will appear as if he's sold out to his fans. He's now crafting his image, in other words.

Did he always do this, one wonders. Was his hardscrabble past exaggerated for effect? These are the suspicions cynics have always had about him. He doesn't do much to deflect such cynicism in poems like 'swimming pool.' On the other hand, he didn't need to feature this poem here. If he didn't, we wouldn't have known about his refusal to be snapped by Monfort. Smug or not, he was always upfront about things like this.

In 'as you slow down the mermaids look the other way' it seems as if he's waiting to die, going to the track to stop himself thinking of this. We see evidence of his body slowing down in other poems as well – 'checkmate,' 'small talk,' 'last Friday night,' 'from the dept. of health' etc.

The most interesting poem in the collection is 'friend of the family.' Here he suggests he was sexually abused as a boy. Was he? He never talked about it if he was. Why wouldn't he have done so? He talked about everything else. There's a possibility the circumstances are made up but they're so detailed it's unlikely. Most of his 'self-referential' poems are based on fact and this seems to be too.

In the same year we got another major biography, this one simply called *Charles Bukowski*. It was written by Barry Miles. Miles had already written biographies of Jack Kerouac, Allen Ginsberg and Paul McCartney.

His collaboration with McCartney (in Apple's sister company Zapple) led to him doing a recording of Bukowski reading his poetry in the sixties. His book is replete with anecdotes and is also very well written. The main problem with it is that it has no photographs in it. This is all the more surprising considering it was published by Virgin, the company that now publishes Bukowski's books in the UK alongside Ecco. There are also some names missing from the Index that one might have expected to find there: John Dullaghan, Amber O'Neil, Georgia Peckham Krellner, etc.

There are also factual errors, like when Miles says 'I shot a man in Reno' is a poem rather than a story, or when he tells us 'The Fiend' was written in the first person. (It was written in the third). He also tends to use material in Bukowski's fiction as verbatim facts about his life. This leads him to incorporate them into the biographical parts of the book. As we all know, there was a very thin line between Bukowski's life and his work but the line still existed.

These are small caveats. Miles has the voice of a poet in many of the chapters and he captures Bukowski's bittersweet *demi-monde* with empathy.

A film made about Bukowski that year failed to show such empathy. Bent Hamer's *Factotum*, based on his 1975 book of the same name, was beset by many of the problems that had dogged *Barfly*.

The main mistake was having a mainstream star like Matt Dillon (who wasn't too renowned for subtlety in his performances) playing him. Why did Hollywood never choose a character actor to play Bukowski? He didn't look like an A-lister so why should an A-lister play him?

371

Matt Dillon played Bukowski in *Factotum*

Bukowski would probably have turned in his grave to see Dillon playing him. It was bad enough to have to see Ben Gazzara doing so. Dillon was even prettier.

A better choice would have been someone like Eli Wallach or George Carlin if age permitted, someone who looked like he'd lived, who had expressive features. Dillon's face was too blank. It didn't show the '1000 year old eyes' Bukowski was professed to have. A character actor with a pock-marked face - someone like Strother Martin or Jack Elam? - would have had been more suitable. Elam usually played the bad guy in westerns. Bukowski looked like a bad guy in a western. That's where the casting directors should be looking for the next biopic. Otherwise all the films based on his books are going to end up as bland treatises that fail to capture his ruggedness.

Dillon made things worse for himself by ringing Linda one night and asking her how she thought he should approach the part. Linda isn't a film-maker. A wife isn't usually the best person to advise on things like this. Too many other factors are at work.

They talked for four hours. She kept telling him that Bukowski wasn't a slob, that he was very hygienic. That was the worst thing she could have said to Dillon. It sanitized his attitude, which had already been pretty sanitized anyway.

Dillon wasn't familiar with Bukowski's work before coming to the role. He should have gone to the library instead of making the phone call to Linda. He'd read some of his stories but precious little of his poetry. He referred to him in an interview as 'a white haired guy who wrote notes for dirty old men.' (Not *for*, Matt, *of.* And it was just one man. Capitalized). He was also misinformed about his life. He called Jane 'Jane Bukowski' instead of Jane Cooney Baker. But he was on the ball when he said one could learn more from Barbet Schroeder's interviews with Bukowski than from *Barfly*. He was also right when he suggested Warren Oates would have been a good choice to play Bukowski.

Bukowski himself wanted Jack Nicholson to play him in a movie of his life. That wouldn't have worked. Nicholson would probably have got the voice right – neither Rourke nor Dillon did that - but it would have been better to avoid any high profile star altogether. Dillon didn't get the walk right either. (Rourke did his best to do Bukowski's lumbering walk but I agree with the man who said he ended up looking like the 'before' picture in a hemorrhoid cream commercial).

Bukowski wanted Jack Nicholson to play him in a movie of his life

Is there ever going to be a great film based on a Bukowski book besides *Crazy Love*? Paul Verhoeven bought the rights to *Women* many years ago. One imagines that if it was filmed we'd have another hunk playing Bukowski in it. To that extent it's a blessing it hasn't got off the ground.

With a few notable exceptions, Hollywood doesn't know how to deal with writers on celluloid. European directors understand them better, though they often seem content to brand him a communist and leave it at that. Maybe it's better if *Women* doesn't become a film, just like it's better that *Post Office* doesn't, or *Hollywood,* or *Ham on Rye*. (Taylor Hackford holds the film rights to *Post Office*).

Even with the beard and the hangdog expression, the Matt Dillon of *Factotum* looks like any other slacker taking a time out from a privileged life rather than someone a few steps away from 'the row.' The women he hooks up with – Lili Taylor and Marisa Tomei – carry on the charade of *faux*-misery. He trudges from job to job with growing disenchantment and the film drowns under the weight of all the angst. He tries his best to under-act but when you try to do something, by definition, you're acting so the under-acting, by default becomes over-acting.

Come On In! was published the following year. It was another comprehensive collection of poetry that had been stored up in John Martin's war chest for posthumous release. Every new Bukowski book was an event but this one left some question marks about the choice of material. Some of it was obscure and many of the poems fell below the standard of previous collections. Was the well running dry at last? There was still enough of the old Bukowski magic to keep one turning pages but for a lot of the time comfortable living seemed to detract from his inspiration. '

In 2007 we got *The People Look Like Flowers At Last,* another bumper collection of verse. By now one was entitled to wonder just how long this after-death party could go on. Did he ever spend a night without writing? Was it true, as he said, that he could crank out ten poems a night without thinking? How had Martin managed to hold off so much for so long? He seemed to be drip-feeding it to us like a literary sleight-of-hand. Martin had once told Bukowski he believed one of the secrets of Elvis Presley's success was the way his manager, Tom Parker, managed to keep his songs in storage when he was in the army and thereby exploit the appetite for them during Presley's 'missing years.' Bukowski was shocked to be mentioned in the same breath as the pop singer.

'Martin has thousands of poems under cover,' Bukowski told Carl Weissner in 1986, 'He'll never print them all. He won't live that long.' But he did.

The posthumous publications of Bukowski's poetry outstrip almost any writer going. This may not be the best one but it's of a superior quality to *Come On In!* There are poems on everything from Hemingway (whom he defends instead of attacks - for a change – in 'the hatred for Hemingway') to the lonely death of William Holden. 'I never bring my wife' is an ode to reclusiveness. 'Poor night' is a rare poem about writer's block. An oracular tone is evident in poems like 'just another wino' and 'fingernails; nostrils; shoelaces.' His father figures in 'acceptance' where he tells us about a story he once wrote which impressed him. It ended with a horse kicking its owner in the head. Such brutishness probably appealed to him. What's interesting is that it's the only time Bukowski ever received praise from him for anything. He ends the poem by saying the moment where he expressed admiration for the poem was as close as he ever got to him.

The most interesting poem in the book is an extended one called 'rimbaud be damned' concerning a relationship he had with a woman in the 1960s. The most poignant one is 'life at the P.O.' where he microscopes twelve years in the post office into two very telling pages. 'Contributors notes' is a hilarious satire on magazines like the *Sewanee Review* which he despised for their sense of self-importance. In 'an interviewer at 70' he's asked why he isn't as wild as he used to be. He replies that he can't keep on writing poems about spilling beer onto the laps of whores. A good line, but it's years since he did something like that. Sometimes he labors this point in the later collections. His world is medical examinations now, pragmatism, meeting his obligations.

2007 also saw the publication of *The Pleasures of the Damned*, an anthology of his poetry from 1951 to 1993. Devotees had read most of it in other collections already but there was some original material as well. His guts were on the pages as ever, bleeding from every pore. The pen, as they say, is mightier than the sword but with Bukowski they often seemed to be indistinguishable. Rabelaisian musings lock horns with pulp poetry in the crepuscular world where he charms us with his devil's music. Life is absurd for this dime-store existentialist but that doesn't stop us enjoying the ride. As in previous collections, whenever his inspiration fails him, a narrative thread picks up the slack.

A different kind of narrative unfolded that year in Los Angeles when bus tour guide Richard Schiave got a fright just as he was about to ferry some Bukowski fans around buildings associated with him. Before the tour began he spotted a notice in the property section of a newspaper saying 5124 De Longpre Avenue was about to be pulled down to make way for a set of condominiums. He rang a preservationist called Lauren Everett and told her. Together they launched a campaign with the Cultural Heritage Commission to have it preserved as 'an iconic part of L.A.'s history.' It was, after all, within these walls that Bukowski composed *Post Office, Factotum* and God knows how many poems. He'd also met Martin for the first time there, and his future wife. And he did his research for *Women* there – though this involved more humping than writing.

Their efforts were resisted by the property's owner, Victoria Gureyeva. She said Bukowski didn't deserve such an honor because he was a Nazi. Gureyeva was Jewish. Her grandfather was a Holocaust survivor. She knew Bukowski also had Jewish roots and had largely disavowed them. Ben Pleasants corroborated that in *Visceral Bukowski*. These were on his mother's side. Bukowski, allegedly, wasn't proud of them. 'There's a rumor that Hitler's mother was also partly Jewish,' Gureyeva averred, 'Now we have Bukowski. Hitler Number Two.'

John Martin now entered the debate, saying Bukowski was anything but a Nazi. 'He was a contrarian,' he argued, 'He'd say anything to get on people's goat, especially when he was young.' But the fact remained that he took up the Nazi cause, right back to the first story he ever wrote which championed a German pilot. This was a 'contrarian' move even then but that didn't make it any the less real. It was also claimed that the FBI confiscated a lot of pro-Nazi stories Bukowski had written when they raided his apartment in 1942 and that these were destroyed after he became famous. (In work that survives, right down to apparently innocuous poems like 'Adolf' published in *The People Look Like Flowers At Last,* we can witness that strain quite clearly).

Bukowski scholar David Stephen Calonne edited *Portions of a Wine-Stained Notebook* in 2008. This was an anthology of uncollected stories and essays from 1944 to 1990. It had a large wingspan, going from his first ever published story, 'Aftermath of a Lengthy Rejection Slip,' to his last published one, 'The Other.' A fictional account of meeting John Fante was also featured, along with his first 'Notes of a Dirty Old Man' column and various outpourings from the undergrounds. John Martin called it 'the missing link' of Bukowskiana - high praise indeed from the man who discovered him.

Frances - or FrancEye as she started to call herself later on in life - died the following year. She was 87. She'd become something of an eccentric in her later years, letting the hair on her chin grow so long she came to be known affectionately as The Bearded Witch of Ocean Park. That was in Santa Monica. She later moved to Northern California to be near Marina. (Marina lived in Albany). Many people felt Bukowski never gave Frances her just deserts. His cruelty to her was largely a result of the many problems he was going through during the three years he spent with her, both in his job and in himself. Quite apart from these, one would be hard put to imagine a more incompatible couple than this one.

Ecco brought out another Bukowski title that year, *The Continual Condition.* It was a slim collection of verse. It carried a commendation by no less a luminary than Leonard Cohen on the back cover. 'He brought everyone down to earth,' Cohen was quoted as saying, 'even the angels.' It's difficult to imagine a rarefied soul like Cohen being a Bukowski fan but he was. His penchant for profanity may have been more rarefied than Bukowski's but that didn't mean it wasn't there.

This is probably the weakest of the posthumous collections. Somebody once described Bukowski's writing as being like battery acid squirted out of a tommy gun. If so, that acid has lost some of its pungency here. The battery is occasionally flat. 'I'm turning the streets back/over to you/tough guy,' he writes in one poem as he puts Mahler on the tape deck. The storms have been silenced. He's content to sit out the years. If people don't want him anymore they can always read Norman Mailer.

Elsewhere we get the well-travelled tropes of women and track, bars and sex, writing and pain. The title poem is disappointing. 'A fine madness' is an onslaught against sobriety. In 'rejected' he tells us an editor sent him back a story one time because he didn't think a man who's old and ugly, like its central character, could bed four women in the one day. Bukowski then proceeds to have various encounters with four women – in the one day.

Some of the poems seem wrongly titled. ('Agnostic' is really about his hatred of Christmas rather than Christ). Others seem to ramble without purpose. The aforementioned Leonard Cohen once said, 'It's not poetry just because the lines don't reach the end of the page.' Maybe the comment could be applied to Bukowski here, at least in those ones that seem to lack conviction. He had a habit of ending poems suddenly and the tendency seems more in evidence here than usual. Was drink a factor in it, his hand hitting the carriage return prematurely? Sometimes this produced interesting tonal shifts but not here. Even so, bad Bukowski was better than no Bukowski. The collection is almost worth buying for the brilliant poems that finishes it, 'bayonets in the candlelight.' It leaves you speechless.

On went the publications. In 2010 City Lights brought out *Absence of the Hero,* another anthology of uncollected stories and essays, this time from 1946-1992. The book was again edited by David Stephen Calonne. Some of it consisted of outtakes from his 'Notes of a Dirty Old Man' columns but most was new. Calonne unearthed previously unpublished work ranging over four decades, some of it even surprising John Martin.

Pamela Brandes – now Pamela Wood - also brought out a book about Bukowski that year. She called it *Scarlet*, the same name he'd used for the book of poems he gave her when they were together. This had shocked her at the time but she came to realize he hadn't meant to insult her by it. She appreciated the fact that he'd written it in the only way he could, the Bukowski way.

Her book is a real page-turner, an eye-catching account of two zany years they spent together. She says she didn't know how deep Bukowski's feelings ran for her until she read about their relationship in Howard Sounes' 1998 biography of him. This is surprising as his obsession with her is the whole theme of the book. She hooks him in and then widens the leash. He spends much of his time in *Scarlet* searching for her, leaving her frantic messages, driving around lonely streets in frustration as he looks for her. When they break it's because he knows she could never be happy with him.

She's in the controlling position right through the relationship, apart from those moments where he goes bonkers - which any girlfriend of Bukowski's must have expected would happen at some stage. The bottom line is that both of them moved on from what happened between them, finding tranquility in more sober relationships afterwards. Some people have criticized Wood for her 'reincarnation' as a realtor but there's no law that states one has to be a cocktail waitress all their life. What's slightly more disconcerting is the earnest tone she employs when writing about her feelings for Bukowski throughout the book, which stands in marked contrast to her comment in John Dullaghan's *Born Into This* that she never really took the relationship seriously.

The following year was a bumper one for Bukowski-related titles. First off we had Ben Pleasants' satirical novel *The Victory of Defeat*. Pleasants sent me excerpts from this in 2003 when we were in communication. They'd been published in a journal called The *William & Mary Review*. It's a book Bukowski himself wanted him to write so it's not surprising that it's dedicated to him: 'To Charles Bukowski, who told me to write it, but make it funnier.' A comic re-working of many of the events in his life, it features the picaresque adventures of a neo-Nazi apologist called Henry Jokowski.

It begins in Los Angeles in 1941 with our hapless hero frustratedly squeezing out his pimples. 'Poor Henry was a zero,' Pleasants tells us. He's an angry young man who dreams of writing The Great American Novel. An outcast in school, he carries a copy of *Mein Kampf* with him as he's turfed out of his home and goes travelling.

He launches crusades against what he calls 'dumbocracy.' He joins a German-American Association that holds torchlight parades celebrating Hitler's victories in Europe but then the Japanese invade Pearl Harbor and the political goalposts shift.

The FBI pursue him for draft evasion. The only clothes he owns are what he has on his back: a Nazi uniform. Pleasants pulls out all the stops to create a laugh-a-minute yarn that also manages to include dancing girls and the Mafia. Bukowski would have loved it if he lived to see it, especially the saucy passages. Sadly, Pleasants also died shortly after its publication.

Later that year Jory Sherman published *Bukowski and Me: The Beast and the Bastard*. This was a reprint of his book *Friendship, Fame and Bestial Myth*. It was a memoir that documented the differing perspectives they had of their relationship. It lasted over twenty years, beginning when they were both struggling poets, but Bukowski disavowed it.

Writing to Sherman in 1979 he said, 'I don't know why, but somewhere, somehow, you've gotten it into your head that we have a friendship going, that we're comrades. We don't and we never did have. It was always you who knocked at my door and it was always an intrusion. The reason I have not answered your letters is because I'm not interested and never was.' This despite the fact that he'd sent him a copy of *It Catches My Heart in its Hands* in 1962 and inscribed it, 'To Jory Sherman – Before we rush to the sun, a few drinks between us, my friend.' Bukowski seemed to reserve a special coldness in his heart for Sherman for reasons best known to himself. Sherman never knowingly did anything to upset him.

David Stephen Calonne edited *More Notes of a Dirty Old Man: The Uncollected Columns* for City Lights that year too. The following year he wrote a full scale biography of Bukowski, *Charles Bukowski*.

Paul Brody wrote a capsule biography of him in 2013 called *Bukowski, The Dirty Old Man of American Literature.* In the same year we had *Bukowski: an Anthology of Poetry and Prose,* an excellent compilation with contributions from Abel Debritto, David Stephen Calonne, Steve Richmond, Joan Dobe Smith, A.D. Winans, etc.) as well as a host of other writers. The poetry is of an exceptionally high standard. Some of it is ironic, like the one called 'The SASE' by Henry Denander. Here Denander tells us he bought a stamped addressed envelope Bukowski once sent to a magazine called the *Chiron Review*. Obviously the magazine failed to return the envelope (and poem) to him. Denander now buys it on eBay. So the *Chiron Review* is being rewarded for its laxity. (The contribution that was presumably inside the envelope hasn't surfaced).

Linda King brought out a number of books on Bukowski, some of them including the poems he wrote to her. *Bukowski Undigested* appeared in 2008. *Loving and Hating Charles Bukowski* came out in 2012 and was reprinted two years later. It was a rollercoaster ride through the craziness of trying to hold a relationship together with a man who was as much a force of nature as anything else. It's an incredible book written with a lot of passion and humor.

The love letters the pair of them exchanged are like the letters between Henry Miller and Anais Nin, filled with hydraulic energy. This was a relationship doomed to disaster from the get-go but along the way it gave us everything we could have expected from a Bukowski relationship: lust, wit, anger, tenderness, yearning, desperation, devotion, infidelity and 101 other things besides. Even if king's poems couldn't hold a candle to his ones you can see his influence in the ones she includes here.

The ever-busy David Stephen Calonne brought out *The Bell Tolls for No One,* another collection of Bukowski's stories, in 2015. That year also saw the publication of *Bukowski and the Beats,* not to be confused with Jean-Francois Duval's book of the same name from Sun Dog Press. This is a slim volume Bukowski would have hated for its dry academic tone. Subtitled 'A Proletarian Writer's Portrayal of the Degradation and Exploitation of America's working Class', the only interesting parts of it are those where the author, M.J. Poynter, quotes from his books. There are also a number of errors in it which testify to the hasty manner in which it seems to have been cobbled together. Thus we read of 'Earnest' Hemingway, John 'Brayan,' 'duke' boxes instead of juke boxes, and a William Burroughs book called *The Naked Lunch* rather than *Naked Lunch.*

The following year Fourth Estate published *Essential Bukowski,* an abridged collection of previously published poems selected by Abel Debritto. Debritto edited another book that year which was brought out by Canongate Publishing. It carried a title one never expected to see on a book by this author: *On Love.* He uses the term 'love' in a loose manner to accommodate Bukowski's amorphous yearnings in that regard. (At times it doesn't even apply to people but rather objects: a typewriter in 'we get along,' a car in 'eulogy.') The titles of some poems should alert us to what we might call Debritto's 'expanded' definition of love: 'one night stand,' 'love poem to a stripper,' 'love crushed like a dead fly,' 'balling,' 'the end of a short affair,' 'love is a piece of paper torn to bits,' 'prayer for a whore in bad weather,' 'to the whore who took my poems.' In Bukowski's book love definitely seems to be, as they say, a four-lettered word, at least as far as Debritto is concerned.

He has some bitter words to say about Barbara Frye in the poem 'hello Barbara.' In 'a woman who had ants for pets and fed them sugar,' Frances comes in for the familiar Bukowski bile. He's kinder to her in the most well-known Frances poem, 'one for old snuggle tooth' but he makes fun of her sensitivity in 'the dressmaker.' The lukewarm affection he gives her in 'it was all right' is as good as it gets.

There are a number of Jane poems as well. These are very touching. In one of them, 'shoes,' Bukowski suggests she wrote to him from a hospital when she was dying and that he didn't reply. This flies in the face of all the accounts of her final illness we've read up to now. Could he be talking about another woman? It's unlikely. (A negligible poem with the same title is clumsily inserted later on in the book).

Some of the poems addressed to Linda (like 'the shower') may strike readers as being too graphic. A lusty tone also accompanies poems like 'blue moon, oh bleweeww mooooon how I adore you.' Debritto chooses an appropriate poem to close the book: 'confessions.' Here Bukowski again tackles the subject of death. He expresses a fear not so much of dying as leaving Linda behind him. He then plucks up the courage to say the words he always feared, 'I love you.'

Canongate published two other Bukowski anthologies that year, *On Writing* and *On Cats*. The first is excellent even if it's wrongly titled. (It should have been called *Selected Letters on Writing*). *On Cats* has some pleasant reflections but there's nothing sensational here. The tone is tranquil. He knows cats can never be his friends but he enjoys their company. So much so, in fact, that in the next life he says he wants to be one himself. He isn't joking here. He loved their composure, the fact that they can never be rocked by anything. They never experience fear, he says, only anger, and that was something else he admired about them.

The book is a composite of poems and stories. It's a slim volume. Is it justifiable? Maybe for cat lovers rather than lovers of Bukowski. In some ways it smacks of overkill. Completists may wish to add it to their library but Bukowski the cat lover is surely a detour from the main highway of his life. One wonders what might be coming next. *Bukowski at the Track? The Places Bukowski Lived? What Bukowski Ate in the Post Office?*

Another recent Bukowski-related title to appear on the shelves is Daniel Schwartz' *Chuck and Jane,* a conceptual novel that tells us what might have happened if Bukowski met Jane Austen and tried to have sex with her. The idea was good but for it to work it needed a foothold in reality and this it doesn't have. The style is very fluid but there's no attempt to portray anything of Austen in the book. She might as well have been Jane Cooney Baker for all the definition she gets. In fact sometimes she sounds like her. The book is really just an excuse to write about a character like Bukowski and this it does with a lot of humor. Here's Chuck leaving his job in a dog biscuit factory: 'I told Biscuit I couldn't take it. He begged me to finish my shift. I put him in a headlock until his ears turned pink. I didn't say goodbye to the oven.' The writing is of a high quality throughout, more often than not reminding one of Bukowski himself, as in this passage where he writes about writing: 'A poem isn't a mid-forties white male non-smoker with 2.5 children and a trophy wife. Find your muse. Mine's a screaming cunt of a banshee that echoes in my head until my eyes bleed.'

The latest collection of his verse to appear from Ecco is *Storm for the Living and the Dead,* another fascinating anthology of previously unpublished work from magazines even Bukowski enthusiasts may not have heard of – *Signet, Evidence, Intrepid, Kauri, Planet, Lemming, Big Scream, Heads Up, Buffalo Stamps, Second Aeon, Black Mass, Apache Quarterly, Orphans,* etc. So diverse are the poems, one feels oneself being continuously transported back to the time when he was starting out. The same passion is there, the same abstruseness, images conflating in his brain without any order or pattern, which is, of course, the best kind of poetry.

The poems range over various decades, with all the chaos that wingspan entails, and you rarely know what you're going to get as you turn the pages. The bad habits that afflicted his style when inspiration failed him are rarely in evidence here. Even when he appears to have writers block, as in the poem 'I think of Hemingway', he gives us an inspired take on it.

His voice is unrecognizable in many of the contents, like the stream-of-consciousness of 'kuv stuff mox out.' A poem like 'the rope of glass' could have been written by anyone with its straightforward narrative; Bukowski's voice isn't really recognisable. Neither does 'A trainride in hell' show any of the trademark Bukowski style. Where have these poems been until now? In 'sometimes when I feel blue I listen to Mahler' he even writes about himself in the third person. We're well into the book before we find poems on Linda or Jane or horses or the post office or John Fante or his father, or the familiar humor we expect from him, which appears in the potted autobiography, 'a poem to myself.' The book also contains probably the last thing he ever wrote, surely a collector's item, in February 1994, his first fax poem.

This may not be the best posthumous collection of his work out there but it's definitely amng the oddest ones. .

Epilogue

Bukowski seems to be everywhere today but it wasn't always like that. When I started writing the original edition of this book in 2000 I had difficulty finding most of the magazines that published him. Books by and about him were often rare too. In fact when I went to the Dublin branch of Waterstones I discovered they didn't even have an agent for Black Sparrow Books, which was then the main outlet for these. I eventually found a shop on the banks of the Liffey called – appropriately – *Forbidden Planet* where I was able to order them. The shop specialized in graphic novels but it had a Bukowski book in the window and that led me in. For the next year or so I made my way to it with a sense of excitement after getting a phone call to say my latest order had arrived from Santa Rosa. The modern reader has no such difficulties, especially since Ecco has started to produce his work so prolifically.

What will posterity make of Bukowski? He shot from the hip and lip, firing on both barrels to comfort the afflicted and afflict the comfortable, letting his words take him where they would, like his life. Through them he communed with the dark places of the heart and soul.

He once said he'd prefer if someone handed him a lead pipe instead of a poem. At least a pipe was itself. It didn't make any designs on a person. Most poems, on the contrary, had an agenda. They tried to coerce the reader into a point of view, which was a form of tyranny His own work, he assured everyone, had no message to impart, no healing balm. His writing was a mirror rather than a lamp, and a cracked mirror at that. This was no Moses leading readers to any Promised Land, just a fellow loser sharing his load.

A double-fisted drinker who created literary anarchy until the world sat up and took note, Bukowski never made apologies for his cruelty, for his inability to feel the tenderness that had been denied to him in his youth, when he most needed it. His parents sent him out into the world with nothing so nothing, he thought, was what he owed the world back.

He never had time for writing that had to be studied or interpreted. You either got it first time or not at all. He didn't trust the mind, he said, unless it was run by the bellybutton.

He wrote for taxi drivers, for slaughterhouse employees and mailmen, for misfits and malcontents and isolationists and saddle-sore losers - all the people he'd once been himself. Someone once said of Stephen King that he took horror writing away from Transylvania and brought it to the local trailer park. Maybe Bukowski did something similar, except with him the horror was inside his head. His work was narrow from the point of view that most of it is in the first person but that fact also gives it its intensity. His mind is so volcanic you never feel a sense of claustrophobia. From his hermetically-sealed slices of dementia we see a very defined world: the whisky-drenched milieu he alchemized as he slouched towards his nirvana.

He was unfashionable for years because he wrote in language that everyone could understand. The academics felt there had to be something wrong with it on that account. They wanted obscurantism for its own sweet sake. They wanted motifs and symbols and allusions and ambiguity and multi-layered meanings to test their exegetical skills. They wanted *haute cuisine* but Bukowski only offered them fast food. And they failed – or refused - to digest this. What he did was too easy to be good as far as they were concerned. It didn't pass the litmus test because it didn't have the Bullshit Factor.

Writing had to be an obsession, Bukowski told us. It had to be a pact until death between you and your muse. You couldn't do it from nine to five. It had to eat into your sinews. There would be no tiptoeing through the tulips for him, no rarefied psyches floating on gossamer wings. He made it his mission to take literature out of the chamber-rooms and give it back to the people. All too often poetry fell into the hands of those who'd never lived, who knew words but not worlds. He wanted to get back to the time Stone Age man scratched hieroglyphics on walls, to re-invent The Thing Itself.

Hemingway did this with his 'iceberg' style of writing, six-sevenths of the meaning being below the surface. Bukowski left the iceberg above the surface but stained it with his anger. There was no subtlety in his work so there was no need for wrangling between critics about what he meant, no deconstruction of his texts by the revisionists. It was plain for all to see, the muck and the savagery, with here and there a tin can glinting in the sun in a vague hint at some redemptive import. But only if he felt like it.

Careful writing was deathly writing, he told us. You had to stumble before you flew. As it was with horses, so it would be with the printed word. He shied away from the favorites.

He didn't go to war but he used his pen like a bayonet. The blood he drew was sometimes his own.

He had a beautiful spirit inside that not-so-beautiful body. If he'd been born prettier he may never have taken that walk on the wild side that gave him so much of his raw material. Maybe he should have been grateful for the boils, and all the physical and emotional pain they engendered.

His idea of a Utopia, he once told Steve Richmond, would be to build wood houses in the desert, put lots of sand between them and sell them to people who would be free to do anything they pleased. There would be no rich people in this world and no literary pretenders either. Nor would there be a police force. Eligibility for inhabiting it would be determined by dint of the residents' paintings.

Bukowski told us stories about his life, about the trivial things that filled up his days. He didn't stylize the mundane like so many others; he just put it down as it happened. Like the Manny Hyman of *There's No Business*, he told us the world was shit. Some of us appreciated that and some of us didn't want to be reminded of the fact but the way he said it made you listen whether you wanted to or not. His words stuck on the page like glue: hard, viscous and unrelenting. You could look the other way but Bukowski would probably be there too, coming at the same theme from a different angle, taunting you from all corners with his phlegmatic malaise.

He breathed life into poetry by endowing it with his explosive personality, first with surrealism and then with a dogged plainness. Either way he had you. When you finished a Bukowski poem you know you've been somewhere. Exactly where you weren't sure. Maybe you didn't want to be. You had a window onto a life that was all that could be said. Was it art? You didn't care. It touched you. It didn't play tricks with your head like most other poets you knew

He was our last mad writer and to that extent a species the literary world can ill afford to do without.

Scorn not his simplicity.

Play the piano drunk.

Ask the dust.

Works by Charles Bukowski:

Flower, Fist and Bestial Wail (1960)
Longshot Pomes for Broke Players (1962)
Run with the Hunted (1962)
It Catches my Heart in its Hands (1963)
Crucifix in a Deathhand (1965)
Cold Dogs in the Courtyard (1965)
Confessions of a Man Insane Enough to Live with Beasts (1965)
The Genius of the Crowd (1966)
All the Assholes in the World and Mine (1966)
At Terror Street and Agony Way (1968)
Poems Written Before Leaping out of an 8 Storey Window (1968)
Notes of a Dirty Old Man (1969)
The Days Run Away like Wild Horses Over the Hills (1969)
Post Office (1971)
Erections, Ejaculations, Exhibitions and General Tales of Ordinary Madness (1972)
Mockingbird Wish Me luck (1972)
Me and Your Sometimes Love Poems (1972)
South of No North (1973)
Burning in Water, Drowning in Flame (1974)
Factotum (1975)
*Love is a Dog From Hell (*1977*)*
Women (1978)
Play the Piano Drunk like a Percussion Instrument Until the Fingers Begin to Bleed a Bit (1979)
Shakespeare Never Did This (1979)
Dangling in the Tournefortia (1981)
*Ham on Rye (*1982*)*
*Bring Me Your Love (*1983*)*
*Hot Water Music (*1983*)*

The Bukowski/Purdy Letters (1983)
The most Beautiful Woman in Town and Other Stories (1983)
Tales of Ordinary Madness (1983)
There's No Business (1984)
War All the Time (1984)
You Get so Alone at Times that it Just Makes Sense (1986)
Barfly (1987)
The Roominghouse Madrigals (1988)
Hollywood (1989)
Septuagenarian Stew (1990)
The Last Night of the Earth Poems (1992)
Screams from the Balcony: Selected Letters 1960-1970 (1993)
Pulp (1994)
Living on Luck: Selected Letters 1960s-1970s (1995)
Betting on the Muse (1996)
Bone Palace Ballet (1997)
The Captain is Out to Lunch and the Sailors Have Taken Over the Ship (1998)
Reach for the Sun: Selected Letters 1978-1994 (1999)
What Matters Most is How Well You Walk Through the Fire (1999)
Open All Night (2000)
Beerspit Night and Cursing (2001)
The Night Torn Mad with Footsteps (2001)
Sifting Through the Madness for the Word, the Line, the Way (2002)
The Flash of Lightning Behind the Mountain (2004)
Slouching Toward Nirvana (2005)
The Bell Tolls for No One (2005)
Come On In! (2006)
The People Look Like Flowers at Last (2007)
The Pleasures of the Damned (2007)
The Continual Condition (2009)

*Essential Bukowski (*2016*)*
*Storm for the Living and Dead (*2017*)*

Select Bibliography:

Brewer, Gay, *Charles Bukowski* (Twaynes United States Authors Series, 1996)
Calonne, David Stephen (ed), *Sunlight Here I Am* (Sun Dog Press, 2003).
  - Portions from a Wine-Stained Notebook (City Lights)
  -Absence of the Hero (City Lights, 2010)
Charles Bukowski (Reaktion Books, 2012)
Celine, Louis-Ferdinand, *Journey to the End of the Night (*John Calder, 1988)
Cherkovski, Neeli, *Bukowski: A Life* (Steerforth Press, 1999)
  - Whitman's Wild Children (Steerforth Press, 1999)
Christy, Jim, *The Buk Book* (ECW Press, 1997)
Dardis, Tom, *The Thirsty Muse* (Abacus, 1990).
Debritto, Abel, (ed) *On Love* (Canongate, 2016)
  - On Cats (Canongate, 2016) *On Writing* (Canongate, 2016)
Dorbin, Sanford, *A Bibliography of Charles Bukowski* (Black Sparrow Press, 1969)
Fante, John, *Ask the Dust* (Panther, 1985)
Fox, Hugh, *Charles Bukowski: A Critical and Biographical Study* (Abyss Publications, 1969)
Harrison, Russell, *Against the American Dream: Essays on Charles Bukowski* (Black Sparrow Press, 1994)
King, Linda, *Loving and Hating Charles Bukowski* (Wild Ocean Press, 2014)
Locklin, Gerard, *A Sure Bet* (Water Row Press, 1996)
Miles, Barry, *Charles Bukowski* (Virgin, 2005)

Norse, Harold, *Memoirs of a Bastard Angel* (William morrow, 1989)

Pivano, Fernanda, *Laughing with the Gods* (Sun Dog Press, 2000)

Pleasants, Ben, *Visceral Bukowski* (Sun Dog Press, 2004)

The Victory of Defeat (2011)

Polimeni, Carlos, *Bukowski for Beginners* (Writers and Readers Publishing, 1998)

Poynter, M.J. *Bukowski and the Beats* (CreateSpace, 2015)

Richmond, Steve, *Spinning off Bukowski* (Sun Dog Press, 1996)

Schwartz, Daniel, *Chuck & Jane* (2017)

Sherman, Jory, *Bukowski & Me* (Rebecca J. Vickery, 2011)

Smith, Jules, *Art, Survival and So Forth: The Poetry of Charles Bukowski* (Wrecking Ball Press, 2000)

Sounes, Howard, *Locked in the Arms of a Crazy Life* (Rebel Inc., 1998)

- *Bukowski in Pictures* (Rebel Inc., 2000)

Vinnines, Melanie (ed), *Bukowski: An Anthology of Poetry and Prose* (Silver Birch Press, 2013)

Weizmann, Daniel (ed), *Drinking with Bukowski* (Thunders mouth Press, 2000)

Winans, A.D. *The Charles Bukowski Second Coming Years* (Beat Scene Press, 19960

Wood, Pamela, *Scarlet* (Sun Dog Press, 2010)

VHS Material

The Bukowski Tapes (Bukaroo)

*Bukowski at Bellevue (*Visionary*)*

Audio Cassettes

The Home Recordings, 1969-1970. (Bukaroo)

Odds and Ends (Bukaroo)

The Screaming Life of Bukowski (Bukaroo)

There Goes the Neighborhood (Bukaroo)

DVDs

There's Gonna be a Goddam Riot in Here: Bukowski live in Vancouver (Monday Media)

CDS

Bukowski: King of Poets (Chinaski Records)

Solid Citizen: Bukowski Live in Hamburg, 1978 (Chinaski Records)

The Life and Hazardous Times of Charles Bukowski (Chrome Dreams)

Index